[d i g i t a l]
LIGHTING &
RENDERING

BY JEREMY BIRN
SERIES EDITOR: GEORGE MAESTRI

New Riders
201 WEST 103RD STREET
INDIANAPOLIS, INDIANA 46290

Digital Lighting & Rendering

International Standard Book Number: 1-56205-954-8

Library of Congress Catalog Card Number: 00-100411

Printed in the United States of America

First Printing: July 2000

04 03 02 01 00   7 6 5 4 3 2 1

Interpretation of the printing code: The rightmost double-digit number is the year of the book's printing; the rightmost single-digit number is the number of the book's printing. For example, the printing code 00-1 shows that the first printing of the book occurred in 2000.

Trademarks

Warning and Disclaimer

Publisher
David Dwyer

Executive Editor
Steve Weiss

Series Editor
George Maestri

Development Editor
Linda Laflamme

Managing Editor
Jennifer Eberhardt

Project Editor
Linda Seifert

Technical Editor
Dan Ablan

Cover Image
Jeremy Birn

Cover Design
Aren Howell

Interior Design & Production
Kim Scott
kim@bumpy.com

Proofreaders
Teresa Hendey
Bob LaRoche
Debra Neel

Indexer
Lisa Stumpf

Contents at a Glance

TABLE OF CONTENTS

3 Three-Point Lighting

4 Shadows

7 Exposure

8 Composition and Staging

9   Materials and Rendering Algorithms

DEDICATION

To my parents.

ABOUT THE AUTHOR

Jeremy Birn is a freelance animator, teacher, author, and 3D artist. He works in and around Hollywood, California, and at his home in Marina Del Rey. Jeremy works with several programs, including Softimage 3D, Alias Power Animator, and more recently Alias | Wavefront's Maya and Avid's Softimage | XSI.

AUTHOR ACKNOWLEDGMENTS

I got the idea to write this book when George Maestri's landmark title *[digital] Character Animation* was released by New Riders Publishing. Seeing how well he covered the art of 3D character animation in a non-software-specific way, I thought I could do a similar book to cover the other half of the creative work in 3D. I was very pleased when acquisition editors from New Riders phoned me to ask about writing for them. I was even more pleased that my book was to be a part of the *[digital]* series founded with George Maestri's title, with George reading and commenting on all of my chapters.

Another New Riders author, Dan Ablan (of *Inside LightWave 3D* and *Inside LightWave 6* fame) read my chapters, shared his greater experience as an author, and verified that all of my terminology (based on experience with Alias, Softimage, and Maya) would jive with LightWave users.

Thanks also to Discreet Logic for sending me 3D Studio MAX, along with their connection to Mental Ray. And thanks to Softimage for all of the betas of Twister, Sumatra, and finally the Softimage | XSI software they sent me while I wrote this book.

In writing the software notes and web links that appear throughout this book, I received an enormous amount of help on the Internet, especially from the regulars on the 3dRender.com Discussion Group.

Henrik Wann Jensen (graphics.stanford.edu/~henrik/), the pioneer of Photon Mapping, was very supportive in reading and correcting some of my explanations of rendering algorithms and global illumination techniques in Chapter 9.

Two artists whose work I admired on the web, Jeremy Engleman (art.net/~jeremy) and Eni Oken (www.oken3d.com), were both generous in providing high-resolution art to print in the book, along with extra screen shots and behind-the-scenes information to share how they created their work.

I rendered the majority of the figures in this book on my Intergraph TDZ 2000. Some of the earlier images, scenes, and models were created in the SGI lab of the Art Center College of Design in Pasadena, and a few images were also rendered at The California Institute of the Arts in Valencia.

Finally, thanks to everyone at New Riders Publishing, for their patience with my progress through the writing schedule(s), for their decision to allow all of the pages to be printed in full color, and for their tireless work in putting together what I hope will be a popular and memorable book.

NEW RIDERS ACKNOWLEDGMENTS

New Riders would especially like to thank author Jeremy Birn, for a book done splendidly. It took a while, perhaps, but it was certainly worth the wait.

New Riders would also like to thank *[digital]* series editor George Maestri, for his continued support and enthusiasm for the *[digital]* series.

A Message from New Riders

As the reader of this book, you are our most important critic and commentator. We value your opinion and want to know what we're doing right, what we could do better, in what areas you'd like to see us publish, and any other words of wisdom you're willing to pass our way.

As the Executive Editor for the Graphics team at New Riders, I welcome your comments. You can fax, email, or write me directly to let me know what you did or didn't like about this book—as well as what we can do to make our books better. When you write, please be sure to include this book's title, ISBN, and author, as well as your name and phone or fax number. I will carefully review your comments and share them with the authors and editors who worked on the book.

Please keep in mind that I didn't write this book and am probably not the best person to bring technical issues to. If you run into a technical problem with how the book explains something, it's best to contact our Customer Support staff, as listed later in this section. Thanks.

For any issues directly related to this or other titles:

Email: steve.weiss@newriders.com
Mail: Steve Weiss
         Executive Editor
         Professional Graphics & Design Publishing
         New Riders Publishing
         201 West 103rd Street
         Indianapolis, IN 46290 USA

Visit Our Website: www.newriders.com

On our website you'll find information about our other books, the authors we partner with, book updates and file downloads, promotions, discussion boards for online interaction with other users and with technology experts, and a calendar of trade shows and other professional events with which we'll be involved. We hope to see you around.

Email Us from Our Website

Go to www.newriders.com and click on the Contact link if you

- Have comments or questions about this book

- Want to report errors that you have found in this book

- Have a book proposal or are otherwise interested in writing with New Riders

- Would like us to send you one of our author kits

- Are an expert in a computer topic or technology and are interested in being a reviewer or technical editor

- Want to find a distributor for our titles in your area

- Are an educator/instructor who wishes to preview New Riders books for classroom use. (Include your name, school, department, address, phone number, office days/hours, text currently in use, and enrollment in your department in the body/comments area, along with your request for desk/examination copies, or for additional information.)

Call Us or Fax Us

You can reach us toll-free at (800) 571-5840 + 9 + 3567. Ask for New Riders. If outside the USA, please call 1-317-581-3500 and ask for New Riders. If you prefer, you can fax us at 1-317-581-4663, Attention: New Riders.

For Inquiries into Academic Sales or Reselling Opportunities

Please call (800) 428-5331 for information on purchasing New Riders books.

TECHNICAL SUPPORT AND CUSTOMER SUPPORT FOR THIS BOOK

Although we encourage entry-level users to get as much as they can out of our books, we appreciate keeping in mind that our books are written assuming a non-beginner level of user-knowledge of the technology. This assumption is reflected in the brevity and shorthand nature of some of the tutorials.

New Riders will continually work to create clearly written, thoroughly-tested and reviewed technology books of the highest educational caliber and creative design. We value our customers more than any-thing—that's why we're in this business—but we cannot guarantee to each of the thousands of you who buy and use our books that we will be able to work individually with you through tutorials or con-tent with which you may have questions. We urge readers who need help in working through exercises or other material in our books—and who need this assistance immediately—to use as many of the resources that our technology and technical communities can provide, especially the many online user groups and list servers available.

- If you have a physical problem with one of our books or accompanying CD-ROMs, please contact our customer support department.

- If you have questions about the content of the book—needing clarification about something as it is written or note of a possible error—again please contact our customer support department.

- If you have comments of a general nature about this or other books by New Riders, or if there has been a delay in your receiving a response from other New Riders sources, please contact the executive editor.

To contact our customer support department, call 1-317-581-3833, from 10:00 a.m. to 3 p.m. US EST (CST from April through October of each year—unlike most of the rest of the United States, Indiana doesn't change to Daylight Savings Time each April). You can also access our tech support website at http://www.mcp.com/support.

Thanks again; we appreciate your business!

1

INTRODUCTION

T O HELP YOU MAKE better 3D renderings, this book fuses information from several fields. In these pages you will find concepts and techniques from professional cinematography, design principles from traditional visual arts, practical advice based on professional graphics production experience, and plain-English explanations of the science behind the scenes.

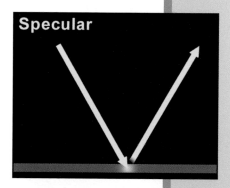

1.1 CINEMATOGRAPHY

When you want to make the most of the camera and lights in your 3D scene, it helps to study techniques developed and used by professional cinematographers shooting live-action films. This book gleans many concepts and techniques from cinematography to help you answer questions like these:

- How do you reproduce the recognizable qualities and color temperatures of natural light sources? (See Chapter 5, "Qualities of Light" and Chapter 6, "Color.")

- How can you apply principles and techniques developed by Hollywood lighting designers to your 3D scenes? (See Chapter 3, "Three-Point Lighting.")

- How do you simulate the exposure process of a real camera and the natural side-effects of a cinematographer's exposure controls? (See Chapter 7, "Exposure.")

Artists working in a new medium need to learn from older media, but they also need to grow and develop on their own. Although learning from cinematography is important, it would be a mistake to assume that 3D rendering is merely a computerization of the same art form. This book explains many situations where imitating the same lighting set-ups used in live-action would not yield the same results, and it also covers many techniques that are not possible in live-action cinematography.

It took decades after the invention of motion pictures before filmmakers developed the cinematic conventions that we now take for granted in well-filmed movies. As film production matured, cinematographers actually began relying to a greater extent on principles that had existed for centuries in painting and illustration; early films had suffered because many of the first camera operators were technicians unschooled in other visual arts.

Computer graphics, like early motion pictures, are still frequently created by technicians instead of artists, and the difference is visible. Being an expert user of a 3D program, by itself, does not make the user into an artist any more than learning to run a word processor makes someone into a good writer. Just as a writer needs to know what to say, a 3D artist needs to know how to compose an image and which lighting and shading are needed in a shot. Fortunately, the infant art form of computer graphics has vast pools of knowledge to draw from in cinematography and in the classical visual arts.

1.2 CLASSICAL VISUAL ARTS

The classical visual arts, especially painting and illustration, are the source of most rules, conventions, and expectations with regard to creating and composing images. You can help your work by taking advantage of established aesthetic guidelines and 2D design principles to answer questions like these:

- What kind of composition and perspective will create the most appealing rendering, best guide the viewer's eye, and complement your 3D scene? (See Chapter 8, "Composition and Staging.")

- What visual functions do you want your shadows to serve in your composition? (See Chapter 4, "Shadows.")

- What kind of color scheme will be used in the scene, and how will your color choices be interpreted by your audience? (See Chapter 6, "Color.")

Several chapters in this book focus on visual arts topics as a source of aesthetic principles to help plan, improve, and complete your work.

1.3 SCIENCE

Understanding relevant aspects of optics, physics, computer science, and human perception can improve your work in 3D graphics. It pays to know what's going on behind the scenes so that you can answer questions such as:

- What optical and physical principles are being simulated by your software, and which aren't being simulated correctly? (See Chapter 9, "Materials and Rendering Algorithms.")

- How will people perceive your images, and how do you influence a viewer's perception? (See Chapter 6, "Color," and Chapter 8, "Composition and Staging.")

An artist should never be afraid to get his hands dirty with his work; just as a sculptor gets to know every facet of his stone, a 3D artist needs to know his renderer. This book is written for end-users of 3D software—not for programmers—but it nonetheless strives to cover in plain English many of the calculations and algorithms your 3D rendering software is using behind the scenes. One of the keys to taking control over your medium is to understand how it works, and to learn it well enough to break its rules.

1.4 PRODUCTION TECHNIQUES

In the real world of professional graphics production, you need to get your work done quickly and efficiently, and you need to work with your clients, bosses, and co-workers. Throughout the book information is drawn from professional graphics production experience to help answer questions such as the following:

- How do you work efficiently with clients to create 3D renderings that you are both happy with? (See Chapter 2, "Lighting Workflow.")

- How do you use multilayer and multipass rendering to deliver the most versatile elements to a compositor? (See Chapter 10, "Compositing.")

- What tricks do you need to develop the most realistic texture mapping based on real-world surfaces? (See Chapter 9, "Materials and Rendering Algorithms.")

- What techniques are most effective for integrating your 3D renderings with a real scene, and how do you prepare on location for the lighting match? (See Chapter 10, "Compositing.")

The professional production information in this book is written to be useful to other professionals, students, and hobbyists alike.

1.5 WHO SHOULD READ THIS BOOK

You should read this book when you have at least a working knowledge of how to use a 3D rendering package and are interested in taking your 3D rendering further.

- For professional users of 3D rendering software, including 3D artists, animators, and technical directors, this book is designed to help with real-world production challenges and to contribute to the on-going growth of your work.

- For intermediate to advanced students of computer graphics, this book will help you develop more professional production skills.

- For dedicated 3D hobbyists, this book can help you improve the artistic quality of your 3D renderings and learn more about professional approaches to graphics production.

This book is written to be clear, but not condescending. Every effort has been made to define terms, the first time they are used, and to illustrate every concept and technique with figures and sample renderings. However, this is not an introduction to 3D graphics. This book is designed to complement, rather than to replace, your software's manuals and help files.

1.6 SOFTWARE REQUIREMENTS

Digital Lighting & Rendering is not limited to one specific brand of software. This book covers art, techniques, and concepts that will be applicable to your 3D rendering work, no matter which brand of 3D rendering software you choose.

1.6.1 3D RENDERING SOFTWARE

No single program is going to support every feature, function, and rendering algorithm described in this book. Hopefully you won't mind learning about a few functions that aren't in your particular software yet. Although different programs have different features, the similarities in how you create a well-lit rendering outweigh the differences, making the content of this book applicable to multiple 3D rendering packages.

You've probably heard the saying "It's not what you've got, it's how you use it." If you do a professional job of texturing, lighting, and composing a 3D rendering as described in this book, nobody will know or care if you are using a lower-cost software package. On the other hand, if you don't work on your lighting, if you never think about color schemes, if you leave your shadows and composition to chance, then the most expensive software in the world won't help you make a decent rendering. Naturally, to have the best of both worlds, to be a skilled user running powerful professional tools, is an ideal most people aspire to.

The techniques, concepts, and layouts detailed in this book are applicable in any 3D rendering package. Coverage of specific features and terminology has been carefully edited to work with multiple programs and platforms. Most sections show several alternate approaches or workarounds to achieve every effect described. With an awareness of the art and computer graphics principles that go into a rendering, and a little bit of "creative problem solving," you can accomplish great work in almost any rendering package.

1.6.2 2D SOFTWARE

Besides 3D rendering software, you will also need 2D paint, image-processing, or compositing software to complete many types of texture mapping, histogram analysis, and compositing processes described in this book.

Any good 3D system should be complemented with 2D software capable of at least basic creation and manipulation of texture maps. Ideally, a program with a histogram display, support for a full range of image-processing filters, and still or motion compositing capabilities will round out your system.

Reading this book may teach you some things about your software and about other software used in the industry. But software is not the subject of this book. This book is about what you can create.

1.7 CREATIVE CONTROL

You probably learned this lesson in dining at seafood restaurants:

If it smells like fish, it is not good fish.

A similar principle applies in computer graphics:

If it looks like computer graphics, it is not good computer graphics.

When an image is well-lit and well-rendered, the technology behind the image does not call attention to itself. Viewers will notice only a compelling image, a realistic scene, or an innovative new visual style. When viewing a great rendering, the fact that a computer was used in creating the image will not be the first thing that strikes a viewer's mind.

When you, the artist, are truly in control of your 3D rendering, then it is your hand that the viewer will see in your work, rather than the impression that a computer has made the picture.

The goal of this book is to help you take control over the lighting and rendering process so that every aspect of your rendering is the result of your own deliberate and well-informed decisions. Each chapter will deal with an issue or aspect of lighting and rendering a 3D scene, discuss how it works, and show how you can make it work better.

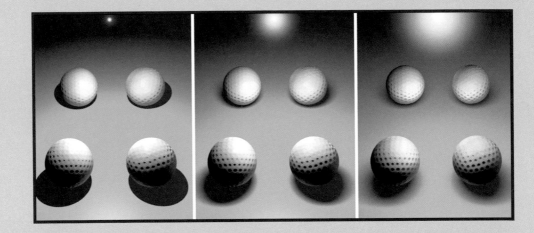

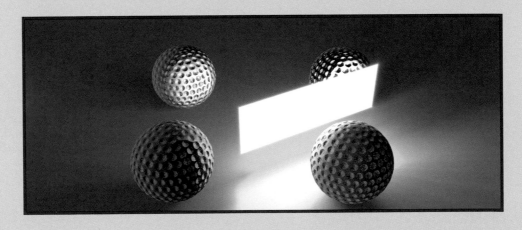

2

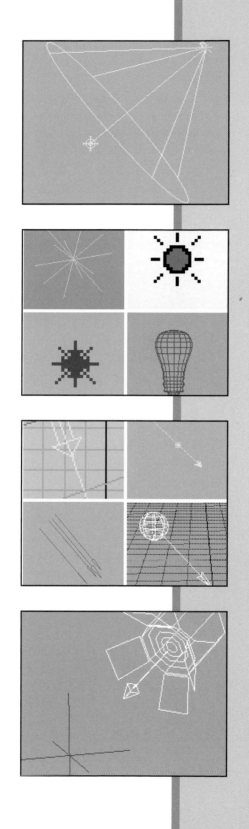

Lighting Workflow

A GREAT RENDERING can be generated through random experimentation, happy accidents whose results you want to keep, or as a result of last-minute decisions and modifications. Most often, however, your best renderings will be produced when you are in full control of your software and when you have developed a workflow to consistently achieve professional results. Your workflow is the set of habits and processes you use to compose, test, and revise your renderings in a professional environment. This chapter discusses a basic workflow, focusing on maintaining control of your lighting.

2.1 GETTING STARTED

A well-lit scene takes advantage of the full range of tones in your palette. When lights are kept under control and limited to specific areas and surfaces in your scene, then you can render a variety of tones, including both light and dark shades within your scene. To take advantage of a full range of tones, you need to adjust your monitor so that you can see the whole palette; then adjust your software to get rid of any uncontrolled light.

2.1.1 ADJUST YOUR MONITOR

If your monitor is adjusted poorly, you might find yourself under-lighting or overlighting every scene and using only one range within the available palette. Some users trap themselves by adjusting their monitors to make very dark tones visible and then use only the lower 25% (or less) of the available palette.

Before you start lighting, take a moment to make sure you are seeing an accurate representation of your scene. Although no two monitors show an image exactly the same way, you can at least make sure that you meet a basic minimum requirement. That is, you should at least be able to see the difference between a full range of shades of gray on your monitor. The brightness and contrast on many monitors are adjusted so that you cannot see the first or last digit on the chart in Figure 2.1.

Some programs have their own color-correction controls that make an image appear different when viewed inside of that program from when viewed in another window or application. Turn off any automatic color-correction that would create this kind of difference, so that your renderings and texture maps will not appear to shift colors between applications.

Being able to distinguish between a full range of grays on your monitor is only a minimum requirement. If you are doing renderings for any specific kind of output—such as output to motion-picture film, video, or a color printer—you will have to make specific display adjustments to preview the actual appearance of your final output medium.

Although controls for adjusting a computer display vary between brands of monitors, color-matching software, and video cards, a basic approach to calibrating your display works with most systems. To calibrate your display to a specific output device, use the device to print or output a test image containing a broad range of tones and colors. Then, display the test image on your computer's monitor and compare the file on the computer to the output copy. Viewing the monitor image and final output side by side, adjust your display until the tones and colors on your monitor match the final output as closely as possible.

2.1 View the file GrayScale.gif while adjusting your monitor.

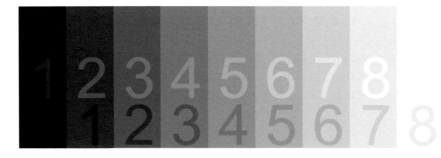

If you don't know the specifics of how your work will be output, fine-tuning your monitor in this way might not be possible before you render. In this case, you might need to use a paint or image-processing program to adjust your images after they are rendered, to precisely control the final output on a specific printer or film recorder.

2.1.2 START IN DARKNESS

To be in control of your scene's lighting, start in total darkness so that you can deliberately add all the light that will appear in the scene. When you shoot a film on location, starting in total darkness isn't always possible because there is usually some natural light in an environment. Fortunately, however, computer graphics are like a well-built sound stage, in that it is easy to start in total darkness for complete control. All you need to do is turn off any other light in your scene, such as default or ambient light, which could rob you of control over the lighting of each individual area of the image.

2.1.2.1 THE AMBIENT LIGHT PROBLEM

The parameter called ambience (also called *global ambience* or *ambient light*) in most programs is an unrealistic effect that is not similar to its real-life namesake, and can impair your control over lighting the scene.

In real life, ambient light is the widely distributed, "indirect" light that has bounced off (or been transmitted through) objects in your scene. Ambient light illuminates even the areas not directly lit by another light source. Shadowed areas of a real room are sometimes made visible only by the ambient light. Real-life ambient light is tinted as it bounces around the environment and adds different colors to different sides of objects, based on colors it has picked up from the environment. Real ambient light varies in intensity in different parts of the environment and adds different tones to objects from different angles.

In 3D graphics, the "ambience" in most programs just means an amount of flat, uniform brightness added to objects in the scene, making objects visible even where no light source illuminates them. This is usually done without any calculation of an appropriate tone or direction of indirect illumination, and produces unrealistic shading that is uniformly applied. Global ambience adds the same color and intensity to all sides of an object, without regard for its position. You can see the unshaded ambience in the shadow area in the left frame of Figure 2.2. Focus on the lower-right area of the ball. The dents are not even visible in the area lit only with ambient light because the ambient light does not provide any shading based on the angle of the surface.

2.2 Global ambience (left) is an unrealistic effect that robs the scene of shading and depth.

In general, global ambient light will rob your scene of richness and variety, especially in areas not illuminated by other light sources. To get the most local control over your lighting, and the best quality of shading, turn off any global ambience in your scene. If you can choose a color for your global ambience, pure black is a very good choice. This way, there will be no light added to the scene other than the lights that you deliberately position and control.

> **NOTE**
>
> An exception appears in software from Alias|Wavefront, where the type of light called "ambient" can actually produce shading based on its position. When ambient shading is fully activated, the ambient light functions similarly to a point light, except that it does not cause specular highlights. Only if no ambient shading were used would this light pose the problem of flat, global ambience. With ambient shading, it makes a good fill light.

After you have turned off global ambience, you can light a 3D scene to take advantage of the full range of tones that would be available when shooting a scene on film. Images shot on film can use a range of tones from pure black to pure white, limited only by the latitude of tones available on the film stock. Making this level of contrast possible, some portions of a filmed image can fall off into blackness where there is too little light to be visible relative to a scene's exposure. Global ambience in your 3D scene would take away the option to leave an area completely unlit, because the global ambience would be added to all parts of the scene.

> **NOTE**
>
> See Chapter 7, "Exposure," for much more detail about exposing a 3D scene.

2.1.2.2 ALTERNATIVES TO GLOBAL AMBIENCE

Some people seem to be addicted to the bad habit of using a uniform global ambience because they are worried that areas of their scene will fall off into a stark blackness without it. They think that using a small amount of global ambience is a harmless cheat. In reality, other techniques are better for adding secondary illumination to quality-oriented renderings.

Many artists add their own *fill* lights to a scene to provide secondary lighting that is more controllable than global ambience. A fill light can be any kind of light source (such as a spotlight or directional light) that is dimmer than your main light source and is used to brighten an otherwise unlit area. The right side of Figure 2.2 is lit with a set of fill lights that add shading and color variation to the ball, producing richer, more realistic shading than global ambience provides.

Definitions of ambient light vary between programs. Software that includes radiosity or other global illumination models may use a more accurate calculation for the addition of ambient light, instead of adding a uniform global value. If this alternative is available, and does not require an unreasonable amount of time to compute, it can add an enormous improvement to the secondary lighting in your scenes.

> **NOTE**
>
> See Chapter 3, "Three-Point Lighting," for more information about using fill lights.

> **NOTE**
>
> See Chapter 9, "Materials and Rendering Algorithms," for more about radiosity and other modes of energy transfer.

2.2 ADDING LIGHT SOURCES

Most software offers several different kinds of lights that you can add to your scene. Some of the figures in this section are designed to make the individual light as visible as possible, and even highlight the light sources with visible glow effects. In most cases, however, a viewer won't be able to tell which kinds of lights you have used in a final rendering. You can choose types of light as a matter of convenience; after you know where you want to apply and confine your illumination, you can use whichever tool will make the light easiest for you to control.

2.2.1 POINT (OMNIDIRECTIONAL) LIGHTS

Point source lights have slightly different names and icons in different programs, as shown in Figure 2.3, but by any name these lights do the same thing: A point light simulates rays shining out from one infinitely small point in space.

Point lights are sometimes called *omni* or *omnidirectional* lights, because they emit light uniformly in all directions, like a bare light bulb or glowing star in space. The illumination and shadows aim out away from the light in all directions, as shown in Figure 2.4.

In real life, you aren't likely to find any light that is uniformly omnidirectional. Most sources emit more light in some directions than others.

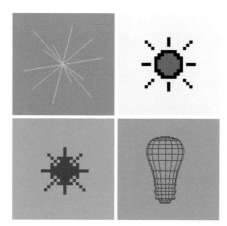

2.3 Icons for a point light in LightWave 3D, a radial light in Electric Image, a point light in Maya, and a point light in Softimage all perform similar functions.

If you are adding point lights to your scene to simulate real light bulbs, for example, remember that most real light bulbs have an opaque metal socket that blocks light from one end, and many are mounted in some kind of a fixture or shade that limits their directionality.

Even though point lights start out as omnidirectional, you can give them a throw-pattern that is uneven, like a real light bulb, to aim more light in some directions than in other directions. You can do this is by applying a texture map to the light, or by grouping the light with 3D objects that will cast shadows. Figure 2.5, for example, shows a point light positioned inside a model of a lampshade; this limits the light to functioning much like a spotlight. The light is blocked by the geometry because it is set to cast shadows.

2.2.2 SPOTLIGHTS

Spotlights are a basic staple of most lighting designs in computer graphics. Spotlights are a popular choice of many artists because they can be controlled conveniently to aim light at a specific target, as shown in Figure 2.6.

2.4 A point source emits light evenly in all directions.

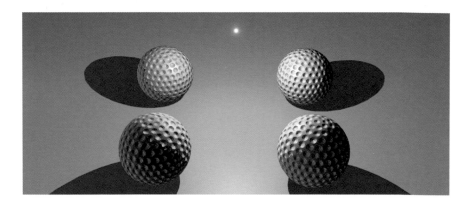

2.5 Shadows and other factors can limit a point light.

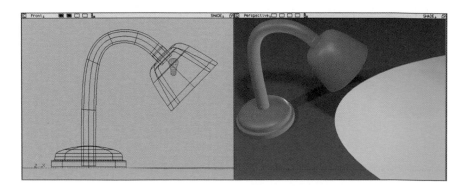

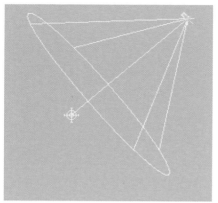

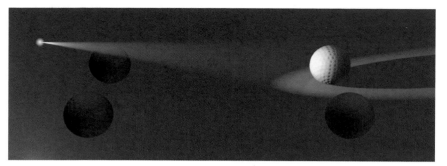

2.6 A spotlight can aim light at a specific target.

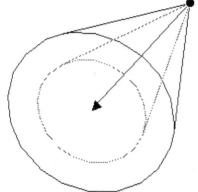

A spotlight simulates light radiating from a point, much like a point light. A spotlight, however, limits the illumination to light within a specified cone or beam of light only. The rotation of a spotlight can determine where the beam is aimed. You can also link a "target" to the light so that the light is always oriented toward the position of the target. You can also group a spotlight with a 3D object, such as a model flashlight or car headlight assembly, so that the beam of light will be aimed as if the light were radiating from the object. Figure 2.7 shows some of the popular representations of spotlights in different programs, usually displaying an outline of the cone's position and some indication of the direction in which the light is aimed.

Spotlights are staples of visual effects in your renderings. A spotlight has extra controls and options not found on other types of lights, as shown in Figure 2.8. Options such as projecting an image map from a light, or making a beam of light visible as if shining through fog, are often best controlled with the beam of a spotlight.

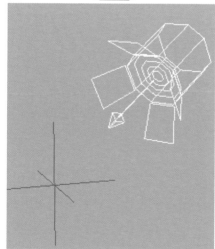

Other common spotlight parameters enable you to control the width of the cone (usually specified in degrees) to vary between a narrow beam and a broader one. The amount of *softness* of the cone (also called *spread* or *falloff*) allows the intensity of the light to diminish more gradually as it approaches the edge of the beam. A softer edge on a spotlight's beam will make the light's individual location less obvious and will avoid creating a harsh "circle" of projected light, as shown on the left side of Figure 2.9. This enables you to more subtly lighten or darken areas with a spotlight. With a very soft-edged beam, for example, you can aim a spotlight from within a room to brighten the general area around a window and curtains, or aim a spotlight with a negative brightness at the corner of a room to darken it.

2.7 Icons show how spotlights are aimed in Alias Power Animator, Electric Image, and Softimage.

Because spotlights can be aimed and controlled so conveniently, some artists rely on them to simulate light from almost any source and light most of their scenes entirely with spotlights. Even when a light needs to shine in multiple directions, such as the light from a table lamp, two or more spotlights can be positioned together and aimed in different directions. In Figure 2.10, the light from the lamp is created by aiming one spotlight upward and another downward. There isn't necessarily anything wrong with this, although the advantages and uses of other light types should not be overlooked out of habit.

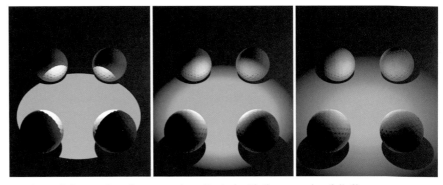

2.8 Extra controls are available with spotlights, shown here in 3D Studio MAX.

2.9 A spotlight cone's softness can be adjusted with the spread or falloff.

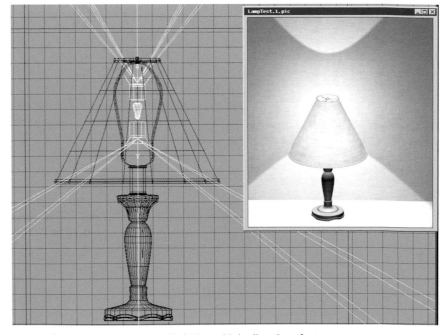

2.10 Multiple spotlights can cast light in multiple directions from a source.

2.2.3 DIRECTIONAL LIGHTS

The farther a light is from the subjects being lit, the more the illumination and shadows of the different objects in the scene will become parallel. A nearby point light lights the objects on the left side of Figure 2.11. Each object is lit and shadowed at a different angle, based on the object's position relative to the point light. In the middle of Figure 2.11, the point light has been moved a greater distance away from the subjects, and the illumination and shadows have become closer to parallel. A point source would have to be infinitely far away for the shadows to be perfectly parallel; for all practical purposes, however, a very distant light source such as the sun can cast shadows that appear parallel in an ordinary terrestrial environment. On the right side of Figure 2.11, a *directional* light has been used rather than a point light, to simulate a point light at an infinite distance.

Directional lights are variously known as "distant," "direct," "infinite," or "sun" lights in different programs, and have different icons (see Figure 2.12). A directional light sets a single vector for all its illumination and hits every object from the same angle, no matter where the object is located. All the shadows cast by a directional light are cast in the same direction and are orthogonal projections of each object's shape.

It does not matter where a directional light is located relative to the objects being lit. The only thing that matters in placing a directional light is which way it is pointed. The actual angle used by a directional light is controlled differently in different programs. Some implementations use the rotation of an icon to aim the directional light. Other types of directional lights use a vector from the icon to the target or the

2.11 A nearby point light (left) creates illumination from a greater range of angles than a distant light (right).

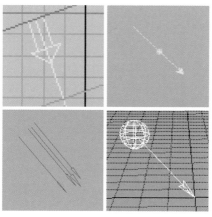

2.12 A 3D Studio MAX Target Direct Light, Infinite Lights in Power Animator and Maya, and Directional Lights in Softimage, all serve the same purpose.

global origin. Some directional lights simulate the sun's angle, based on a specified date, time, and location.

Because a directional light is not as easy to aim or confine to a local area as a point light or spotlight, it is most useful as a part of your secondary or fill lighting, and not as the main light on a subject. A set of directional lights from different angles can be used together to provide fill light, even if the individual lights from each angle are very dim. Directional lights can fill very large areas with illumination that appears to be ambient or atmospheric, such as filling in daylight from the sky, providing a quick, effective alternative to global ambience. Refer to Figure 2.2; the fill lights used on the right side are directional lights.

2.2.4 AREA LIGHTS

A standard point or spotlight emits light from an infinitely small point in space, not simulating the size of a physical light source in real life. A point light does not have a scale in any dimension. This means that a point light, as shown on the left of Figure 2.13, creates crisp, hard-edged shadows, and creates a sharply defined terminator on smooth surfaces. For a more accurate simulation of real light, *area* lights have a definable scale, so all rays of light are not emitted from exactly the same point. The middle and right panels of Figure 2.13 show the results of scaling an area light to a larger size.

If an area light is scaled very small, its illumination will appear similar to a point light. A larger area light, as shown on the right in Figure 2.13, will make the light appear softer, creating softer shadows and creating illumination that can "wrap around" nearby subjects.

The quality of light and shadows achievable with area lights can make them an excellent choice for some realistic renderings. Because they can add to your rendering time, however, some people find that on a specific system area lights can be more useful when rendering the occasional

NOTE

Area lights are not supported in all renderers. Chapter 5, "Qualities of Light," discusses other techniques used to achieve similar soft lighting effects.

2.13 A point light (left) creates sharper illumination than a spherical area light (middle), which gets even softer when scaled to a larger size (right).

high-quality still image than in longer animation projects where many frames need to be rendered quickly.

Area lights are implemented differently in different programs. In some programs, area lights are listed as a separate type of light, as a separate choice from spotlights, point lights, and other types previously described. In other programs, the property of functioning as area light is an option available on existing spotlights or point lights. Having a spotlight with the option of lighting from an area provides the benefit of being able to conveniently aim an area light with a spotlight's cone.

2.2.4.1 SPHERICAL AREA LIGHTS

The area light in Figure 2.13 is scalable in all three dimensions. This is sometimes called a *spherical* light, because it simulates light coming from a spherical region of space, similar to a glowing bulb or round light fixture. This can be especially useful for lighting anything that appears very close to a large light source. A spherical light can be uniformly omnidirectional, so the rotation of the light has no effect on your output. A spherical light can be used to replace a point light, when the illumination needs to appear more diffused or you want your light to cast soft-edged shadows.

2.2.4.2 FLAT AREA LIGHTS

Area lights are commonly available in flat shapes such as discs and rectangles. A light emitted from a two-dimensional area can use less rendering time than light emitted from a three-dimensional area, although the number of samples may be adjustable with either approach. A rectangular area light, as shown in Figure 2.14, is similar to an illuminated ceiling panel, a plane scalable in width and height, that illuminates objects with a naturally soft, diffused light. In addition to simulating light from ceiling panels, other common uses for flat area lights are simulating the reflected illumination from brightly lit walls and ceilings and providing a soft, realistic light source for portraits or still-life renderings.

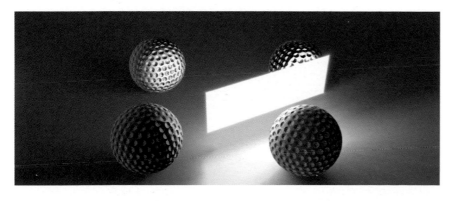

2.14 A rectangular area light resembles a panel of soft light.

Aiming or rotating a flat area light changes your results, because light coming from the edge of the flat area light is more likely to create sharper shadows and be dimmer; light from the face of the light, on the other hand, will be brighter and more diffuse.

2.2.4.3 LINEAR LIGHTS

A *linear* light is a type of area light that is similar to a fluorescent tube and can be scaled in only one dimension. Giving it a length can soften the shadows and extend its illumination in one direction. Figure 2.15 shows a linear light illuminating a scene. Notice how the aiming of the linear light affects the output: The shadows of the objects along the length of the light are very soft, but shadows from the end of the light are more focused.

You can use linear lights to simulate light from fluorescent tubes, laser blasts, or any other sources that appear to be lines of light. Even when a line shape is not specifically needed, linear lights (rather than flat or spherical area lights) are sometimes used for general soft lighting in a scene because they do not add as much to your rendering time as the other types. A linear light can produce an appearance very similar to a flat or spherical area light, but can render more quickly because it needs to be sampled only along one axis rather than two or three.

2.2.4.4 MODELS SERVING AS LIGHTS

In some programs, a 3D model in your scene can be designated to function as a sort of area light source. With this feature, even nontraditional shapes of light, such as a neon sign, can be used as true light sources, as shown in Figure 2.16. In most programs, however, effects such as neon signs are usually faked by rendering a bright-looking object and also by positioning some other kind of light near the sign to illuminate the surrounding area.

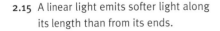

2.15 A linear light emits softer light along its length than from its ends.

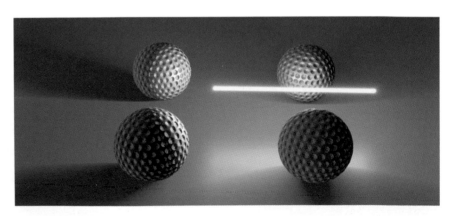

2.16 Your own model can provide a custom light shape.

2.3 TESTING YOUR LIGHTS

Lighting is 5% setting up and 95% revisions and adjustments. While you add lights to your scene, it is inevitable that you will test render the scene several times—and make revisions and adjustments—before you have a final product you (and your client) are really proud of. Efficiently managing all your tests and revisions is an integral part of producing high-quality renderings and meeting deadlines.

In a scene with several lights, you need to know what each specific light is doing for you, and which light to adjust if you don't like the shading of a surface. You need specific test renderings to evaluate your lighting and to make sure that each light is really doing its intended job.

To save time and to isolate problems, not all your test renders need to be attempts to output a whole scene at once or to create a final-looking product at full quality. You can use several techniques in your workflow to make tests that clearly show you just the information you need to control your lighting.

2.3.1 ISOLATING A LIGHT

To see exactly where one spotlight is aimed, or just how a backlight or rim light glints off the edge of an object, sometimes you want to render a test that isolates the illumination from just one light. To set up this rendering, just hide or deactivate all the other lights in the scene. Also be sure to turn off any "ambient" or "default" light added by your software, if you haven't already. Now you can produce a rendering that shows exactly what a particular light does for you, with blackness in every other part of the shot.

Figure 2.17 shows two lights from the same scene in isolation. If you are adjusting one particular light, especially a light that will contribute a subtle effect, isolating a light can give you a good look at what you are adjusting. Isolating a light is a good habit to get into any time you are focusing your attention on a specific problem you need to fix with a light, or for setting up any specific effect you want a light to achieve in a scene. Tests with only a single light also render faster than renderings with more lights visible.

Lights rendered one at a time reveal where each source contributes illumination to your scene. If you haven't been keeping track of which surfaces each light illuminates, you may be surprised by the results of rendering some of the lights in your scene in isolation. You may have underestimated how far a light can travel, and might not know that a small point of light on one side of a room is actually casting light and shadows on the opposite side of the room. Rendering that light in isolation would show its full effect, and thus enable you to fix the problem (for example, by adjusting the light's falloff distance or attenuation).

Viewing lights in isolation allows subtle effects to be set up with precision. If you are creating a rim of light to glint off the edge of a character's head and outline his profile, for example, it is easier to initially position and adjust the light in isolation, viewing the rim of light against black, than to try to position it when the subtle effect is mixed with the results of several other lights.

Beginning users often have some lights in their scenes that are not accomplishing their intended results. If surrounding geometry accidentally blocks a shadow-casting light, for example, it might contribute little

NOTE

Load an old scene that you created before reading this book, and test each of the lights in isolation. You might be surprised by how each light contributes to your rendering, and how you could have controlled or adjusted them differently for a better effect.

2.17 Two lights from the same scene in isolation.

or no light to a rendering. Test rendering a scene that already has several lights active would make it easy to overlook this problem. A beginning user might go back and make the light brighter, render again, and then when he still doesn't see enough illumination from the blocked light, he might add another light to the scene. He would have rendered the scene several times without locating the actual problem, and he would have left an unnecessary shadow-casting light in his scene, slowing down future renderings.

The process of "debugging" this kind of lighting problem is made faster and more efficient by viewing lights in isolation. If a test rendering were lit only by the light that was being blocked, the problem of a light being shadowed by its own fixture could be quickly isolated and fixed (for example, by excluding the fixture from the light's illumination or by moving the light.)

2.3.2 FALSE COLOR LIGHTS

Often, you will be lighting the same subject with multiple lights. When two or more lights are hitting a subject, all their illumination may start to overlap and blend together, creating room for confusion in diagnosing any problems with a test rendering. You can avoid a slow trial-and-error adjustment process and complete your rendering faster if you can see exactly what each light is contributing to the illumination of the scene, while still viewing how multiple lights overlap.

Looking at the rendering on the left side of Figure 2.18, you can get the general impression that there are two lights, one from the left and one from the right, illuminating the vase. To differentiate between the overlapping lights, an easy test is just to give each light a bold, false color, as seen on the right side of Figure 2.18.

If you were looking at only the normally colored rendering in Figure 2.18, you might not be able to tell whether the dimmer light was also spilling onto a part of the wall. With the false colors, the dimmer light is given a red color, making the red spill on the back wall easy to locate.

A false color test can be seen as a variation on rendering each light in isolation one at a time, but produces renderings that still show how light from two or more sources interact or overlap.

2.3.3 FLIPPING BETWEEN VERSIONS

If you ever find yourself unsure whether an adjustment has made a difference or are left wondering "what did that just do?" after trying some function, it is a good idea to compare the two test renderings in a

2.18 False colors make it easier to identify the contribution from each light source.

flipbook. Very subtle differences or adjustments, which you might not be able to accurately perceive when viewing two renderings side by side, can be noticed as a movement or shift in the image when you flip between them in the same window.

Most 3D programs that support animation can be configured to display multiple rendered frames in sequence, enabling you to flip from one frame to another in a window. You can compare any two versions of a lighting setup by rendering one "frame" of animation before the change, and another frame after the change. Using a flipbook, or animation-playing utility, you can flip back and forth between the two (or more) frames. If you don't have a flipbook-type utility, a paint program that supports layers will also allow an image layer to be toggled between being visible and invisible, to facilitate flipping between two renderings.

Seeing changes in the same window helps to locate any shift or change between two versions, or to confirm whether the versions are identical. A flipbook also gives you another way to see how a specific light contributes to the scene. By flipping between two renderings, one including the light and the other with the light turned off, you can determine how the light affects the scene.

It is important that the lighting be the only thing changing in your flip-book. If you are lighting a scene you have already animated, either freeze the motion or do multiple renderings from the same frame of the animation, and then assemble the renderings as frames in an animation.

Because adjustments to your lighting could involve a series of test renderings, you might end up appending many frames to your "animation" in order to flip through all the versions you have tested.

2.3.4 PAINT PROGRAM COMPS

A 2D paint program can become a useful tool for experimenting with your 3D scene. Try bringing multiple versions of your rendering into a paint program. You might like the result of fading halfway between two test renderings, and then going back into your 3D program to adjust your actual lights to intermediate values or positions. Or you might try erasing one portion of the top layer to see what the changes would look like if only applied to a part of the scene. Of course, you would still have to go back to implement the changes you liked into your 3D scene, but this experimentation is quick and easy in comparison to revising and rerendering every change in 3D.

A powerful technique in refining your lights is to render each light in isolation, as described earlier, and then to bring each of the isolated single-light renderings into the paint program. Then you can layer the separately rendered lights together, previewing what looks like a complete rendering with several lights, as shown in Figure 2.19.

To layer together the separate renderings of lights, you can use an *additive* operation between the images. Additive layering just means that the color values from one image are added to the color values of another image so that the sum is a brighter result, with all the lighting from both renderings. No alpha channels or masks are needed, because black areas

2.19 Separately rendered lights are composited.

NOTE

You can find an additive layering function labeled Add in Photoshop's Apply Image dialog box as well as in the Simple Additive Compositor in 3D Studio MAX's Video Post module.

NOTE

Rendering in multiple passes is discussed in detail, along with more reasons to render lights in isolation, in Chapter 10, "Compositing."

add nothing to the brightness, having no effect on your results. Only areas where a light brightened an object will add to the additive composite.

Plain additive compositing is only one of the ways to layer together lighting passes. You can also use a blending mode called *Screen*, as shown in Figure 2.19. Screen and Add are similar. Screen has the advantage of not clipping tones that have reached white so quickly, but Add is a more accurate preview of how the lights would be combined in 3D.

After your results look like a single rendering produced with all the lights, you can manipulate the different layers of lighting. Using functions in your paint or compositing program, you can change the brightness or color of any light's layer, or fade it halfway out of the scene, or completely turn it off.

All these changes and tests can be done almost instantly, and you will see these changes applied to the whole scene, including shadows and reflections, with no delay required to do any rerendering. This technique is useful to anyone testing lights and experimenting with a scene, but it will seem even more important if you render your scenes in multiple passes.

2.4 LIGHTING IN PRODUCTION

A project goes through several stages when moving from script to screen, and the point at which lighting becomes involved in the process varies in each production. In some productions, lighting sometimes seems to be an afterthought in a schedule. This is an unfortunate situation, but it is a reality. In some live-action productions, computer-generated imagery itself sometimes seems like an afterthought, and lighting is often not the most high-profile part of the process.

In other words, you can't always begin the process of lighting as early as you would like to. You need the 3D scene to exist first, you need to know the camera angles and poses of the subjects, and you may need to wait for live-action footage to be filmed and digitized before you can design integrated lighting. At the time when lighting can begin, people are usually very anxious to have the lighting done right away, to begin rendering, and see the work.

2.4.1 INTEGRATED TASKS

In some production companies, lighting is a separately delegated task. Instead of having one artist work on all the aspects of a rendering, a studio may pass a project through an assembly line of specialists. The entire job of one person (or one department) within this process is to light 3D scenes.

At smaller companies, however, a single person commonly handles all the aspects of how a scene will be rendered. This person generally sets up the materials, shaders, textures, lighting, and renderer settings, and may have also worked on the modeling and animation. In computer graphics, these jobs actually overlap so much that the effects of adjusting lights in a scene are sometimes indistinguishable from the effects of all the other tasks. Many looks attributed to "qualities of light" in real life are governed in computer graphics as much by shading or material settings as by the light sources themselves.

You never directly see your light sources. Apart from visual effects such as lens flares and light beams, the only way you see the lights in your scene is through the changes they produce on your objects. If modeling or shading problems prevent some objects from responding to light convincingly, your scene might look badly lit, no matter what you do with the lights. Sometimes it is better to fix problems at their source than to waste time trying to light a scene that does not respond realistically to light.

2.4.1.1 GEOMETRY

Some models might never look well lit, no matter what you do with the lighting around them. The geometry itself can have errors or omissions that prevent your subject from responding to light in a convincing way.

Often, the most critical areas of a model's lighting are around its corners and edges. The right frame of Figure 2.20 looks better lit than the left—a highlight defines the top edge of the tape dispenser on the right. In

2.20 The lighting is the same in both images, but looks better on the right because of the beveled geometry.

contrast, the left side looks less solid and less well defined by the lighting. In reality, the lighting is exactly the same on the left and right, but the model on the right is beveled.

Look at any objects that have angles in them, such as a tabletop or television set. The corners may appear to be right angles from a distance; up close, however, you can see that they are actually beveled or curved in some way. As you look at the small, beveled edges of an object from different angles, you see that these corners can often catch a highlight or form bright defining edges. If there were no bevel to catch the light, illumination hitting the object from a 45-degree angle would disappear. In Figure 2.21, the shape of the simple bevel makes a difference in the right frame.

Even with the same lighting and the same material settings, this small difference in the geometry makes a big difference in the rendering. Except for real-time applications where very few polygons can be used in your scene, avoid razor-sharp intersections of planar surfaces in your models, and bevel everything.

2.4.1.2 SHADING

Your materials, shaders, and textures are also factors that determine how a model responds to light. It is technically possible to light an untextured subject or environment. In some cases, a test without textures can help you better see what shading the lighting is creating. Final textures and surface attributes can make an enormous difference to the look of your lighting, however, so you usually want to get textures and attributes of your models adjusted first, before spending much time on lighting.

If an object is set to be reflective or transparent, that can limit its response to light; therefore, although light may be hitting it, it may still look black. If an object is in an all-black environment, setting it to be

2.21 The bevel catches light from different angles.

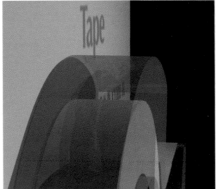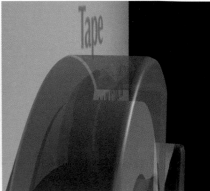

reflective will generally just make the model appear darker. If a surface is set to be transparent, but there is no other object or environment to see through the surface, it will also appear darker.

If you have a transparent or reflective surface that is not responding well to light, there are several ways to bring it under control. When the object is surrounded by other models or given an environment to reflect, it will appear brighter and more convincing. Increasing the brightness of specular highlights on the surface to much-higher-than-normal values can add glints of light to a surface, even if it is highly transparent or reflective. Very few objects are as perfectly reflective or transparent as can be created in the computer. Often, reducing the transparency and reflectivity is the best fix. Give the objects bump maps, or map some dirt and scratches onto the surface, as shown in Figure 2.22.

If your objects include any specularity or shininess, viewing the scene from a different camera angle will change the location of the highlights or specular shading on an object. The exact size, location, and intensity of areas hit by any light should always be test rendered, using your final shading, to confirm that the lights are illuminating areas as you want them to. No amount of knowledge or estimation can replace visually inspecting your results.

A well-lit scene depends on more than just the lights. Revisions to many different aspects of your scene can help improve and perfect your lighting. Whether you are doing a project all by yourself, or you are a small part of a large studio production, pay attention to the other parts of the production process, including the modeling and texturing, that are prominent components of a well-lit scene.

> **NOTE**
>
> Chapter 9, "Materials and Rendering Algorithms," discusses the use of texture in much more detail.

2.22 The shading is improved with some texture and dirt.

2.4.2 THE REVISION PROCESS

If you are working professionally, chances are that someone has to approve your work and will have the authority to request changes in your lighting. Depending on the organization of the production and of your company, the person approving your work may be a client, a director, creative director, art director, your supervisor, or your boss. Ideally, you should be able to have one and only one person to whom you ultimately answer. If more than one person is giving you creative input, the suggestions could contradict each other or be inconsistent.

An "approval process" for your work can be scheduled between you and the client, to define clearly when each test or version of your work will be shown. The goal in scheduling the approval process is to avoid redoing too much work: You can get feedback on test versions or portions of the product before you commit to a final rendering. You don't want to wait until the end of your production schedule, when you have completed your work, to hear from your client that he or she is not happy with some aspect of your lighting and needs it to be changed.

2.4.2.1 PREPARING FOR A CRITIQUE

One vital issue to communicate is the schedule you are planning for the production. Your clients should know what kind of test or stage they will see on each specific date. Before each scheduled critique, make sure that your client understands what is (or is not) included in whatever version or test rendering you will show.

In many situations, you can be forced to show tests to your client that are not in the same output medium as your ultimate product. An image destined for film might initially be previewed on a computer monitor, for example, or a 3D animation that is going to be composited and fully integrated with a live-action shot in a television program might be previewed in isolation or (more crudely) superimposed in front of a background plate.

Prepare your clients for what they will see. If they think that they are going to see something closer to a final product than what you have to show, a crisis of confidence might result if they are disappointed with your work.

Make sure that the client understands whether he is looking at a color-accurate proof, as well as any differences in resolution, aspect ratio, printing process, or other possible discrepancies between the test and the final product.

Make sure your client understands exactly what can (or cannot) be changed later in the production. If your company is going to deliver the shadows in the scene as a separate element, to be composited later with live-action footage, for example, it will be possible to change the darkness or opacity of the shadows during the compositing, but it might not be as easy to change the angle or direction of the shadows after they are rendered. The client should know which aspects of the scene need to be corrected now, and which can be adjusted later.

You can never be too clear about setting the context of the discussion. It can be a good habit to start any presentation with clear statements such as "This is what we are working on now…" or "These are the things we will still be able to change later."

2.4.2.2 STAYING ORGANIZED

Clients often change their minds about issues in ways that might make you go back to previous versions of a scene. Don't assume that your data becomes worthless the first time it is rejected; otherwise, you might find yourself trying to re-create some aspect of it at a later date.

A client or supervisor might also need his memory refreshed as to how the scene is evolving, or as to how you have responded to previous notes. Be prepared at any time to show the client any previous version of the work that you have discussed, in case it is needed as a point of reference or comparison.

Don't lose track of which scene you used to create an image, especially for an image that you may have shown to a client or taken notes on. All your test renderings can end up as a big directory of image files. You will also be creating scene files with different filenames for each version of your 3D scene data. It is vital to keep track of which version of your scene is used to create each rendering, either by giving them the same name or number, or by writing down a log, documenting which pictures are rendered from which 3D scenes.

If you are also developing or using different versions of texture maps, the same need for tracking versions also applies to the maps. An old scene that is reloaded might not work well if texture maps it had used are missing or have been replaced with newer versions.

2.4.2.3 TAKING NOTES

When taking notes during a critique, don't assume that every word you hear will be technically accurate, or that it will exactly match computer terminology. Suppose, for example, that the client tells you that "the skin should look more translucent." Don't assume that you have to reach for a setting or shader labeled "translucency." The impression of translucency might come from a texture-mapping change, such as seeing more of the color of the veins under the skin, or from a lighting change, such as making sure that the extremities of the subject are lit more warmly when seen in front of a bright background.

Sometimes, a note will only sound like a rendering note, but will in fact turn out to be unrelated to the lighting and shading. Imagine, for example, if the client had said the character's skin should look "softer." This might be an issue in shading or texturing the skin, and might be helped by the lighting. It could also be a modeling issue, however, requiring you to create more "give" to show the skin pulled inward around straps or belts in her costume. It might even be an animation issue, if the deformation of the skin makes it look too rubbery, or if it does not fold or compress when touching other objects.

To help pin down vague comments and impressions, it is handy to have photo reference or reference footage of related subjects on hand. If the client can say "Make it look like this picture" or point to a specific phenomenon on videotape, it can add more to your understanding than a verbal agreement alone.

2.4.2.4 DEFENDING YOURSELF

You may be presenting your revisions to a person whose entire job is to have opinions about other people's work. For him not to have an opinion would be as serious a neglect of duty as if you showed up without graphics. If you don't want to be stuck reworking something, don't call attention to it or ask about it. Never volunteer to show multiple versions of something and ask for the client to choose, unless there is time in the schedule to make many additional revisions and variations.

It is essential to remember that lighting and rendering are only one part of the project you are working on. A critique may go by with comments being made only about the modeling or the animation and without a word about the lighting or texturing. If your job is just the lighting and texturing, this is a very successful critique. On the other hand, if you also did the modeling and animation for the production, and you know that things will be revised once or twice, you may find that changing around lights and colors is an easier way to keep your client busy than allowing speculation about how you could rebuild your models or restage your scene.

One answer you should never give, to any request, is "That's impossible." Predicting extra costs or lengthy production delays is a better way to avoid doing something. Suggesting alternative routes that might better fit the client's budget and schedule is even more helpful. You could be embarrassed when you figure out how to do it the next week, or when the client asks elsewhere and eventually finds what he wants.

2.5 EXPERIMENT

No matter how busy you are, be sure to find time to experiment. It seems as though the software used in the industry changes in some way every few months. New algorithms are available. New techniques are possible. New hardware continuously forces users to reevaluate previous standards and brings more functions and processes into reach.

Working in computer graphics puts every artist in the "Alice-in-Wonderland" situation of having to run very fast just to stay in the same place. Keeping up with today's technology requires that you rethink and revise even your most tried-and-true techniques and to invest the time in testing new ones.

Early in a production, before your actual scene is ready to light, it is possible that some aspects of your work can be tried in an empty scene or tried without all the final models. If you need to light a smoke or rain effect, for example, you can develop and test it in front of a background of a similar color without waiting for a final scene to become available or slowing down your tests with the actual models.

Even after a project is delivered, before you put away your files, load up the scenes (no matter how sick you are of them) and experiment with a few more renderings. You may want to render a high-resolution print of the scene for your own portfolio, or experiment with other ways the scene could look, without matching your client's expectations.

If possible, work on personal projects, no matter how brief or simple, to stretch what you can achieve. You may have some "downtime" between major projects to do your own work. Perhaps you are fortunate enough to be reading this book while you are still a student; if so, you can experiment with each of the techniques and concepts covered here.

Experimentation not only benefits your production and your career, it is essential to your own personal growth. You may look back on your work at some point and discover that you have gained more from a series of inconsequential personal projects and experiments than from any of your professional production work.

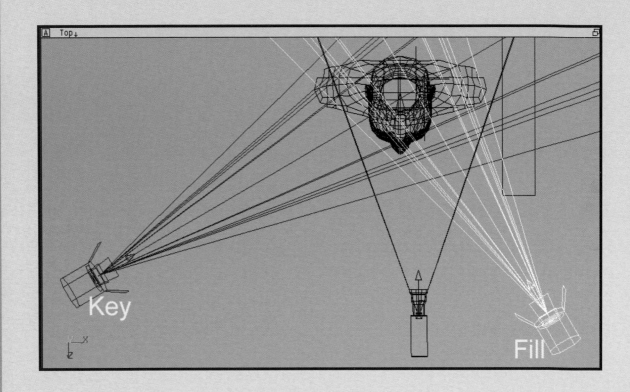

THREE-POINT LIGHTING

O NE OF THE MOST POPULAR and attractive ways to illuminate any subject is with a classic Hollywood lighting scheme called *three-point lighting*. Three-point lighting is a design that makes it easy to "model" your subject with light, to convey its full three-dimensional form through your rendered image. Variations on three-point lighting can cast a favorable light on anything from a small prop to a movie star. Learning to use the three points as described in this chapter will give you an understanding of major roles that lights can play in almost any lighting design.

3.1 MODELING WITH LIGHT

Before discussing the specific decisions and light positions that create three-point lighting, it is important to understand the underlying issues and goals that have made three-point lighting such a popular framework for cinematic lighting design.

Beginners sometimes think that a subject is well lit just because it is brightly lit, and that all it takes is enough light to make the entire subject visible. In reality, even when a subject is brightly lit, important aspects of its form will not be visible without effective shading from different angles. Figure 3.1 is certainly bright enough, for example, but the shading is not adequate to reveal the three-dimensional forms of the models.

One of the main goals of three-point lighting is *modeling with light*. To model with light is to illuminate a subject so that your two-dimensional output shows the subject's full three-dimensional form.

Figure 3.2 shows the same objects as Figure 3.1, but they are better modeled with light. You can see that one surface is a sphere, and the other is the flat end of a cylinder. Your audience would have missed this distinction in Figure 3.1.

Most scenes are not as extreme as Figure 3.1, but the figure makes the point that overly uniform lighting can flatten a subject, hiding the actual curvature and modeling. This kind of "flattened" look is sometimes seen in a photograph taken with a camera's built-in flash, or in video news coverage where a light is mounted directly on top of the camera.

Figure 3.2 has more variation of shades used in lighting the subjects. Light that is brighter on one side, with dimmer light from other angles, can prevent flat, uniform lighting and can add the shading needed to model with light. For the best modeling, study the shading on your surfaces and make sure that there are no overly flat, uniform areas.

3.1 No modeling is visible in these forms.

3.2 The new lighting reveals the forms.

One way to study the shading of your subject is to imagine your subject defined by different *planes*. Planes are just portions of the surface with their own angles, and you can imagine flat planes existing even as a part of curved, organic forms. Figure 3.3 shows a human head rendered with distinct planes rather than smooth shading. (Even before the advent of computer graphics and polygon meshes, illustrators talked about the "planes of the face" as a way to break down the forms that need to be shaded—building an object out of polygons only makes the analogy more convenient.)

To model a surface with light, different values have to be assigned to the different planes of the surface. In Figure 3.3, each plane of the face is given a different shade by the lighting design, with the illumination varying as you look from one plane to the next. As you move on to the left side of the subject's face, where the brightest light doesn't reach, a second light continues the shading and adds more variety to the surface.

Figure 3.4, on the other hand, shows a mistake that is common in computer graphics. It uses a flat "ambient" shade to fill in the unlit areas. This creates regions of uniform shading on the parts of the head not illuminated by the main light. In the areas such as the neck, you can't see any difference between adjacent planes of the head, meaning that they are not modeled with light.

In areas where the shading doesn't vary, where moving from one plane to another doesn't move you into a different tone of illumination, you

3.3 The planes of the face are each illuminated with different tones.

3.4 In the ambient-lit area, the planes are not distinct.

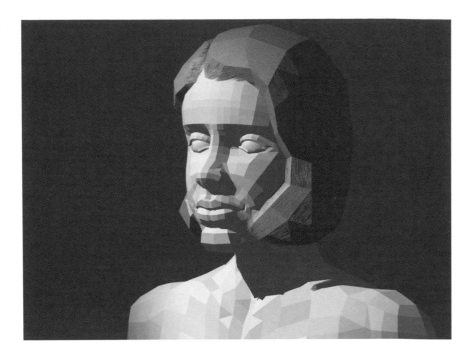

NOTE

Refer to Chapter 2, "Lighting Workflow," for a more complete explanation of why adding a uniform global ambience hurts your lighting.

will not see all the "modeling" that could be shown in a shaded form. Avoid the flat, dead spaces of ambience, or uniform lighting, and use lights to shade your subject with varied gradients.

Three-point lighting, as described in the following sections, is a reliable approach to modeling your subject with light. In setting up a three-point lighting design, keep the goal of modeling with light in mind with each adjustment, and look at the modeling indicated in each test rendering.

3.2 THE THREE POINTS

The three "points" in three-point lighting are actually three "roles" that light can play in a scene, each serving a specific purpose:

- **Key light.** This light creates the subject's main illumination and defines the dominant angle of the lighting. The key light is usually brighter than any other light illuminating the subject and is usually the light that casts the darkest, most visible shadows in your scene.

- **Fill light.** This light softens and extends the illumination provided by the key light and makes more of the subject visible. The fill light can simulate the effect of reflected light or of secondary light sources in the scene.

- **Backlight.** This light creates a "defining edge" to help visually separate the subject from the background. The backlight can glint off the subject's hair (backlights are sometimes called "hair lights" for this reason) and add a defining edge to show where the subject ends and the background begins.

In reading these definitions, don't confuse "backlight" with "background" light. A backlight is not designed to illuminate the background, only to create a defining edge around the rim of your subject. None of the three points discussed so far need to light your set—they are usually used to light your main subject, such as a character or product, and other lights can be used to light the environment around it.

For a quick preview of the three points, Figures 3.5, 3.6, and 3.7 show the points being added one at a time around a 3D head. Figure 3.5 is lit with only a key light. The key light illuminates a portion of the subject, but the opposite side still falls into darkness. In Figure 3.6, a fill light is added on the opposite side of the subject, continuing the shading over the whole surface. In Figure 3.7, a backlight has been added, producing a defining edge around the character. This small rim of light is all that needs to be lit by a backlight to separate the subject from the background.

Three-point lighting is actually a flexible set of principles that can be changed and adapted into a wide range of lighting designs. No single "recipe" for a successful lighting treatment will suit every shot. Each time you apply three-point lighting, you need to make variations and decisions specific to your scene. The following sections discuss how to choose positions and settings for your key light, fill light, and backlight.

3.5 The key light adds the dominant light to the subject.

3.6 The fill light continues the shading around the model.

3.7 The backlight creates a defining rim to separate the subject from the background.

3.3 KEY LIGHT

Every three-point lighting scheme has a key light. As the main, brightest light in the scene, the key also establishes the dominant angle for the illumination of your subject. Choosing an angle for your key light is one of the most important decisions in lighting your subject.

Lighting angles described in this chapter are relative to the position of the camera. Three-point lighting works best when you set up your shot and camera angle first, before positioning your lights. If you later change your mind and decide to shoot your scene from a completely different angle, the lighting would also have to change. Viewing your scene from the point-of-view of your camera, you can add and adjust your key light.

Putting the key light too close to the camera angle can flatten the form, as shown in Figure 3.1. But moving the key too far to the left or right can be harsh and distracting in its own way, and might not fully illuminate the face.

Think of a character's nose as a sun dial, and watch which way its shadow points. If it points downward toward some part of the mouth, as in Figure 3.8, this is a normal way of seeing a person. Viewers are used to seeing people in environments with overhead light. To aim the shadow in this expected way, the key was positioned above and to one side of the subject, as shown in Figure 3.9.

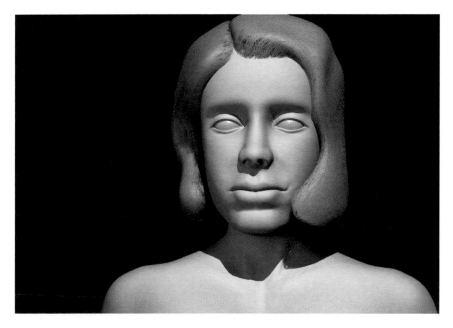

3.8 The nose shadow points toward a part of the mouth in the most normal lighting.

If the nose shadow shoots off sideways, bisecting the cheek, as in Figure 3.10, this is less flattering and sometimes makes the lighting a distracting element in the scene. This can happen when the key light is positioned too far to one side, as shown in Figure 3.11.

3.9 A common key light position is over the subject and at least a little off center.

3.10 The nose shadow telegraphs the sideways angle of the lighting.

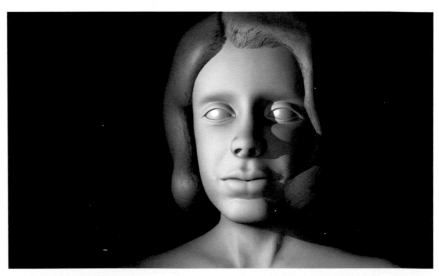

3.11 The key light from the side creates the sideways nose shadow.

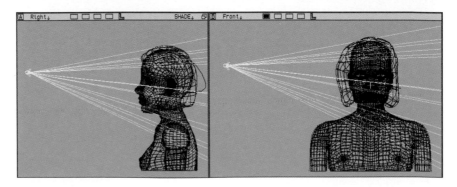

An extremely unnatural effect occurs when the key light is positioned low, aiming upward at the subject, as in Figure 3.12. At a summer camp, you may have tried aiming a flashlight upward and holding it directly under your face. This can be a terrific technique when telling ghost stories. You can turn an ordinary person into a frightening, ghostly apparition, just by positioning your key light as shown in Figure 3.13. Unless the source of the light is visible in the scene—for example, if the character is standing over a fire or holding a lantern—low-angle light can make the audience notice something very unusual about the lighting. Be selective in using this effect.

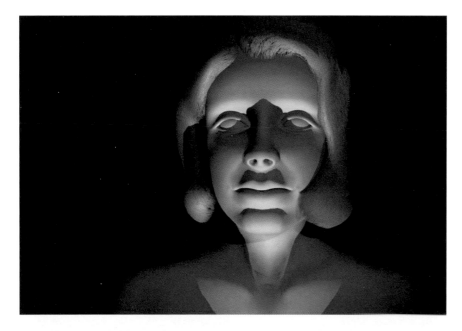

3.12 Low-angle lighting is sometimes called "Light from Hell."

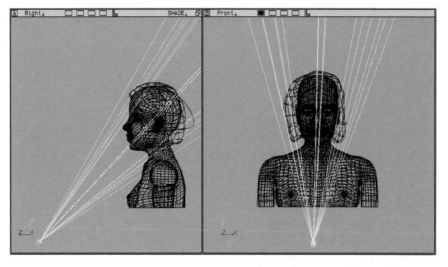

3.13 The key light from below creates unnatural lighting.

Raising the key light too high above your subject can create dark shadows within the eye sockets, hiding her eyes in shadow, as shown in Figure 3.14. With the key light angle in Figure 3.15, even if the eyes were made visible by fill light, the "raccoon eyes" look could still be noticeable, and is not very attractive.

Positioning the key light all the way behind your subject could put your subject into silhouette, as shown in Figure 3.16, and cast shadows down toward the camera. This departure from standard three-point lighting places the key light behind the subject, as shown in Figure 3.17. Even though the key light is in a position that normally would be used for a

3.14 The "raccoon eyes" look comes from very high-angle lighting.

3.15 The key light is positioned at an unnaturally high angle above the head.

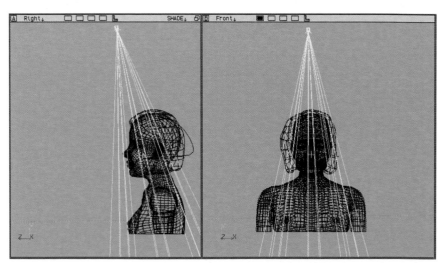

3.16 An upstage key can cast a character into profile.

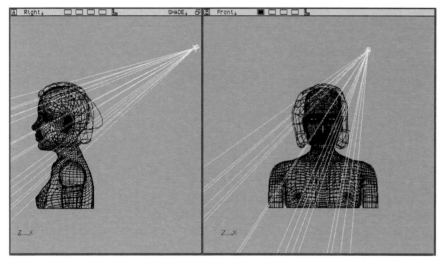

3.17 The key light is positioned behind the head.

backlight, it can be called an "upstage key." This can be a very dramatic effect. Remember, however, that lighting effects can sometimes be distracting in a story or can compete with the character's performance for the audience's attention.

Of all possible choices, positioning the key about 15 to 45 degrees to the side (left or right) of the camera, and about 15 to 45 degrees above the camera, seems to be a "happy medium" for most standard three-point lighting setups, and is a useful starting point in lighting many scenes. When trying for a "normal" lighting setup, you can usually stay within the range of angles shown in Figure 3.18.

One exception to these guidelines is that when shooting a character in profile, you may want to rotate your key and fill lights so that the character's face is fully lit, as shown in Figure 3.19.

In animated productions, you have to anticipate the movements of characters with your lighting. It is a good idea to test render different frames from any animated shot, including tests of the lighting at any "extreme" poses of the head. When a character turns and looks sideways, you might want to check that you have adequate light to define the profile.

Ordinarily, moving the key light more than 100 degrees away from the camera angle would make it function more as a backlight or rim light. In a profile shot or in an animated shot in which a character turns into profile, however, you can position the key light to keep the character's face in the light, as shown in Figure 3.20.

3.18 Typical key light angles are relative to the camera angle.

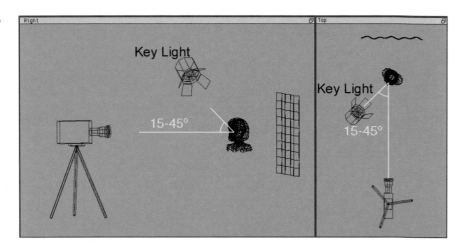

3.19 The key light can be moved to face a character in profile.

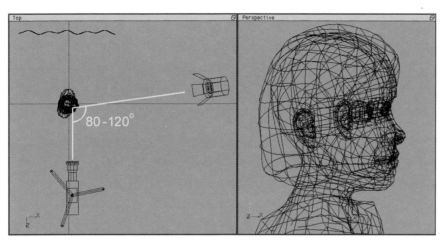

3.20 The key light can move much farther from the camera angle to light a profile shot.

Your actual lighting should be influenced both by the angles that best light your subject and also by the apparent light sources in your scene. Within a normal range, a specific lighting angle can be chosen to match the environment around the character. Outdoors, the time of day might suggest an angle for the light from the sun and sky. Indoors, a lamp or a window might light a room, and you would want the key light to appear to come from the same general direction. The angles suggested in this section are general guidelines that should not override your own judgment of what seems appropriate to your scene.

3.4 FILL LIGHT

In real life, some situations "provide their own" fill light, because illumination from the key light is reflected by other surfaces in the scene, adding additional illumination to the subject. By taking advantage of this in photography—and sometimes in live-action film and video—terrific results can often be achieved using just one light to light a scene. If it reflects off other surfaces, a single source can provide all the direct and indirect illumination needed for some live-action shots. In a standard scanline renderer or raytracer, without radiosity, this "indirect" illumination is not calculated. A renderer that does not calculate any indirect illumination can produce a scene such as Figure 3.21, in which the brightly lit wall on the right side does not appear to bounce any light back onto the subject.

To achieve the same illumination in computer graphics, you may need to add a dim fill light at a generally opposite angle from the key, to simulate reflected light. Figure 3.22 has an added fill light to roughly simulate indirect illumination in the scene.

NOTE

To learn about indirect illumination, types of renderers, radiosity, and simulating radiosity, see Chapter 9, "Materials and Rendering Algorithms."

3.21 A subject without indirect illumination or fill light falls off into unnatural blackness.

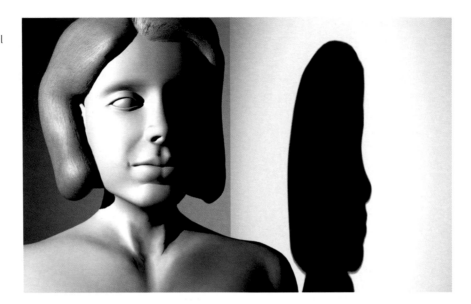

3.22 This use of fill light simulates indirect illumination.

The fill light in the case of Figure 3.22 is just a dim spotlight added on the other side of the subject, as shown in Figure 3.23. For the most true-to-life results, you would position the fill light behind the wall that is being brightly lit, to simulate light bouncing directly off the brightest spot of the wall. The direction of your fill light does not have to be precise or numeric, however; sometimes the key and fill are both more useful when cheated toward the front of the subject.

A fill light is usually most useful when placed at a generally opposite angle from the key. If the key comes from the upper left of the frame, for example, the fill should generally come from a lower angle, to the

right. Instead of putting the light all the way to the opposite side, however, you may achieve better results if you move the fill light closer to
the camera angle, so that the areas lit by the key and fill overlap. Making
the areas lit by the key light and the fill light overlap guarantees that you
will have continuous shading across the entire surface. Figure 3.24 shows
a good "normal" range of fill light angles, with the fill coming from only
slightly above the camera angle, but somewhere between 15 and 60
degrees to the left or right of the camera angle. These are very loose,
general guidelines.

A good rule of thumb is that, while your key light is above your subject,
the fill light should be lower than the key. The heights can range from a
position just below the key, down to the level of the subject's head. If
the fill light were actually lower than the subject's head, on a side of the
subject lit primarily by the fill light, the subject would be receiving

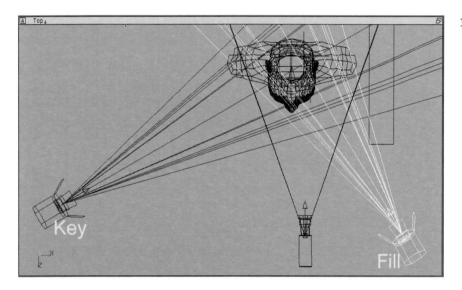

3.23 This fill light loosely approximates the direction of the side wall.

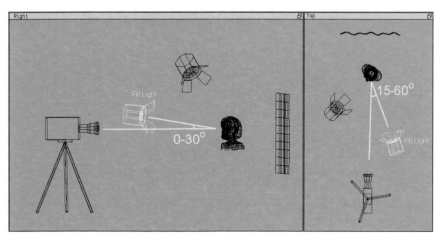

3.24 A fill light comes from a generally opposite direction.

unflattering low-angle light. The logic behind this convention is that, although most key light sources are overhead, such as the sky, sun, and ceiling fixtures, the secondary (fill) illumination often comes from light reflected off the ground or walls, or from dimmer light sources such as table lamps.

An unnatural degree of symmetry is a problem in computer graphics in general and is something to watch out for in positioning your fill light. Just as you don't want your scene as a whole to look too symmetrical, don't put your fill light in a position that is exactly mirror reflected over the camera axis from your key.

Fill lights are not only positioned to simulate reflected light. The position and direction of a fill light may be influenced by any secondary light sources visible in a scene. If there is some apparent light source, such as a desk lamp, that could motivate your fill light, try to make your fill light come from that direction.

Because there are several different reasons to add a fill, there will be times when several fill lights are needed in a scene. You might have fill lights for simulating or enhancing the reflected light, other fill lights motivated by secondary light sources in the scene, or other lights just broadening or softening the illumination from the key light.

There are very few cases when you would skip the fill light altogether. Sometimes you might render without fill light when raytracing transparent objects, such as a wine glass, that can be lit on both sides by one key light. Some stylized renderings might use very high contrast and no fill, or might use a simple two-tone shading style requiring only a key light.

A scene rendered with radiosity, or other lighting models that support indirect illumination, might rely on computer-simulated bounce lighting rather than a fill light. Even in live-action productions, where naturally reflected light is present, however, fill light is still often added to extend or modify it. Even when using radiosity, you should also consider adding fill lights whenever needed to soften, extend, or modify reflected light.

3.5 KEY-TO-FILL RATIOS

The brightness of your fill light is important to the tones and contrast in your scene. Too much fill light could compete with the shading from the key light, flattening the subject, as seen on the left side of Figure 3.25. Too dim a fill light can leave a dark side of your model undefined, as shown on the right side of Figure 3.25. A reasonable amount of fill light, shown in the center, is noticeably dimmer than the key light, but still bright enough to fully light the subject.

The difference between the brightness of your key light and the brightness of the fill light is called the *key-to-fill ratio*. When your key light is twice as bright as your fill light, for example, it is a 2:1 key-to-fill ratio. In Figure 3.25, the left side uses a very low 1.5:1 key-to-fill ratio, the middle uses a moderate 4:1 key-to-fill ratio, and the right uses a very high 24:1 key-to-fill ratio.

In plain English, what the key-to-fill ratio measures is the level of contrast in the scene's lighting. You want to know how much brighter the brightly lit parts of the scene will be than the dimly lit parts.

It is the illumination at the subject that is being compared by your key-to-fill ratio, not at the light sources. Be sure to take into account any *attenuation* (also known as "decay" or "falloff") that will reduce the brightness of a light before it reaches the subject. If a light has decayed to half its original brightness where it illuminates your main subject, for example, use half of its brightness setting in your key-to-fill ratio.

> **NOTE**
>
> A warning is required about two confusing terms. You will sometimes hear the phrases *high-key* or *low-key* used in reference to an environment's lighting. These terms might sound as if they are describing the opposite of their actual meaning. High-key refers to a bright environment, with a lot of fill light, and therefore a low key-to-fill ratio. Low-key means a dark-looking environment, without much fill light, and therefore a high key-to-fill ratio.

3.5.1 LOW KEY-TO-FILL RATIOS

Figure 3.26 uses a low key-to-fill ratio of about 3:1. Even though the key light represents the sun, you can imagine that the light-colored table and walls could be providing a high proportion of fill light by reflecting much of the sunlight that illuminates them. The extra fill light in the scene helps to simulate reflected light, as well as adding to the impression that the leaves are somewhat translucent.

3.26 "Still Life with Spider Plant," by Jeremy A. Engleman, was rendered with a low key-to-fill ratio.

Here are some situations in which you would expect to see a greater proportion of fill light, and might choose to use a low key-to-fill ratio:

- Interiors with white or highly reflective surfaces, such as a kitchen or bathroom, would naturally have a low key-to-fill ratio, because of the amount of reflected light created in that kind of room in real life. After adding even one bright light to such an environment, you expect the illumination to be reflected onto almost every surface, and it could look unnatural to have any completely dark shadows in the room.

- Cloudy, overcast, or snowy days block the direct sun, and also provide more scattered or reflected light from different sides of the sky. If a typical outdoor scene uses the sun as a key light and the sky as the main source of fill, the dimmer sun and brighter sky can lead to a very low key-to-fill ratio in those weather conditions.

- Some productions, such as a comedy or children's program, use consistently low key-to-fill ratios, such as 2:1 to 4:1, to maintain a bright, cheerful mood. Enough fill light is added to illuminate every corner of the characters and the sets, and even the shadows are not very dark.

- A lower key-to-fill ratio is preferred in designing images for output to television than might be used for print or film. Conventional televisions cannot display as full a range of tones as can be projected on film. Lighting for television requires more fill light in some areas just to make the areas bright enough to be visible.

Be careful when your key-to-fill ratio drops much below 2:1. If your fill lights are bright enough to rival or overpower your key light, there might not be enough variation in tone to shade your subjects and model with light. Before you add too much fill light to any scene, stop and think if you are really happy with the key light's position and settings. When your key light is not working for you, it is better to go back and fix it than to get trapped masking the problem with unnecessary fill levels. If you don't like the main shading and shadows from your key light, you should fix your key light; don't waste time adding more and more fill to hide the key light's effect.

If you are using several fill lights, keep track of the total brightness as they add up, to make sure they don't accidentally add up to more illumination than your key light. If two fill lights both illuminate the same planes of your subject, add together the brightness of both to calculate the proportion of fill light. If a fill light overlaps with the key light, also add the fill's illumination to the key's side of the ratio. With overlapping lights taken into account, your key-to-fill ratio can be expressed as "key + fill : fill + fill."

3.5.2 HIGH KEY-TO-FILL RATIOS

Higher key-to-fill ratios, such as 8:1 or more, can create a dramatic look for darker, more shadowy scenes with a lot of contrast between bright and dark. The starkness of falling off to black on one side of a character's face may be appropriate for some environments—such as Figure 3.27, which was set in a moving subway train. High key-to-fill ratios can sometimes create dramatic images with a lot of visual impact.

3.27 A high key-to-fill ratio can look dramatic or moody.

The impression of a "dark scene" in a movie does not have to come from an underexposed piece of film, but more often can come from a high key-to-fill ratio. When you want to create a "dark scene," the scene can still show some well-lit detail in selected, controlled areas, to show the important elements in the scene in sufficient light. You can take advantage of the full range of brightness available in your palette and use a high key-to-fill ratio, making some areas of the scene well lit and other areas much darker.

You can actually build a greater sense of darkness through contrast than through underexposure. Careful control over your illumination is the secret to lighting a dark scene, not just making everything dim and murky. The shadows fall off into blackness in Figure 3.28, for example, with very little fill light. This creates the impression of a dark scene even though some areas of the scene are brightly lit.

When you light a scene with very little fill light, make sure that any important actions or parts of a character's performance are still visible in the key light. If it is important that the audience see something, even if other parts of the scene are murky, make sure that the important detail or area is lit well enough to see.

Some situations in which you would expect less fill light, and might choose to use a high key-to-fill ratio, include the following:

- Night scenes frequently have high key-to-fill ratios. At night, you will still have a key light coming from the moon or an artificial light source, but there is no natural source of fill light from the sky.

- Scenes in horror movies, or dramatic and suspenseful scenes frequently benefit from a high key-to-fill ratio. Using less fill light means that more of the scene is hidden in darkness, which is frequently useful in building suspense. A film genre called *film noir* was known for this look.

- Work rendered for film can show a greater range of brightness than work rendered for video. A key-to-fill ratio of 8:1 is already a fairly high-contrast, dramatic-looking scene for television; in film, however, a more stark shot might use 16:1 or higher, when appropriate.

Don't assume that bolder and more attention-grabbing lighting will always be better lighting, or that half-lit characters are always a more "artistic" choice. Many productions benefit more from lighting that subliminally enhances a scene than from lighting that calls attention to itself and distracts the audience from the story.

3.28 The high key-to-fill ratio means high contrast between shadow areas and bright areas.

High key-to-fill ratios can also make your key light look harder, when there is less fill to soften its falloff. Especially in computer graphics, harsh lighting treatments can sometimes look unnatural.

3.6 BACKLIGHT

Backlight is a convention inherited from black-and-white cinematography. Lack of color forces photographers and cinematographers working in black-and-white to accomplish even more with lighting than is necessary in color, and backlight is a terrific tool for visually separating a gray actor from the gray wall behind him. In color, backlight is still useful, especially in cases of dark-haired subjects against a dark background. Backlight is not used quite as frequently in color, however, and is considered more of an optional, stylistic device. Figure 3.29 shows the same scene without backlight and with it, and shows that the difference is greater when viewed in black and white.

You should think before adding backlight to every scene. Often there is already enough contrast between the subject and the background, so you might not need an extra defining edge from a backlight. In some scenes, a bright light behind the character might not seem plausible. Whether extra backlight will be "cheated" into a scene is a decision that depends on the visual style of the production and on the importance of the distinction between the foreground and the background.

3.29 A black-and-white subject can merge into a background (top left) until it is better defined with backlight (top right). In color, the subject is easier to distinguish without backlight (lower left), and backlight adds less to the rendering when used (lower right).

3.6.1 RENDERING BACKLIGHT

Backlight can sometimes be challenging to simulate in computer graphics. To render Figure 3.29 with a noticeable rim of light wrapping around the subject, multiple backlights were used, as shown in Figure 3.30. All the light positions are relative to your camera angle, positioned, and test rendered so that they illuminate the visible edge of the subject. Be sure to test render your scene from the final camera angle when setting up backlight.

It is okay for your backlight to be very bright. Sometimes it can even be brighter than the key. Because it is behind the subject, only highlighting the edge of the visible surface, the backlight does not compete with the shading of the key light.

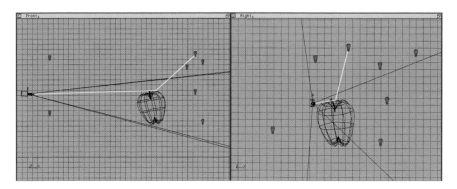

3.30 Multiple backlights are sometimes needed to create a rim that wraps around the subject.

In some situations, the effect of backlight can be diminished or completely hidden in computer graphics, when light from the same angle would have been more effective in real cinematography. To compensate, you may need to make your backlight proportionately brighter or to adjust the subject's shading and the light's position. You need to be especially careful if you have a backlight positioned directly opposite the camera (behind the subject, for example) as in Figure 3.31.

In real life, a bright light directly behind a person is still visible as a glowing edge around the person's hair, skin, and clothing. This is because real skin, hair, and clothing tend to be surrounded by a layer of translucent fuzz. The fuzz layer is made of tiny translucent hairs, fibers, and other particles that can catch and diffuse light and seem to glow when lit brightly from behind. Even nonhuman subjects can be covered with dust, liquid, or other thin layers that respond better to backlight than a conventionally shaded surface in 3D graphics.

When the backlight is directly behind an object in your 3D scene, it often has no visible effect on the way that object renders. On the left side of Figure 3.32, for example, the lower ball does not appear to receive any illumination from the bright light that is directly behind it. On the right side of Figure 3.32, a fuzz layer is roughly simulated with translucent fur from a fur shader. Adding fur to all your objects is slow,

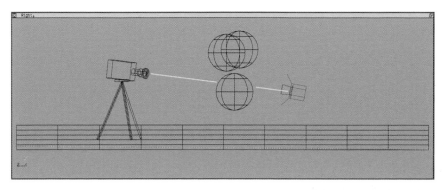

3.31 A light positioned directly behind a subject can be more effective in live action than in computer graphics.

3.32 Most 3D objects will hide a light placed directly behind them (left), unless a translucent layer is added (right).

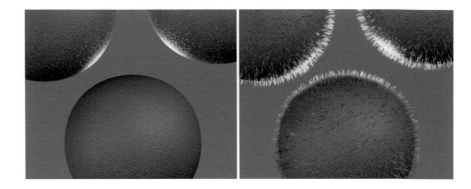

difficult, and often impractical; and most 3D scenes that need backlight will not have a realistic fuzz layer on each object.

To avoid blocking the backlight completely, it is safer to move the backlight higher up and toward the camera, as seen in Figure 3.33, so that it is not completely behind your subject.

NOTE

See Chapter 9, "Materials and Rendering Algorithms," for more information about highlights, specularity, and shading models.

If you want backlight to trace around the edge of a curved surface, not just create one hotspot at a point on the edge, it helps to create your backlight with diffuse, not specular, illumination. Reducing the specular brightness of the subject's material can help extend the defining edge, as shown in Figure 3.34. Blinn shading can sometimes work better than Phong at diffusing a backlit highlight, if you have a choice of shading models.

If a single backlight does not give you a long enough rim of light, you sometimes need to use several backlights in a row behind your subject. To produce the image on the right side of Figure 3.34, three backlights were used, as shown in Figure 3.35.

Using a row of lights as a backlight is a pragmatic variation on three-point lighting. Adjustments such as this are sometimes necessary to solve problems and achieve the results you want.

3.33 Moving a backlight higher and toward the camera can make a bolder defining rim.

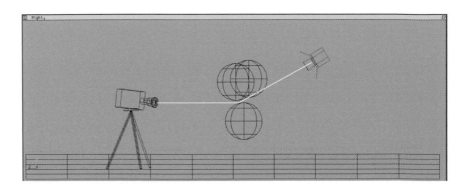

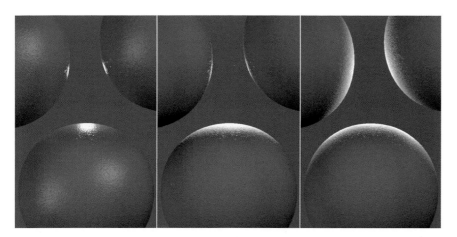

3.34 Tight specular highlights (left) don't make as effective a defining rim as diffuse shading (center) and using multiple backlights (right).

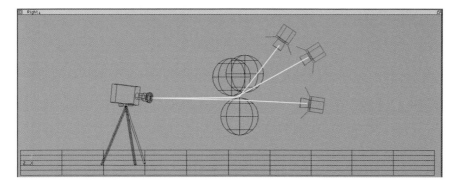

3.35 Multiple backlights extend the illuminated rim.

There is no fixed recipe for three-point lighting, only a series of options and decisions. None of the specifications or suggestions in this chapter should limit or discourage your own experiments and departures from the norm. Hopefully, the concepts behind three-point lighting should raise your awareness of some of the issues and concerns in lighting a subject, so that you can better devise your own lighting schemes for your own scenes.

3.7 SUMMARY

This chapter introduced a number of important concepts that you will need to know as you read the rest of the book or do any other work with lighting:

- Three-point lighting is generally used to solve a common problem: how to fully represent a three-dimensional form with a two-dimensional image. Producing shading that solves this problem is sometimes called "modeling with light."

- In a well-lit scene, every light exists for a purpose. Three of the possible purposes for a light are to serve as a key light, fill light, or backlight.

- Like all rules in art, the conventions of three-point lighting are flexible guidelines, ready for you to exploit and manipulate.

3.8 EXERCISES

Watch a movie on video so that you can freeze it at a few specific scenes. For each paused scene, see whether you can answer these questions:

1. Where is the key light? Fill light? Is any backlight used?

2. Is there an apparent (or assumed) light source motivating the key, fill, and backlight? Do you think some of the light was "cheated" into the scene—light that wouldn't logically exist in the time and place of the story?

3. Does the scene have a high key-to-fill ratio? How does the level of contrast affect the scene? Does the key-to-fill ratio make sense in that scene's environment?

4. Find a shot with a character standing in front of a background or in front of another character. Is the lighting in the foreground different from the lighting in the background? Does the lighting help to separate the foreground from the background in any way?

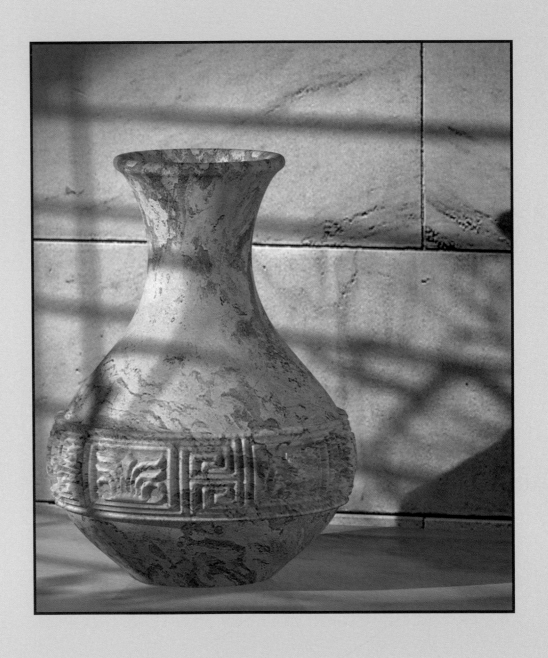

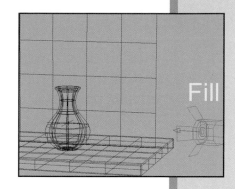

Fill

[CHAPTER]

4

SHADOWS

S HADOWS ARE an important part of your lighting design, as vital as illumination itself. The quality of shadows in your rendering can add realism to your scenes, add richness to the tones and shading of your image, tie elements together, and improve your composition. Shadow rendering in 3D graphics is also a key technical area to master. Making the best choices of shadow-casting algorithms, building up a bag of tricks to cheat and manipulate your shadows, and knowing how to optimize your shadows for the best possible rendering speeds are essential skills that every 3D artist should possess. This chapter explores both the visual and the technical side of shadows in 3D graphics.

4.1 THE VISUAL FUNCTIONS OF SHADOWS

People commonly think of shadows as obscuring and limiting vision. Although objects can be hidden in shadows, shadows also can reveal things that would not be seen without them. Here are some of the visual functions that shadows serve in cinematic images and computer graphics.

4.1.1 DEFINING SPATIAL RELATIONSHIPS

Shadows serve a practical purpose in most scenes by showing the spatial relationship between objects. They show where an object is planted on the ground or how far an object is located above the ground. Without shadows in the left frame of Figure 4.1, for

4.1 On the left side, you cannot tell how close the large upper ball is to the back wall. The most basic use of shadows is to show spatial relationships between objects.

example, you can't tell exactly where each ball is located. With the addition of shadows, the right frame reveals more information about the balls' relative positions and depths than the left frame. The shadows show when a ball is on the ground, when it is in the air, and when two balls are near each other.

4.1.2 REVEALING ALTERNATIVE ANGLES

A well-placed shadow can reveal a new angle on a subject, one that otherwise might not be visible. When your shadows cast a crisp, clearly defined image of your subject, as in Figure 4.2, you can think of the

4.2 The shadow reveals a new angle on the character.

shadow as a sort of rendering unto itself. The shadow in the figure reveals a character's profile, which would otherwise not be seen in the rendering.

Many programs enable you to view the scene from a light's point of view, as an aid to positioning and aiming the light. The outline of what you see—the profile of the subject from the light's point of view— shows you the shape that will be rendered as the shadow. This is especially important if you are using dark, hard-edged shadows. Every shadow does not have to project such a distinct shape, because often shadows will be softer or more subtle; when the shadow will be crisp and prominent, however, pay attention to the shape you are defining.

4.1.3 ADDING TO YOUR COMPOSITION

Shadows can play an important role in the composition of your image. A well-placed slash or other shadow can "break up" a space, adding variety to what otherwise would be a monotonous, continuous surface, as seen in Figure 4.3. A shadow can lead the viewer's eye to a desired part of the rendering or can create a new design element to balance your composition.

4.1.4 ADDING CONTRAST

A shadow can add contrast between two elements that might otherwise appear similar in tone. If you were rendering a red object against a red background, for example, as shown on the left side of Figure 4.4, the layers could be hard to distinguish without shadows. On the right of the figure, shadows add depth and definition to the rendering by increasing the contrast between the foreground and background.

4.3 A slash breaks up the space and adds to the composition, making the image on the right a more attractive rendering.

4.4 Shadows add contrast between the foreground and background.

4.1.5 INDICATING OFFSCREEN SPACE

A shadow can also indicate the presence of offscreen objects. The sense of "offscreen space" is important to many renderings, especially when you are telling a story. A shadow can appear to have been cast by objects not visible onscreen, to indicate that there is more to the "world" you are representing beyond what is seen in the shot. The shadows in Figure 4.5 suggest a great deal about the other elements in this environment.

4.1.6 INTEGRATING ELEMENTS

Computer graphics are often used to create fanciful or implausible scenes, scenes that juxtapose elements not normally seen together or that might not seem logical. By cementing the relationship between objects, shadows can also create a kind of integration between the elements in a scene, as seen in the commuting hippo in the subway car in Figure 4.6. If one of the objects is a moving character, the interaction of moving shadows will even further emphasize that the figure and the setting are both in the same space.

When asking the audience to accept a scene that would otherwise strain its credibility, convincing shadow interaction can add an important piece of reality to help sell the illusion. If a production is supposed to be completely photorealistic, a single element such as a missing shadow could be all it takes to make your work look "wrong" to the audience. Shadows serve the interest of adding realism and believability, even if there is no other reason for them in the composition.

4.5 The shadow indicates what is offscreen.

4.6 Shadows help integrate otherwise incongruous elements.

4.2 WHICH LIGHTS NEED TO CAST SHADOWS?

In a scene with several different light sources, how do you decide which lights need to cast shadows and which lights do not? Start answering the question by thinking about which visual goals, outlined earlier, you want your shadows to accomplish. Will one light that casts shadows be enough? Are there other places in the scene where more shadows should appear? Are shadows strongly motivated by some light source, so that realism is at stake if a shadow is omitted?

4.2.1 SINGLE-SHADOW SCENES

One approach that can work well for some productions is to turn on shadows from your key light, but to set your fill lights not to cast shadows. Some animators apply this convention almost automatically. It can work well in a simple shot within a character animation, for example—when all you really want is for a character to cast a shadow onto the ground, but you don't need to build up any great complexity in your shadow area. The subject in Figure 4.7 casts a single shadow. The result is clean and simple, and no more shadows seem necessary.

4.2.2 SHADOWS FROM FILL LIGHT

In addition to the primary shadow from your key light, at times you will also need a secondary shadow from your fill light. The ball on the left

4.7 A single shadow from the key light is often enough.

side of Figure 4.8 does not look fully "attached" to the ground, for example, because it does not cast a shadow. Because the ball is in an area where the key light is already being blocked by another object, it is being lit only by the fill light, which does not cast shadows. On the right side of Figure 4.8, turning on shadows from the fill light fixes the ball's position, even though it is in the shadow area.

When an important part of your scene takes place in the shade (in an area where your key light is already blocked), secondary shadows may become necessary from your fill light, backlight, or other lights. Flat, dead-looking shadow areas, as seen on the left side of Figure 4.8, do not have as much shading or variation as the areas of the image outside of

4.8 Without secondary shadowing (left) the ball casts no shadow.

the shadows. Secondary shadows, such as shadows from your fill light, help make sure that the illumination and shadows within your shadow areas will be just as completely rendered as the other areas of your scene.

4.2.3 SHADOW CLUTTER

At times, being able to avoid unwanted shadows is a blessing; most live-action cinematographers would kill for the capability to eliminate any unwanted shadow at the push of a button. Setting all your lights to cast shadows could slow down your rendering, but more importantly, it could clutter the scene with unnecessary multiple shadows or call attention to the number of light sources in a scene with shadows heading in different directions. Figure 4.9 shows multiple shadows that add unnecessary, distracting lines to the rendering.

Don't assume that the presence of many raytraced shadows in a scene automatically adds to the realism. Sometimes the shadows in a real scene are so soft and subtle that you barely notice them, and leaving a shadow out of your rendering could look more natural than covering every surface with overlapping shadows.

4.2.4 OMITTING SHADOWS

If your scene is not required to be completely realistic, omitting shadows is a stylistic decision that doesn't necessarily hurt your production values. Many hand-drawn illustrations and cartoons are created without shadows,

4.9 Multiple shadows can create unnecessary clutter.

for example, and usually the shadows are not missed. In Figure 4.10, removing the shadows did not lower the overall rendering quality; it only gave the scene a cleaner, punchier, slightly more "illustrated" look. Other aspects of the lighting—including the matched dark and light areas and the illumination by the bar of light along the hippo's side—help integrate the elements, even without shadows. Only when you look at the area immediately around the feet do you consciously miss the presence of shadows.

Especially in scenes that already have tightly controlled, selective lighting, the added complexity of shadows might only clutter the image, and a slightly simpler rendering, such as Figure 4.10, could be a more engaging way to present some subjects.

One reason that scenes without shadows can still look natural is that viewers can't always tell whether a dark area of your rendering is a cast shadow or whether that area is unlit for another reason. In the computer, shadows are strictly defined as the areas of 3D space from which a light's illumination has been blocked by an intervening object. In common English, however, people use the word more broadly, referring to almost any dark or unlit area as "shadows." Many people would say there is a shadow on the unlit side of the character's face in Figure 4.11, for example. Even though technically shadows were not used in the rendering, the prevalent dark areas still create the impression of a "shadowy" scene.

4.10 Without shadows, the image still holds together, but changes in style.

4.11 No shadows appear, only a shadow area.

4.2.5 SHADOW AREAS

Darkness, unlike light, does not need a source. People cannot tell where darkness comes from or from what direction it arrives. In many scenes, all the dark or unlit areas seem to blend together visually. All the adjacent dark tones, whether they are darkened by a shadow or were not being illuminated in the first place, collectively form the visual *shadow areas* in a rendering.

A shadow area is an image that includes not only what is strictly defined as a shadow—where the light has been blocked by something—but also other areas that are unlit. In Figure 4.12, for example, the areas

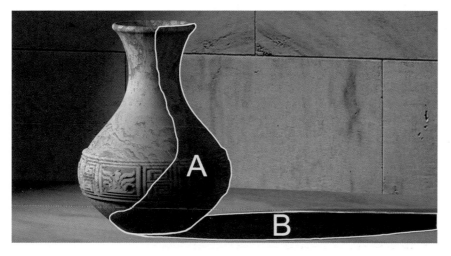

4.12 Areas A and B are both perceived as shadow areas, but only area B is a "cast shadow."

labeled A and B are both parts of the shadow area of the image. Area A is dark because that side of the vase faces away from the light and would be unlit even if there were no shadows rendered in the scene. Only area B is technically a cast shadow.

4.3 SHADOW BRIGHTNESS

Shadows that are too dark or too light can look unrealistic, or even distracting, as in Figure 4.13. In real life, light reflects between surfaces; therefore, shadows opposite a brightly lit surface do not become completely dark, and any brightly lit area shares some of its illumination with nearby darker areas.

Most photographs balance between adjacent dark tones in an image so that the tones mesh together to integrate the shadow areas. There are several different approaches to controlling the brightness of your shadows, and some of the most obvious are not necessarily the best.

4.3.1 THE SHADOW COLOR SETTING

In many programs, a setting in a light's control panel offers an apparently simple solution to lightening your shadows. By turning up the *Shadow Color* (sometimes called *Umbra Brightness*) setting, a portion of the light is allowed to leak directly into the shadow area. The parameter lightens only the cast shadow (the cast shadow was labeled Area B in Figure 4.12), without filling in the unlit sides of objects (Area A from Figure 4.12). This creates a potentially unnatural effect, as seen in Figure 4.14.

Figure 4.14 shows the cast shadow being lightened by raising the shadow color on the key light, and yet the unlit side of the vase remains

4.13 A too dark shadow area can look unnatural.

dark. This does not create a cohesive shadow area, and it looks unnatural because reflected light in the room would naturally illuminate both the cast shadow and the unlit side of the vase.

Using the Shadow Color setting on a light to adjust the brightness of the shadows can pose other problems. When the shadows cast by a light are not completely solid, a portion of the shadow-casting light is allowed to pass through any surface, including solid walls and tabletops. This can create unnatural effects, as seen on the left side of Figure 4.15 (where the circle of light cast down from the lamp appears on the floor under the table). On the right side of the figure, the shadow color is at 0, making a more realistic rendering.

In real life, the shadow of a solid object, such as a tabletop, is completely opaque, allowing no light through. The reason that you don't normally see completely black shadows under tables in real life is not because the

4.14 A shadow color lightens the cast shadow without lightening the unlit side of the object.

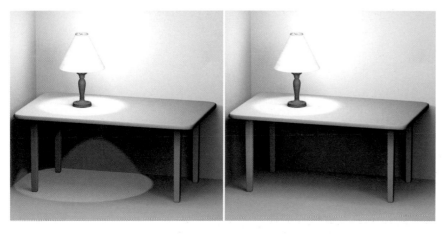

4.15 A shadow color allows light to leak through solid objects.

light from the same source has leaked through the tabletop, but instead because light has reached the shadow area from other angles.

4.3.2 AMBIENCE TO BRIGHTEN SHADOWS

Activating global ambience in your scene will brighten the entire scene, including all the shadow area, as shown in Figure 4.16.

There are problems with using ambience to control your shadow color. Global ambience adds a flat, uniform level of illumination to your shadow areas, with no variation of shading to model your subject with light. Detail, curvature, and variation, such as the carved pattern on the side of the vase in Figure 4.16, can be hidden or poorly represented by flat, ambient illumination.

4.3.3 FILL LIGHT TO BRIGHTEN SHADOWS

A more realistic way to control the brightness and tone of your shadow areas is with a fill light. In Figure 4.17, a fill light adds a matching tone to both the cast shadow and to the side of the object that was unlit. The tones are balanced, so the overall shadow area is more consistent and believable, and variation of shading is added to the shadow area.

Figure 4.18 shows the more realistic setup using a fill light to lighten the shadow area.

Sometimes shadows look richer and more interesting when they are rendered in a color that contrasts with the surrounding area or main light color. In Figure 4.19, for example, the fill light lighting the shadow area is tinted blue, and the main shadow-casting light is tinted yellow.

4.16 Ambience lightens the shadow area with flat, unrealistic shading.

4.17 A fill light shades the shadow area more naturally than increasing the shadow brightness or ambience did.

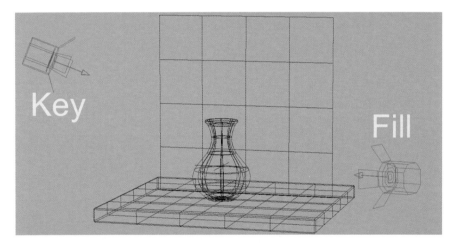

4.18 The fill light is positioned to illuminate the shadow area.

4.19 A colored fill adds complementary color to the shadow area.

4.4 SHADOW ALGORITHMS

Many rendering programs enable you to choose between two popular techniques to calculate shadows:

- A *raytraced shadow* is calculated by a process called *raytracing*. Raytracing traces the path that a ray of light would take from the light source to illuminate each point on an object. Raytracing software can accurately determine whether any intervening objects would block a part of the light to create a shadow.

- A *depth-mapped shadow* (sometimes called a *shadow-mapped shadow*) uses a precalculated *depth map* to determine where shadows will be rendered. A depth map is an array of numbers representing distances, computed by the software before it starts to render the scene itself. With points measured in each direction the light shines, the depth map stores the distances from the light to the nearest shadow-casting object found in each direction. During the rendering, the light will be cut off at the distances specified by the depth map so that the light does not shine farther than the distance stored for each angle. This makes the light appear to be blocked by other objects, without the renderer needing to check the geometry of the scene while rendering each point.

NOTE

For more information about raytracing and other rendering algorithms, see Chapter 9.

Depth-mapped and raytraced shadow techniques can produce similar-looking output, so often your audience cannot see any difference. You can choose an algorithm based on rendering speed, the type of light casting the shadow, whether transparent objects are casting shadows, and the accuracy or softness of the shadows you require.

4.4.1 RENDERING SPEED

Raytraced shadows often take longer to render than depth-mapped shadows. To render each point of a scene with raytraced shadows, the renderer needs to check through the scene for shadow-casting objects between the light and the point being rendered. This process can take a while—especially for complex scenes.

A depth-mapped shadow can often render much more quickly than a raytraced shadow, because the geometry in the scene needs to be scanned only once (for the initial creation of the depth map). To render an image with depth-mapped shadows, the renderer can immediately look up each light's cutoff distance from the depth map, without needing to search the scene's geometry for shadow-casting objects while rendering each point.

4.4.2 TYPES OF LIGHTS

It is much easier for rendering software to render depth-mapped shadows from a spotlight than from an omnidirectional light. A depth map needs to store data for each angle a light shines, which can be more easily achieved for the limited range of angles defined by a spotlight's cone than for angles all the way around an omnidirectional light. Many programs make depth-mapped shadows available exclusively on spotlights. The programs that do allow depth-mapped shadows from omnidirectional lights require additional memory and time to render these shadows.

Raytraced shadows may be your only choice when casting shadows from lights that are not spotlights. Because not every program supports raytracing, some software allows only shadows from spotlights.

4.4.3 TRANSPARENCY SUPPORT

A raytraced shadow can appear lighter where the light has passed through a partially transparent surface, and darker where the light has been completely blocked by an opaque surface. When a raytracer encounters an intervening object that is transparent, it can block some of the light or can even recolor the light that will arrive in the shadow area. On the left side of Figure 4.20, the raytraced shadow is shaded to show the transparent parts of the model.

Because a depth map stores only a distance at each angle (not a brightness or color), it cannot represent a light being partially blocked at different distances by transparent objects. Depth maps are "all or nothing," usually creating the same shadow for a transparent object as for a completely opaque object, as seen on the right side of Figure 4.20.

Notice that the roll of tape inside the dispenser actually becomes darker with the depth-mapped shadow, because the shadow-casting light is not

4.20 A raytraced shadow (left) accurately represents transparency, but the depth-mapped shadow (right) does not.

illuminating it through the transparent plastic. When lighting with depth-mapped shadows, you sometimes need to add extra lights or exclude transparent surfaces from casting shadows to correct for this kind of problem.

Raytraced shadows can pick up the shape and color of a transparency map applied to a model. A transparency-mapped stained glass pattern is picked up in its shadow in Figure 4.21, for example. Depth-mapped shadows cannot do this, although similar output may be faked by projecting a colored pattern directly from the light source.

4.4.4 RESOLUTION

A raytraced shadow computed at each point in your rendering is very accurate. At whatever resolution you render a scene, a raytraced shadow can continue to be crisp and detailed.

The level of detail and accuracy in a depth-mapped shadow is limited to the resolution of the depth map. The resolution of the depth map is usually adjustable with a Shadow Map Size or Map Resolution setting. Raising the resolution of your shadow map can make a sharper and more accurate shadow, but also requires increased memory and rendering time.

Figure 4.22 shows a depth-mapped shadow with a resolution too low for the size of the area covered by the light. This shadow is broken up into square samples, although other rendering software may interpolate between samples differently, so that a low-resolution map looks softer rather than more blocky.

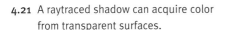

4.21 A raytraced shadow can acquire color from transparent surfaces.

4.22 Too low a resolution for a depth map can cause inaccurate shadows.

If you need crisp shadows over a wide area, raytraced shadows can be your best choice. Depth maps work best when they are used on spot-lights with a limited cone angle or covering a limited area. When a depth map is spread out over a large area, its resolution may need to be increased, although this uses more memory. A depth-map resolution of 512 uses one megabyte of your system memory per light, and a map resolution of 1024 uses four megabytes per light (if your software uses a typical four bytes per depth value).

If you choose to use depth-mapped shadows, you should follow a few guidelines to get the best results with a reasonable depth-map resolution:

- Focus the shadow-casting light on a specific, limited area of your scene that the depth map has enough resolution to cover.

- Adjust any spotlights that cast depth-mapped shadows to have as narrow a cone as possible, while still lighting the subject.

- If you need to illuminate and cast shadows over a large area, con-sider spacing out multiple lights to cover each part of the region instead of using just one light to illuminate the whole space. This will avoid depth map problems and also add desirable variation to the lighting of a large area.

- Some programs have an option to allow the light to overshoot the edge of its cone. If you need a light to cover a broad area, but the shadows themselves are only in a part of that area, you might con-sider such an option. This way, the cone can concentrate the depth-mapped shadows to a limited area, but the light spreads additional illumination without shadows in more directions.

- Another way to light a wide area with depth-mapped shadows is to light the scene with a light that does not cast shadows and then to add depth-mapped shadows in different locations, focused efficiently around your subject, with *shadows-only* lights, which are described later in this chapter.

- As a rule of thumb in most productions, if you are tempted to use a depth-map resolution higher than about 1024, you will usually be better off using raytraced shadows instead.

4.4.5 SOFTNESS

Crisp, hard-edged shadows are a convenient cliché in computer graphics; in real life, however, shadows are not always perfectly focused. In real life, the softness of shadows depends on the size and distance of the light source. A small or distant light source casts crisp shadows, such as the shadows from the sun or a bare light bulb. A larger light source, such as a panel of fluorescent lights or an overcast sky, casts soft shadows. Both depth-mapped and raytraced shadows can be made soft, but they are softened using different algorithms that do not produce equally realistic results.

A depth-mapped shadow can be made soft by blurring or interpolating the samples within the depth map. The amount of blurring to the shadow is set by adjusting a Softness, Sample Range, or Filter Size adjustment. A higher number means more blurring, and also takes a little more time to compute. A soft depth-map shadow is shown on the left side of Figure 4.23.

Raytraced shadows can be softened by using an area light, linear light, or any larger, more diffuse light source. Activating a Raytraced Soft Shadows option in some programs can also produce a similar diffusion of rays. As shown on the right side of Figure 4.23, raytraced soft shadows grow softer with distance from the object casting them. This effect is

4.23 A depth-map shadow (left) is blurred to make a soft shadow, but a shadow raytraced from an area light (right) begins in focus and diffuses with distance from the subject.

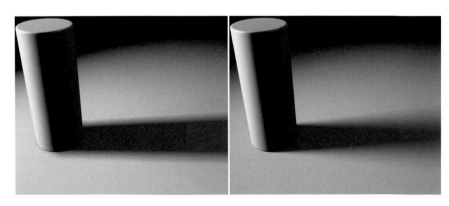

what occurs in nature when light is emitted from a more diffuse area rather than a single point source.

Raytraced soft shadows can add greatly to your quality of shading, but come at a prohibitive price in terms of rendering time. The renderer works slowly because it has to sample and interpolate the shadow from several different points, sometimes doing as much work as if you had used an array of 9 or 16 lights in place of the one with soft shadows. Depth-mapped soft shadows remain a reasonably quick technique in comparison to raytraced soft shadows.

NOTE

Chapter 5, "Qualities of Light," contains a more detailed discussion of the uses and rendering of soft light sources.

4.5 FAKING SHADOWS

In some cases, adding one extra light that casts shadows to your scene can slow your rendering as much as adding 20 more lights that do not cast shadows. Shadow calculation is usually the slowest (or most "computationally expensive") part of rendering a light.

A number of techniques used in graphics production create "fake" shadows that look the same as a "real" shadow. These fake shadows, however, do not fully calculate at each frame based on intervening objects blocking the light. Therefore, when you really need the appearance of a shadow, but can't afford the computational expense of the calculation, you should consider these techniques.

4.5.1 ADDING A LIGHT WITH NEGATIVE BRIGHTNESS

One simple way to fake shadows is to add a light with a negative brightness. In many programs, a light with a negative number for its brightness or color can be used to darken an area of your scene, functioning similarly to a soft shadow in that area. Here's how to step it up:

1. Start with a scene that has no shadows. Without any tricks to fake shadows, the lack of shadows is obvious, and the connection between the vase and the ground is unconvincing.

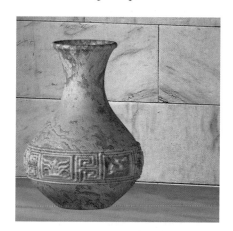

2. Aim a spotlight at the area where you would like to fake a shadow, near the bottom of your object. Do not set this or any other light in the scene to cast shadows.

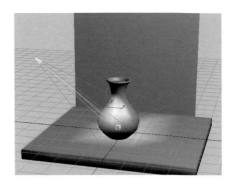

3. Test render and adjust your spotlight so that it brightens the area that a real shadow would normally darken. Exclude any object from the light that would not be receiving a shadow. In this case, the vase is excluded from the light.

4. Adjust the brightness (or multiplier) of your spotlight to a negative number so that it darkens the area rather than lightens it. The result will look very similar to a shadow, with far less computation required.

Most commonly, negative lights are used to subtly darken areas, such as darkening an area under a table or reducing the amount of light in the corner of a room. They also provide an attractive way to simulate soft shadows without slowing down your renderings.

4.5.2 USING 3D MODELS AS SHADOWS

In some renderings, you can use a 3D model to represent a shadow, as seen in Figure 4.24. This is an especially popular solution in real-time video games and simulations, when there is often no time or hardware capability to calculate true shadows. A few dark-colored polygons beneath a character or vehicle offer a simpler solution for representing a shadow.

The same technique of using a flat object to represent a shadow might also be used in some animations that are stylized to produce a cartoon look (if a detailed shadow shape might not be necessary). A simple circle might be constrained to move beneath a character if it would better fit with the drawing style than a complex shape. Generally this technique is used when the only shadow visible will be a shape cast onto a flat ground, not wrapping onto any other shapes or surfaces.

4.5.3 REDUCING THE NEED FOR SHADOWS

The simplest and most effective way to reduce your need for shadows is by carefully aiming and controlling your lights to avoid lighting your desired shadow areas in the first place. Just making sure that the area is outside a spotlight's beam or beyond the attenuation range of the light or excluded from a selectively linked light source can save you and your software a lot of time.

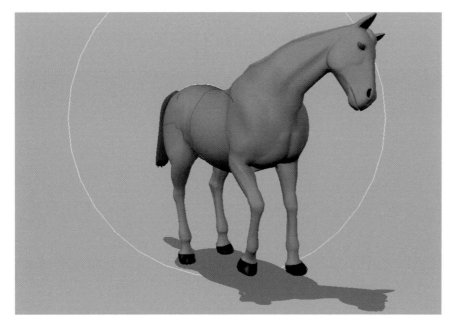

4.24 A polygon mesh can be generated to look like a shadow, generated here by Poser (from MetaCreation).

A lampshade on a lamp is usually thought to cast a shadow, for example. As shown in Figure 4.25, however, replacing the light bulb with a set of lights, one pointing upward and one pointing downward, can create the two cones of light that escape from the shade, without a need for shadow computation. The third light is a dimmer, omnidirectional light that doesn't need to cast shadows, either. This third light adds the effect of light passing through the translucent shade. This combination of lights, when properly aimed, can replace a shadow-casting light source and speed up rendering. It can also provide more direct control over the light from the lamp.

4.5.4 SHADOWS-ONLY LIGHTS

Sometimes, you want a particular light source to cast shadows, but don't want to add any more light to the scene. This is a job for a *shadows-only light*, a light that casts shadows but does not add any illumination. At the top of Figure 4.26, for example, lights are added around the two balls, adding both light and shadows. The shadows are added at different angles by the different lights. If you wanted to keep the shadows, but get rid of the extra illumination, the lights could be turned into shadows-only lights, as shown at the bottom of the figure.

4.5.4.1 POSSIBLE USES FOR SHADOWS-ONLY LIGHTS

In real life, there is no such thing as a shadows-only light. Shadows are places where part of a light's illumination is blocked; so if there is no

4.25 Carefully aimed lights avoid the need for shadow calculation.

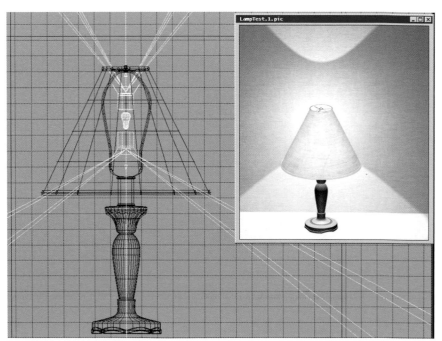

Although ordinary lights (top) add illumination as well as shadows, "shadows-only" lights (bottom) cast shadows without adding any light to the scene.

illumination, there are no shadows. Shadows-only lights are a special-purpose tool in computer graphics. You might find them handy in a variety of special situations:

- Shadows-only lights enable you to "cheat" and render scenes with shadows at implausible angles. Although this might seem to be unrealistic (as in Figure 4.26), the effect is seen in some paintings—if an artist painted from life as the sun moved through the sky, for example—and can be useful as a gag or stylistic device in your 3D scenes.

- Even if several different lights at different angles light your subject, a shadows-only light can enable you to render a single shadow at an angle of your choosing.

- Using a separate shadows-only light for your shadows enables you to create shadows as rich or dark as you need, even if there are bright lights around the scene that do not cast shadows.

- To make more efficient depth-mapped shadows that cover only small areas, you can illuminate the whole environment with nonshadow-casting light, and cast shadows in specific areas with shadows-only lights.

You might not use shadows-only lights every day, but they are a powerful tool to have available, just in case you need them.

4.5.4.2 SIMULATING SHADOWS-ONLY LIGHTS

Unless your software has a specific option or function for creating a shadows-only light, it is usually most effective to create a shadows-only light with the following steps:

1. Create a standard light source, such as a spotlight or point source. Turn on shadow-casting from this first light source so that it casts the shadows you want in your rendering.

2. To get rid of the illumination from the first light, create an exact duplicate of the first light, and leave the copy in the exact same position. Without moving either light, modify the copy in two ways: Turn shadow-casting off, and negate the value of the brightness or multiplier. (To "negate" the number, you change a 1.0 to a −1.0, or a 5 to a −5, and so on.)

The result of the setup is that the second light takes away the illumination of the first light and also takes away illumination from the area that was in the first light's shadow. Together, your pair of lights serves as a shadows-only light source, and any visible illumination of the subject can come from a completely different source. Note that there will be no illumination in the scene from this pair of lights. You need to add another light to the scene to see anything illuminated. Shadows-only lights can be simulated in this way with either depth-mapped or raytraced shadows.

4.5.5 KNOWING WHEN TO FAKE

Use your own judgment as to whether you need to use any cheats or manipulations for your shadows. With computers getting faster, and production schedules always placing demands on your own time, it might not be worthwhile to spend extra time setting up a fake shadow just to speed up a rendering.

On the other hand, learning to think on your feet, and cheating or manipulating any aspect of your rendering, are valuable skills. You are always better off knowing 10 ways to achieve something than to be boxed in to a single type of solution.

Some cheats and tricks are useful not just for saving rendering time, but for giving you more convenient and direct control over your output, to enable you to create the most appropriate shadow qualities for your scene.

4.6 EXERCISES

When you pay attention to your shadows, the improvement to your renderings can be worth the effort and experimentation you invest in them. To focus on shadows, ask yourself some questions about the use of shadows that you see in movies and photographs that you admire, and in your own work.

1. Rent a movie and pause it at some specific frames. Where do you see shadows? Are they all cast from the same light? Are the shadows hard or soft? Does the darkness of the shadows seem to match the level of contrast in the scene?

2. Examine a close-up picture of a person. Do shadows fall on the person's face? Can you tell the angle of the lighting from the shadows?

3. Look at some of the renderings you have created previously. Do the shadows serve any of the visual functions mentioned in this chapter? Are the quantity, darkness, and softness of the shadows appropriate to the scene? Do detail and shading appear in the shadow areas?

5

QUALITIES OF LIGHT

WHAT MAKES ONE light different from another? Different light sources, such as sunlight and moonlight, lamplight and firelight, each add a unique and recognizable look to a scene. The traits that make each kind of light source look unique are called *qualities of light*. This chapter explores the five qualities of light that you need to notice and understand in the real world, and how to convincingly simulate them in your 3D renderings.

5.1 DESCRIBING LIGHTS

An almost unlimited number of adjectives can be applied when describing light, and any of them could be referred to as a "quality of light." This chapter explores in detail the following five qualities of light:

- Softness

- Intensity

- Color

- Throw

- Animation

This is not a definitive list of all words that could be called qualities of light. Instead, these five areas are my recommended outline of the recognizable attributes of a real light source that are worthy of study when examining a real light, and that are important to reproduce in your 3D scenes.

Many other words that people might call a "quality of light" actually fall into one of the five categories listed here. The quality of being "dappled," for example, describes a light's *throw*; a "flickering" light describes its *animation*; and a "warm" light describes its *color*. More about all these qualities follows in this chapter.

A successful interpretation of the five qualities of light can add a real light's distinctive look to your 3D renderings and help separate you from your competition.

5.2   SOFTNESS

One very important quality of light that is often reproduced poorly in computer graphics is *softness*. It is possible to simulate either hard or soft light in your renderings.

The most commonly used light sources in computer graphics produce *hard* light. Hard light is light that is sharply focused, as if it originates from a very small or very distant source. Hard light is recognizable because it casts very crisp shadows and usually creates small, tight highlights. Figure 5.1 is lit by a standard spotlight with raytraced shadows, producing very hard light. Notice that the illumination cuts off sharply between the light and dark areas of the rendering, and there is a bright, focused highlight on some of the objects.

5.1 This scene is illuminated by hard light.

Soft light is slightly more difficult to re-create in the computer than hard light, but it occurs just as frequently in real life. Soft light is light that has been diffused or scattered in some way. Light from a light bulb could be made soft by passing through a cloth lampshade, for example, or light from the sun could be softened by an overcast sky. Soft light is recognizable because it casts diffused, soft-edged shadows rather than crisp ones and illuminates surfaces with broader, less-focused highlights and shading. Figure 5.2 is lit with an area light, producing very soft lighting.

5.2.1 HOW HARD OR SOFT SHOULD A LIGHT BE?

Both hard and soft lights exist in real life, so you should learn to use an appropriate amount of softness in each lighting design. Some of the times when you would want to use hard light are as follows:

- To simulate illumination that comes directly from a small, concentrated light source, such as a bare light bulb hanging in a room.

- To mimic direct sun on a clear day.

- To illuminate space scenes. Because the light reaches objects without being diffused through an atmosphere, you can use very hard light.

- To call attention to an artificial light source, such as when a spotlight is focused on a circus performer.

5.2 This scene is illuminated by soft light.

- To project shadows with clearly defined shapes, such as when you want your audience to recognize a villain by watching his shadow on a wall.

- To light inhospitable environments. Hard light is generally very harsh and makes people uncomfortable.

On the other hand, you would use soft lighting as follows:

- For natural light on cloudy days, when you would not get very bold shadows.

- For indirect light, such as light that has reflected off walls or ceilings, which is generally very soft.

- For light that has been transmitted through translucent materials, such as curtains or lampshades.

- To make a scene more inviting. Soft light tends to make many environments look more comfortable or relaxing, and can make most subjects look more natural or organic. Most interior lighting fixtures in a home are designed to either diffuse the light or bounce the light to soften the light from a light bulb.

- On characters when they are portrayed favorably or made to look beautiful. Close-up shots of many movie stars, especially female lead actresses in Hollywood movies, are frequently soft lit.

- To help renderings look more realistic, and less like computer graphics. Technical limitations have historically made extremely hard light a staple of most 3D renderings, and using soft light avoids this recognizable cliché.

5.2.2 RENDERING SOFT LIGHT

Most common types of 3D light, such as standard point lights and spotlights, originate from an infinitely small point in space, not diffusing the light at all, and produce a hard light. Several options are available for rendering soft light, however, and you can simulate soft light with almost any rendering software.

5.2.2.1 AREA LIGHTS

An area light is one of the most powerful tools for creating soft lighting in computer graphics. Area lights represent a naturally diffused, soft light source that comes from a specified area rather than a single point. The larger the size of an area light, the softer the light and shadows will be, as shown in Figure 5.3.

5.3 The shadow of the apple shows the softness increasing with the area light size.

Even though they can produce very attractive output, area lights are not a practical everyday rendering solution for a majority of people working in computer graphics. It can take a prohibitively long time to render scenes with area lights casting shadows, putting them out of reach of most animators rendering on tight deadlines.

NOTE

The use of area lights and linear lights is discussed in more detail in Chapter 2, "Lighting Workflow."

5.2.2.2 SIMULATING AREA LIGHTS

Soft lighting is not limited to the lucky few with the software and hardware capable of using the most sophisticated rendering algorithms. You can achieve results similar to an area light by following these steps:

1. Start with your subject lit by a single spotlight, as shown in Figure 5.4.

2. If possible, use depth-mapped shadows with soft edges, as in Figure 5.5. The result of this doesn't look much like an area light yet, but it helps eliminate the hard edge of the shadow.

3. Reduce the brightness (or multiplier) of the light to about 20% of its former value.

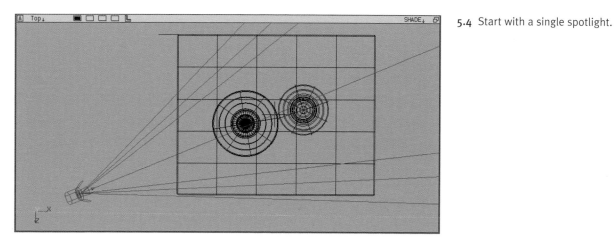

5.4 Start with a single spotlight.

4. Make four more copies of the light, with exactly the same settings. Space the copies slightly apart from one another, as shown in Figure 5.6.

5. Render the scene. The result in Figure 5.7 is similar to an area light, although the scene rendered much more quickly.

The soft shadows can be made smoother and more continuous by increasing the number of individual lights in the row, although this can add to your rendering time.

As with an area light, the shadows in Figure 5.7 become more diffused with distance from the subject. The shadow near the base of the lamp is focused, while the shadow on the back wall is diffused.

5.5 One spotlight does not produce very soft lighting.

5.6 A row of lights softens and diffuses the illumination.

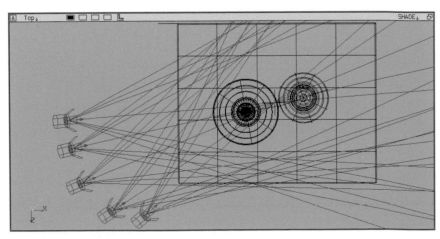

5.7 A "simulated area light" can produce very effective soft lighting.

5.2.2.3 THE VISUAL CUES OF SOFT LIGHTING

In addition to the option of using multiple lights to simulate a soft light source, several different parameters in your scene can help create a softened look. Follow these tips to imitate some of the visual cues usually presented by soft light:

- Avoid tight, specular highlights. Set your materials or shaders to render broader, less-crisp highlights.

- If you are simulating very soft light, such as the reflected light from a wall, do not make that light cast any specular highlights at all. Many programs have an option on the light to disable specular highlights.

- Add additional fill lights to extend the illumination of the key light and prevent the key light from cutting off suddenly at any edge.

- Avoid hard-edged shadows. If area lights or other raytraced soft shadows aren't available, use depth-mapped shadows from a spot-light, which can be softened.

- Adjust the falloff or spread angle of a spotlight's cone so that the edge of the cone of light fades away softly.

By paying attention to visual cues such as these, Figure 5.8 was rendered without the use of any area lights.

The illumination on the bather's back is as soft as you would expect with a large window nearby. The softness results from using multiple light sources to soften and distribute the light, combined with appropriate surface adjustments on the objects. Figure 5.9 shows the location of the careful lighting arrangement of 24 point- and spotlights.

Using these techniques is not just a "workaround" to avoid area lights, it is actually the most common solution to soft lighting used in professional productions. To date, most shots using computer-generated imagery in feature films have been rendered without any extensive use of raytracing,

5.8 "The Bather" rendered by Jeremy A. Engleman (art.net/~jeremy).

5.9 "The Bather" layout in LightWave 3D shows the multiple light sources.

radiosity, or area lights; instead, they have been rendered using spotlights and depth-mapped shadows for most shadow casting.

As a part of a complete lighting design, your choice of simple, effective, controllable tools does not necessarily hurt your production values. In fact, using whichever software functions enable you to render and test-render your scene efficiently is the best approach to building more ambitious projects, without straining your system or your patience with more expensive rendering techniques.

5.3 INTENSITY

One of the most noticeable qualities of light is its intensity (or "brightness.") In Chapter 3's discussion of three-point lighting, the intensity of the light was the primary determiner of whether a light was a key light or a fill light, and what role it would play in illuminating your subject.

You can control the intensity of a light by the brightness of its RGB color, or by a separate "brightness" or "multiplier" setting. Some programs also include global or grouped lighting controls, which modify the intensity of all or several lights at once with a single setting.

Whether you are seeing a scene lit by the sun or by a candle, your eyes adjust to the brightness of the environment. When properly exposed, a film or video recording can use just as bright a tone to portray the light from a candle in a dimly lit room as it uses to represent sunlight in another scene.

Most 3D programs do not include a simulation of a camera's exposure settings, which would adjust a real camera to function in brighter or dimmer environments. As a result, in computer graphics, your light's intensity is used more directly toward the brightness of the final output, instead of being relative to a camera's adjustments.

Because a light's appearance changes in every differently exposed scene, the same type of light, such as a common household lamp, often needs to be given a different intensity in each scene in which it appears. If you had rendered a scene that was lit only by the lamp, you would probably choose a fairly high intensity, as shown in Figure 5.10.

If the same lamp were next to a sunlit window, however, the brightness of the lamp's illumination would probably have to be adjusted to be much dimmer, to realistically represent the same bulb, as seen in Figure 5.11.

5.10 A single lamp can be adjusted to appear very bright to simulate a light-sensitive exposure.

5.11 When the sun is a dominant light source, the same lamp needs to appear much dimmer.

This means that the intensity of lights in most computer software is not "portable" data, like other object attributes, and should be rethought before it is copied into different scenes. It also means that no chart or library of presets would be useful in matching the brightness of a specific kind of light source as it would appear on film (if your renderer does not also simulate the camera's exposure process).

NOTE

Chapter 7, "Exposure," explains much more about the brightness of lights in your 3D scene.

5.3.1 ATTENUATION

In addition to lights appearing at different intensities relative to different exposures, another factor that can change the intensity of illumination from a light is the distance between your subject and the light. In real life, the illumination an object receives from a light decreases as the object moves farther away from the light source. If you hold your hand next to a light bulb, it can be very brightly lit. If you move your hand a few feet away, however, the illumination on your hand falls off to a more moderate value. The decrease in intensity as you move away from a light is called *attenuation*.

As light radiates from a point in real life, illumination attenuates in an *Inverse Square* pattern. Inverse Square attenuation means that the illumination reaching a point on an object equals the intensity of the light at the source, divided by the square of its distance from the object, which could be written like this:

Illumination at an object = Intensity ÷ Distance ^2

Note that, according to the Inverse Square equation, there is no "cutoff" distance. A light can illuminate any object in the scene, no matter how far away, if the light is bright enough. The intensity keeps getting cut in half, diminishing to much lower values, without ever being forced to hit zero. Even though the light could keep going forever, from a practical standpoint, at some distance from the light its illumination will cease to make a visible difference in your scene.

With Inverse Square falloff, the intensity of the light will also control the size of the area it visibly illuminates. A brighter light will illuminate a bigger part of the scene. If a light is very dim, it will visibly brighten only a small area and can quickly cease to be visible.

5.3.2 ATTENUATION IN COMPUTER GRAPHICS

Most software enables you to adjust a light's attenuation in some respects. The controls are also called "falloff," "distance falloff," or "decay."

5.3.2.1 INVERSE SQUARE

Although it is closest to representing light in real life, Inverse Square is not the most user-friendly type of attenuation. The fact that an Inverse Square falloff pattern varies the light by such a great extent means that it is prone to creating hotspots near the light and underlit areas farther away, as shown in Figure 5.12. The fact that a real light does not have any absolute cutoff distance makes it computationally expensive to calculate every light's illumination all the way to the far corners of the scene, even where the light is too dim to make a visible difference.

As a result of these problems, Inverse Square is not the only attenuation pattern used in computer graphics, nor even the most common. Some programs do not even offer an Inverse Square falloff pattern, and others make it optional.

5.3.2.2 LINEAR ATTENUATION

A linear attenuation pattern makes the gradient between light and dark progress more evenly than in real life, as shown in Figure 5.13. A linear falloff means that the distance at which a light will have completely decayed can be set, and illumination will decrease evenly from the

5.12 An Inverse Square falloff concentrates light near its source.

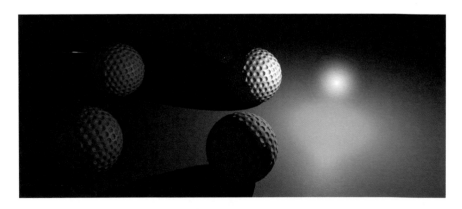

5.13 The linear falloff is easy to control, but not perfectly realistic.

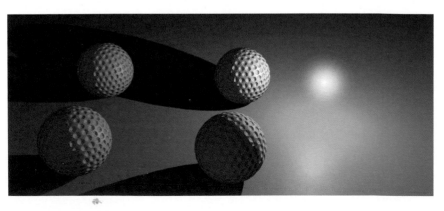

light's full brightness down to zero as it travels from the source out to that distance.

A linear falloff creates very controllable, predictable illumination. After setting a maximum falloff distance, for example, you would know that at half that distance from the light, the light would be half of its full intensity.

Some programs do not give a choice of falloff patterns, so the word "linear" never appears in their interfaces. If a rendering system asks for a beginning and ending falloff distance only, that software is most likely using a linear falloff, even if it is not labeled as such.

5.3.2.3 NO ATTENUATION

It is possible to define lights that have no attenuation. A light with no attenuation would illuminate an object located across the room just as brightly as an object right next to the light. This can sometimes be convenient, because a single brightness level can be chosen without thinking about the distance to each subject. Unfortunately, the result may sometimes look less convincing in your rendering than if you use an attenuating light.

Figure 5.14 does not use any attenuation. You can see that the balls farther from the light are lit just as brightly as the balls close to the light. The result is not as realistic as an attenuating light.

Studying Figure 5.14, notice that even with no attenuation, the ground is still brightest directly under the light. This is not a function of distance, only of angle. The brightness of surfaces still depends on the surface's angle relative to the light, and other brightness differences are created because the light can still be limited by shadows. The result is that there is still some shading and variation visible in the scene, even without attenuation.

5.14 Without attenuation, the light continues at full brightness all the way across the environment.

In some cases, having no attenuation can produce the most realistic output. In a scene with light coming in through a window, for example, the light often does not need any attenuation. If you place a light immediately outside of a set, shining through a window as shown in Figure 5.15, you would probably use no attenuation. Because real sunlight would have already traveled millions of miles to reach the house, those last few feet would make proportionately too little difference to be visible. Using no attenuation would simulate the sun better than using "true" Inverse Square starting at a nearby light. (The light position shown in Figure 5.15 was used to render Figure 5.16 and similar images.)

5.3.2.4 CONSERVATION OF LIGHT

In real life, a light source produces a finite amount of light, no matter how spread out or how concentrated that light may be. A real-life spotlight can be adjusted to a "spot" setting for a narrow beam, for example, or turned to a "flood" setting for a wider beam. Because it is still always producing the same total output of light, the narrow beam would be brighter when concentrated into a smaller beam, and the same light would look dimmer when spread into a wider beam.

The conservation of light is also what is primarily responsible for attenuation. Contrary to popular belief, the rays of light have not "faded away" or been absorbed by the atmosphere. In reality, the more distant object is just receiving a much smaller percentage of the total light output from the source, with the rest of the light having traveled at a different angle and having missed the object. The Inverse Square equation is a simple function of geometry: As the light's cone gets wider with distance, the percentage of the light that would hit an object within the cone decreases as a proportion of the width times the height of the cone.

5.15 Using a nearby spotlight to simulate the sun through a window is a case where attenuation might be unrealistic.

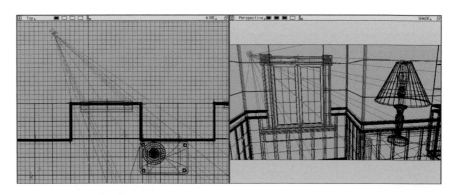

5.4 COLOR

Different types of light sources can be recognized by the different colors of light they typically produce. Most household light bulbs emit light tinted slightly yellow or orange, for example, compared to daylight, which is bluer in color. Reproducing these natural colors of light can produce a more realistic rendering, as in Figure 5.16.

Just as your eyes adjust to a brighter or dimmer environment, your perception of color adjusts to different dominant colors of light. A white shirt will still look white whether you are inside where it is lit by a lamp or outdoors under the blue sky. Cameras and film also are color-balanced for different environments and types of light. A light source in computer graphics does not need to stick to any one hue from scene to scene, but should be given a relative value that can shift with the dominant environment or be adjusted to how you want to portray that light.

As a quality of light, a light's color is one of the ways that a viewer guesses where a light is coming from. In Figure 5.17, for example, light is coming from a junction in the center of the hallway. Although you can't see what's around the corner, the bluish color of the light suggests that somehow this is an opening to the outdoors and that daylight is entering the subway station.

In real life, as in the previous two figures, the illumination in your scene usually has more than one hue. Even if there were only one color of light source in a real scene, different colors from the surrounding environment would still be picked up by reflected light, and this adds a diversity of light colors. Using more than one color of light is usually a good idea in most of your renderings, regardless of whether different kinds of light sources are used in the scene.

> **NOTE**
>
> Chapter 6, "Color," discusses in detail the colors of natural light sources and the process of simulating a camera's color balance.

5.16 Lamplight can appear more yellow in tint; sunlight and daylight are bluer.

5.17 A different color quality suggests that the opening in the center of the hallway might lead outdoors.

Color is more than just another quality of light. Color can set the mood or even change the meaning of your rendering. A great deal of thought can go into an artist's choice of colors and color schemes. Chapter 6, "Color," explores the uses and meanings of color in general, and explains how to reproduce the colors of different light sources under different conditions.

5.5 THROW

Few lights illuminate a subject completely evenly. Instead, there is usually a pattern or shape to the illumination. The *throw*, or "throw pattern" of a light, is the quality of how the light is broken up, patterned, or shaped. The lamp in Figure 5.18 creates two arcs of light on the wall, for example, with an area of duller illumination (from the light transmitted through the shade) in between the arcs.

5.18 The lamp's shade is responsible for its throw pattern.

The ordinary adjustments that you make whenever you aim a spotlight and adjust the width and softness of its cone are already changing the throw pattern of your lights. For more complex patterns, other approaches are possible in most software.

5.5.1 CREATING THROW PATTERNS WITH TEXTURE MAPS

The most powerful option available for adjusting the throw pattern at the light source itself is the option to map a texture or image into the light. A "projector" or "projection image" option essentially turns a spotlight into something similar to a slide projector, projecting an image of your choice into the scene. In Figure 5.19, the light is given a dappled throw pattern that looks as if the light had filtered through trees.

You can design a texture map that blocks light where it is black and that allows more light through with brighter tones. These texture maps applied to lights can create all kinds of throw patterns, simulating light passing through certain-shaped windows or shrubbery, or almost any other throw pattern needed for a light source. The key light used in Figure 5.19 was texture mapped with the map shown in Figure 5.20.

5.19 The dappled throw pattern suggests that sunlight has passed through trees.

5.20 This map on the light functions similarly to a cookie.

5.5.2 GOBOS AND COOKIES

In film lighting, specially cut sheets of wood and metal called *gobos* (short for go-betweens) and *cookies* (also known as a "cucoloris") are used with very much the same result as putting a map on a light. Some cookies are simple geometric forms to reshape the light beam; others break the light into a pattern. Instead of being mounted directly on the light, large gobos can be mounted on their own stands to block, shadow, and reshape light in the scene. A gobo, like any object placed in front of a light, can reshape the light by casting shadows.

In a 3D scene, any shadow-casting object you place in front of a light can be considered a type of cookie. The cookie changes the throw pattern of a light, based on the shape and transparency of the surface blocking the light. Colored transparent surfaces can filter and change light sources, such as when sunlight becomes dappled and greenish by filtering through tree leaves, or light takes on different colors after passing through a stained glass window, as in Figure 5.21.

With raytraced shadows, light shining through transparency-mapped surfaces picks up the transparency map's colors and tones as a part of the throw pattern. With depth-mapped shadows, transparent surfaces might not cast appropriate shadows, but solid objects can still cast shadows that break up a light and thus change its throw pattern. The shadow of venetian blinds on a window can break up any light into a striped throw pattern, as shown in Figure 5.22.

> **NOTE**
>
> Differences between raytraced and depth-mapped shadows were discussed in more detail in Chapter 4, "Shadows."

5.21 A light picks up a new throw pattern from a transparent surface.

5.22 The shadows of venetian blinds create a new throw pattern for a light.

5.5.3 EFFECTS OF THROW PATTERNS

Different throw patterns of light can change the appearance of the objects and the atmosphere in your scene.

The volumetric effect used in Figures 5.21 and 5.22 visibly links the throw pattern on the wall with the light source that motivates it. Activating a volumetric (or "fog") option on your light source shows the effect of the light's throw pattern in space by making the stripes of light visible where they leak through the blinds. Even though volumetric lighting effects are controlled as properties of individual lights in most 3D programs, a volumetric lighting effect is not itself a quality of light. Volumetric or fog effects are designed to simulate smoke or dust in the atmosphere, which should appear to be illuminated with the same throw pattern that illuminates the surfaces of objects.

A striped throw pattern, such as the shadow of venetian blinds, can be an interesting way to define contours of a three-dimensional form. Even though straight slats might cast the shadows, the lines of the throw pattern will become curved when they illuminate a rounded object, as seen in Figure 5.23.

Reproducing various throw patterns of lights is one of the biggest boosts you can give to the realism of your scene. As you look around your home or office, pay attention to the diverse range of throw patterns that can be cast by different light sources so that you can get more ideas for how to enrich your 3D lights with realistic throw patterns.

5.23 A striped throw pattern can define the contours of a three-dimensional form.

5.6 ANIMATION

Many light sources are distinctive because of their animated qualities. Whether it's the flicker of a candle flame, the pulsing lights on top of a fire engine, the sun moving behind a cloud, or the shifting blue glow of a television, you recognize some types of light sources by the distinctive ways that they change over time. Lights can be animated to change in a number of ways, including changing the light's position, animating parameters of the light, or animating shadow-casting objects in front of a light.

5.6.1 MOVING THE LIGHT

Animating the positions of your lights can add an exciting, dynamic shift to a 3D scene. One of the most common situations where you see a moving light source in real life is with lights attached to vehicles, such as a car's headlights. When a car drives past a building, especially when the car turns a corner, headlights are sometimes seen sweeping past the building, casting a changing pattern of light into interior rooms at night, as shown in Figure 5.24. This is especially appropriate if a setting is supposed to look cheap or uncomfortable, like a motel built too close to a highway.

Animating a car's headlights is easy, especially if you don't see the car itself:

1. Set up a few "dummy" or "null" objects in your scene.

2. Group or constrain a pair of spotlights to the nulls, as shown in Figure 5.25.

3. Animate the position of the group including the spotlights to make it drive straight down a road, or animate the position and rotation of the group to make the headlights turn corners.

5.24 A car's headlights create moving light and shadows in a room.

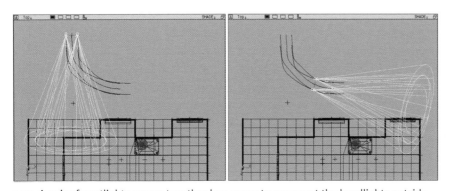

5.25 A pair of spotlights moves together in a group to represent the headlights outside.

5.26 A moving train projects animated lights into the surrounding environment. See the animation Train.mov online at 3dRender.com/light/ Train.mov.

In some scenes, most of the lights in the scene will be animated. A train speeding through a dark environment would introduce a number of moving lights as it travels through the scene, for example, as in Figure 5.26.

Keep these other tips in mind when adding moving lights to a scene:

- A pair of spotlights on top of a police car needs only to be rotated in place to create the effect of the lights accompanying the police siren.

- Rotating lights can be used as a warning outside of loading dock doors that are about to open or when alarms are sounding, and can be applied to doors in space ports or other fictional settings in which someone needs to be alerted to something.

- The sun travels across the sky during the day. Normally the actual motion would require only an animated light if you were simulating a time-lapse (sped-up) shot.

- Helicopters searching a city block with a search light from the air can create an impressive moving light show.

- If a scene is set relative to a moving vehicle, lights such as streetlights can be animated to pass by outside or in the background to simulate the motion of the vehicle itself.

In real life, lights move in many situations. It would be a mistake to animate other parts of a 3D scene but forget to animate your lights.

5.6.2 ANIMATING LIGHT PARAMETERS

Besides moving lights through space, another way to animate lights is to animate the parameters that define the light itself, such as the color, brightness, or other adjustable settings on the light.

The process of animating light parameters varies in different programs, but often there is just a "key" button within the light dialog box or control panel that enables you to record any change to a setting at a particular key frame. The most commonly animated lighting effect is turning the brightness up and down to simulate the light being turned on and off. To animate flashing lights, such as the lights on a marquee, the brightness of each light might be repeatedly changed between zero and full brightness, as shown in Figure 5.27.

5.27 Just animating a light's brightness can create flashing-light effects.

Sometimes turning a light off can be animated over a few frames. Some lights may change color and become redder as the electricity fed to them is reduced. There are other common times when you could keyframe the color or brightness of a light:

- **When a character enters a room.** You could have him turn on a light switch and animate the brightness of some lights in the scene to increase at that moment.

- **To animate traffic lights and signal lights.** Turn on and off individual light sources behind different lenses of the light.

- **To mimic a fire or TV's flickering light.** Don't turn the light all the way off; from frame to frame, just slightly vary the brightness and color for light that comes from television sets or burning fires.

- **For bursts of illumination.** Use animated lights wherever there is a visual effect, such as a laser beam, that could cast a burst of illumination onto the scene.

5.6.3 ANIMATED COOKIES

Because you can use any objects you want to cast shadows and function as cookies, one of your options is to use animated objects. Putting an animated object in front of a light can cast moving shadows and animated throw patterns, even if the light itself is not animated. Just rotating an object, such as a fan blade, in front of a light can create an animated flickering light in your scene, as seen in Figure 5.28. If the light were below the fan rather than above it, a similar flickering light would be visible on the ceiling.

5.28 Animating a fan blade to rotate can create animated shadows.

Animated lights can add greatly to the realism and visual interest of your scene.

With lights moved or attached to moving vehicles, lights that flicker or change on their own, and lights shadowed by moving or changing objects, you have many possibilities to find animated lights in the real world. Throughout the day, watch different light sources and notice the motion or changes in the illumination and shadows around you.

5.7 EXERCISES

Take the time to study the different qualities of light in the real world and double-check them as you adjust the lighting of your 3D scenes. For a particular light, ask yourself about the five qualities from this chapter:

1. **Softness.** Are the illumination and shadows created by the light crisp and hard-edged or more diffused?

2. **Intensity.** Is the light the brightest light in the scene, or does it appear dim relative to other lights in the environment? How bright do objects look at different distances from the light?

3. **Color.** Does the light have any kind of color, from a colored source, or from reflecting off of colored surfaces? If there is more than one type of light source in the scene, can you see any hue difference between them?

4. **Throw.** How evenly does the light illuminate objects around it? Does it cast any kind of shape or pattern into the environment?

5. **Animation.** Is the light completely consistent, or does it flicker or change in any way? Could anything cause the light to move or change?

After you can answer these questions about a light, in the real world or in your own work, you are on your way to richer, more compelling 3D renderings.

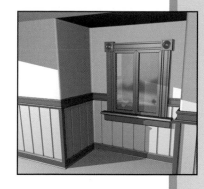

6

COLOR

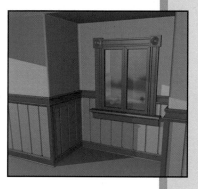

WHEN YOU WANT TO PLAY with your audience's emotions, few tools are more powerful than an intelligent use of color. This chapter explores the visual power of color in your 3D art. The right color scheme can create or enhance a mood, or even change the meaning of an image. But the use of color also has a technical side, and this chapter also delves into digital color reproduction, how to choose realistic colors for different types of light sources, and how colors are reproduced on film.

6.1 FROM PAINT TO DIGITAL

In your first art class, you probably were introduced to a *color wheel* like the one on the left side of Figure 6.1. You were taught that there were three *primary* colors: red, yellow, and blue.

In the field of computer graphics, the primary colors are red, *green*, and blue, instead of red, yellow, and blue. On the right side of Figure 6.1, you can see how colors are distributed differently around the computer's color wheel. For example, orange is much less plentiful on the computer's color wheel, but the shades of blue-green take up more of the spectrum. This means that it sometimes takes longer on the computer to find a precise shade of orange than it does to find a shade of aqua.

6.1 A painter's color wheel (left) uses different primary and secondary colors than the computer.

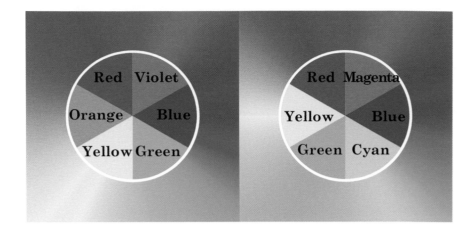

The two color wheels are designed differently to match how colors are mixed in their respective mediums. The traditional wheel (Figure 6.1, left) matches how colors of paint are mixed. Given red, yellow, and blue paint (along with some black and white to control brightness and saturation) almost any color can be mixed, which is why these three are called primary colors by artists. Combinations halfway between primary colors are called *secondary* colors. The secondary colors orange, green, and violet are also shown on the color wheel.

The wheel on the right side of Figure 6.1 is the distribution of colors as they are mixed on the computer, based on the *additive* primary colors that are used in RGB monitor displays, and the *subtractive* primary colors that are used in color printers.

6.1.1 ADDITIVE COLOR MIXING

Red, green, and blue are called the additive primary colors because any color of light can be represented by adding together red, green, and blue light in varying proportions. When red, green, and blue light are combined in equal proportions in a rendering, they form white light, as seen in Figure 6.2.

6.2 The additive primary colors combine to form white illumination.

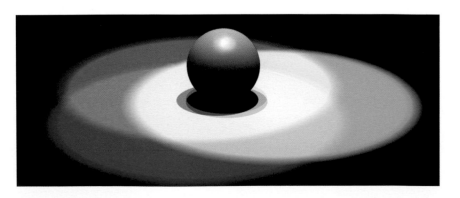

Colors in 3D graphics software are generally stored as RGB (Red Green Blue) colors. RGB colors consist of three numbers, representing the levels of red, green, and blue, respectively, that make up that color. Leading 3D graphics programs render their output in RGB color, as well as using RGB color to calculate the mixing and filtering of colored light.

6.1.2 SUBTRACTIVE COLOR MIXING

Printed output shows color differently than a computer monitor. A monitor starts out black, and emits red, green, and blue light. A printer starts with white paper, and adds a set of subtractive primary ink colors: cyan, magenta, and yellow.

The subtractive primaries are the complements of the additive primaries. *Complementary* colors are pairs of colors that are opposite each other on a color wheel. Each subtractive color serves an opposite function from its complement in that cyan ink absorbs red light (and reflects green and blue), magenta absorbs green light, and yellow absorbs blue light.

In theory, the three subtractive primary ink colors should be all you need to print a color picture. In practice, most full-color printing uses four ink colors: cyan, magenta, yellow, and black (abbreviated "CMYK"). The black can produce crisp text, and also reinforces the shading of the color image. A conventional four-color printed image, created by adding cyan, magenta, yellow, and black dots to the paper, is seen up close in Figure 6.3.

The color you see on your RGB monitor might not exactly match the appearance of a four-color print. Professionals in the publishing industry go to great lengths to calibrate their monitors to match different printers. The process of calibration is often done by sight: A printed image is held next to the monitor, while the monitor displays the same file that

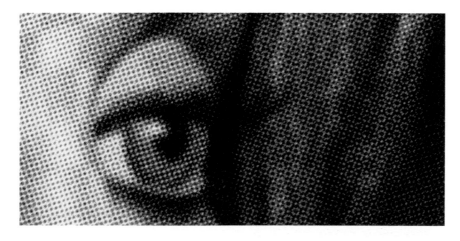

6.3 The subtractive primary colors are used in a four-color printing process.

was just printed. Adjustments to the monitor, and adjustments to display settings on the computer, are made until the computer display matches the printed colors as closely as possible. But even with the best adjustments, some colors appear differently on the monitor than in print, and test-prints are sometimes needed before committing to an important final print.

6.1.3 SATURATION

A color wheel only shows the possible different *hues* of a color, but does not show any changes in *saturation*. Hue is the aspect of a color that tells you its tint or location within the color spectrum, such as red, orange, or yellow. Saturation tells you the boldness or concentration of a color. A highly saturated color will appear rich, pure, and colorful. With less saturation, a color will become paler and less colorful. Colors with no saturation become a shade of gray, as shown on the right side of Figure 6.4.

It is a common mistake in 3D graphics to use too high a color saturation in your objects and lights. In real life, colors are not all as pure and saturated as they can appear in computer graphics. Colors that are slightly polluted, and slightly diluted, often produce more realistic results. For example, the red columns dominate the rendering on the left side of Figure 6.5, and are more realistic on the right side.

Your choice of colors is one of the most important decisions you make in creating an image. Even though your software offers you an enormous palette of possible colors, the art of selecting just the right colors can add greatly to the quality of your work.

6.4 Saturation is highest on the left side of the bar, and is reduced toward the right until the color fades into shades of gray.

6.5 Too saturated a color (left) can be unrealistic.

6.2 COLOR SCHEMES

The most striking images you can create will have a clearly defined *color scheme*, instead of using colors from all over the palette at random. A color scheme is the total set of colors that appear in a rendering. The color scheme creates a first impression, before your audience even interprets the shapes and subjects depicted in the image, and helps set the mood for the scene.

When you add a new color to an object or a light, you are not just setting one color, but are also adding to the color scheme of your image. People will interpret each color in relation to the rest of the color scheme, so forethought is necessary to design the most effective color scheme for your rendering.

You can develop a strong color scheme by choosing a small, consistent set of colors, and coloring every element in the scene with one of these specific colors. Often different kinds of objects in your scene will be given the same colors to maintain your color scheme. For example, in Figure 6.6, the green used in the woman's dress is also used in other parts of the scene, including the wallpaper.

The reuse of the same set of colors "ties together" the image. The yellow of the moon in the upper left of Figure 6.6 is picked up and reused on many objects inside the room, all the way down to the trim on the clothing and furniture in the lower right. Because of the adherence to a limited color scheme, every part of this image is unmistakably a part of the same scene.

6.2.1 COLOR CONTRAST

A color scheme can make use of *color contrast* to make some colors seem to "pop" from a scene, so they jump out and grab the viewer's attention.

6.6 The color scheme helps unify the composition. Scene by Jorge R. Gutierrez (www.mexopolis.com).

Figure 6.7 is a good example of color contrast—it is hard to look at the image without your eye being drawn immediately to the purple figure. The contrast between the purple and the rest of the color scheme makes it pop, not just the color's own hue or saturation.

6.2.1.1 COMPLEMENTARY COLORS

Color contrast is most visible when colors are surrounded by their complements. As noted previously, complementary colors are pairs of colors that are opposite each other on a color wheel. If you refer to Figure 6.1, you'll see that purple is opposite from yellow on the color wheel. This provides a maximum amount of contrast, and makes the purple color appear to be an even stronger and more noticeable color.

The reason complementary colors are called "complementary," instead of just "opposite," is that they work so well together—take advantage of them in your color schemes.

6.2.1.2 EXCLUSIVITY

Color contrast is also increased by concentrating a color in only one area. If purple had been squandered elsewhere in Figure 6.7, such as in a marble texture on the columns, then the purple figure would not carry the same graphic weight or attract the viewer's eye as readily.

Washing a scene with a color of light changes people's perception of the color, by taking away its exclusivity. For example, on the left side of Figure 6.8, the blue looks crisp, solid, and colorful. On the right, the scene is lit only by blue light, so the blue paint no longer pops. The blue

6.7 A limited palette of colors builds a strong color scheme in Lonnie Bailey's "Jester."

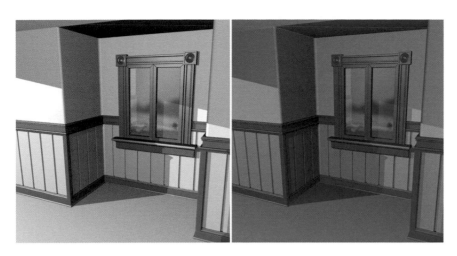

paint blends into what appears to be an oppressive, blue atmosphere, and changes the impression created by the color. On the right, the room no longer looks as colorful.

6.2.2 MEANINGS OF COLORS

Why is the logo of a bank, insurance company, or hospital likely to be blue, while the logo of a fast-food restaurant is likely to be orange? The colors you choose in your color schemes can convey subtle impressions, and trigger different associations in your audience.

6.2.2.1 CULTURALLY SPECIFIC ASSOCIATIONS

Some colors are given meaning through associations within a particular culture. An obvious example is that colors from a nation's flag could be considered "patriotic" colors, or could signify authority, or traditional values, in a particular culture. Colors from another nation's flag might look more foreign, or might not even seem to match as well, as compared in Figure 6.9. Color associations through a nation's art, religion, traditions, and popular culture, can give different colors different meanings in each culture.

You may animate a character playing golf in Miami, Florida, and give him pink golf pants to show him in the spirit of his vacation. Some people will recognize pink as a popular local color in Miami, or may find humor in a golfer's lack of fashion sense. Other viewers might have prejudices about men wearing pink, and misinterpret your intentions. It is a vexing problem that production design elements such as colors will be interpreted by so many different people, in so many different ways. Green may be the color of a popular political party in one country, and a feared paramilitary group in another. White may be the color of

6.9 Colors from a nation's flag are an example of culturally specific interpretations of color.

innocence in one culture, and the color of death in another. If you show your work in public, there is no way to avoid having it interpreted differently by different people.

6.2.2.2 SHARED ASSOCIATIONS

Other colors have more generally recognized associations around the world. Blue is recognized as the color of the ocean and the sky. Pastel blues can make an image appear soothing or calm. Deeper, bolder blues can look solid and majestic. (This could be one reason that so many banks and insurance companies use blue logos, although other theories and associations could also factor into that decision.)

Red may trigger alarm because it is the color of blood and fire. Hot colors, including reds, oranges, and yellows are generally thought to be spicy, exciting, zippy, attention-grabbing colors. A fast-food restaurant might use orange or yellow in its logo and décor to capture this spirit.

Even very subtle tints in a scene's lighting can help create impressions about a scene. A blue-tinted light can create the impression of winter or night air, and make a location or a person look colder. A slightly red or yellow light can make an environment look more warm and cozy, or make a scene look more intimate or personal. (See the "Color Temperature" section later in this chapter for more about colors associated with different light sources and locations.)

Any experience that people have in common can lead to common color associations. In addition to sharing some of the basic colors of nature, the expansion of global media exposes much of the world to a common body of images and color choices, through film, television, art, fashion, and advertising. Thanks to the world's mass media, red is globally recognized not just as the color of natural constants like blood and fire, but of brand names like Coca-Cola.

6.2.2.3 CONTEXTUAL ASSOCIATIONS

Within a narrative film, the meanings of specific colors, like any other symbols, can be redefined. When a shot exists as a part of a story, it will be interpreted differently than if the same image appeared in print or stood on its own. If something is important to a plot, or important to a character within the film, then its presence on the screen becomes a meaningful symbol.

Characters or groups of characters can have their own color schemes in a larger animation, which might be used in their home environment, costumes, props, or even skin colors. Once an audience is subconsciously accustomed to certain colors appearing with your villains, any new element introduced into the film would appear sinister if it used the villains' colors. Like musical motifs, color schemes can follow not just characters, but themes, emotions, or other recurring aspects of a film.

6.2.3 COLOR AND DEPTH

Another way that color choices can affect perception is by serving as a *depth cue*. A depth cue is a hint that viewers will perceive in an image, that helps form an impression about which objects are in the foreground, and which recede into the distance.

6.2.3.1 WARM AND COOL COLORS

Often people perceive colors that are cooler (blue and sometimes green) as being further away, and hot colors (especially red and orange) as being nearby.

Even with no other depth cues, most people will find it easier to see the left side of Figure 6.10 as a frame with a hole in the middle, and see the right side as being a small box in front of a larger square.

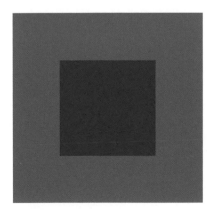 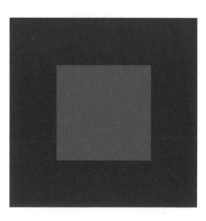

6.10 Other factors being equal, red appears closer than blue.

There are different theories about why this happens. One reason could be that, in natural environments, many subjects are seen against blue sky or green foliage backgrounds, so people naturally consider blue and green colored areas to be "background." People might also focus more attention in nature on warmer brown tones, and red and yellow subjects, such as a red piece of fruit, a wound, or the flesh tones of a person or animal, than on colors of foliage or sky.

Another reason that blue may appear to be further away is due to *chromatic aberration* in people's eyes. Chromatic aberration is based on the same principle through which a prism can split a white light into a full spectrum of separate colors. When light is refracted through a lens, different wavelengths are refracted at different angles. All lenses exhibit some amount of chromatic aberration as they focus light, such that different colors of light are focused differently. The chromatic aberration that naturally occurs in the lenses of human eyes makes them focus to a slightly closer distance to see a red subject than to see a blue subject in the same position.

In a rendering, washing your background with a blue light, and lighting the foreground with red, can effectively increase the sense of depth in a scene. Naturally, this is not something that is appropriate or plausible in every scene. In lighting a section of subway tunnel, colored signal lights could have plausibly illuminated the scene with almost any color, but a red foreground and blue background added punch to the scene in Figure 6.11.

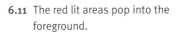

6.11 The red lit areas pop into the foreground.

6.2.3.2 SATURATION

Another bias in depth perception is that colors that are more saturated pop out into the foreground, in comparison to less saturated colors. As any good advertiser knows, a bold, striking color can appear to jump out, while grays, white, and black are less noticeable, and more likely to be perceived as background.

Any fog or atmosphere in an environment, as seen in Figure 6.12, can cause a shift toward less saturated colors with distance. The most saturated green in the image occurs in the plants that are closer to the camera. The saturated green appears to be in front of the less saturated green tones.

The limited focus and resolution of human eyes can also reserve the brightest, purest colors for the foreground. In a soft-focused background, or in subjects appearing small in the distance, the tones from adjacent objects can blend together, diluting any bold, striking colors that could have been visible up close.

6.2.4 COLOR AND DARKNESS

People perceive color differently in dimly lit areas. The impression of darkness in a scene can be enhanced by your color scheme.

6.2.4.1 DESATURATION

The cones in human eyes that are responsible for sensing color are less sensitive in dim conditions than the rods that pick up brightness and

NOTE

If you want to dig deeper into the issues of color theory and perception, and many related issues in 2D and 3D graphics, see Andrew Glassner's excellent two-volume set *Principles of Digital Image Synthesis (Morgan Kaufmann)*. Some college-level math experience is useful in reading this text.

6.12 The more saturated colors appear to be in the foreground in Lonnie Bailey's "Tropical Stream."

darkness. In very dim light, people's perception of color is diminished. When you find your way through a room in the dark, when you can barely make out the shape and locations of objects around you, you probably can't see the color of the objects at all.

Most output media further limits the amount of color visible in dark parts of an image. Color can be reproduced poorly in very dark areas of color prints, color television, and color film. As a pixel dims, or comes closer to black, its hue becomes less visible. If you want to create the impression of darkness in your 3D scene, but don't want to actually under-expose the scene so that your audience can't see the action, choose less saturated colors for your rendering.

6.2.4.2 BLUE FILL

A common Hollywood convention is to use a dim, blue light to illuminate dark areas. This is done most commonly when extra light is "cheated" into an area, where logically the audience would expect darkness. The blue color maintains the impression of darkness, while some light is still being added to the area. In Figure 6.13, for example, the yellow light from the moon is the only motivated light source, but a dim blue fill light washes the rest of the environment, turning the walls of the building blue.

Using blue fill light to signify darkness may have become a convention because a deep blue seems to be the color of a night sky. In early color films, it was still common to shoot "day for night"—filming an outdoor scene in the daytime, but tinting it dark blue to simulate night.

Blue fill light contrasts with the skin color of human actors, partially simulating the desaturation that is expected as an artifact of darkness. In computer graphics, where your subject is just as likely to be a reptile,

6.13 A blue fill light provides illumination while keeping the look of darkness. Scene by Jorge R. Gutierrez (www.mexopolis.com).

insect, or fantasy-colored character, you may find that different color fill lights are sometimes needed to contrast with your character's skin tones.

6.2.5 BLACK AND WHITE

A black-and-white image is more than just a color image with the color removed. Working in black and white carries the added burden of defining and demarcating your figure and ground, sets, props, and characters, all with different shades of gray. Working in black and white often involves manipulating tones in the image, to assign different shades of gray to areas or surfaces of different colors.

In color photography, the extremes of luminance—pure black tones and pure white tones—are not used in spots where a saturated color needs to be reproduced. As shown on the extreme left and right sides of Figure 6.14, areas of a color picture that are either underexposed or overexposed don't show colors as vividly as areas of medium luminance. Because of this, color photography often favors more uniform lighting and shading than can be used in black and white.

If you removed the chroma from most color pictures, and viewed them in grayscale, it might appear that color pictures have less contrast than many black-and-white photographs. The brightest red color in a color picture might only have a midrange luminance if viewed in grayscale. This doesn't mean that color photography is any better or worse than black-and-white, only that it works differently. Color photographers can create images using color contrast as well as contrasting brightness. To replace color contrast, you often want to brighten or darken a subject in a black and white image to establish a contrasting luminance.

Photographers sometimes brighten and darken different subjects with the aid of colored filters. Contrary to popular belief, photographers have been using colored filters on their cameras since long before the advent of color film. A set of colored filters is one of the most important accessories in many black-and-white photographer's camera bag.

Imagine photographing a scene with a red apple, in a tree with green leaves, viewed against a blue sky, as rendered in Figure 6.15. How do you want to reproduce the image in black and white? The scene would not

6.14 The boldest, most saturated colors are possible at medium levels of brightness (center dot), and colors become less saturated in darker or lighter areas (left and right dots).

6.15 Instead of a straight conversion to grayscale, a stronger black-and-white image is created with colored filters.

be well defined if the apple, the leaves, and the sky, were all represented with similar shades of gray. Shooting through a red filter would make the apples lighter than the sky, as seen in the center of Figure 6.15. A red filter would block the blue light from the sky, making the sky darker, even when shot on black-and-white film. But the red filter would allow the red light from the apples through, making them lighter than their surroundings. Conversely, shooting through a blue filter would make the apples darker than the sky, making them stand out better in this particular scene, as seen on the right side of Figure 6.15.

Working in 3D graphics, if your software allows colored transparent objects, then in theory you could achieve similar results rendering your scene through a transparent red object. However, a faster, easier, and more flexible way to simulate the results of camera filters is to process your rendered images within a compositing or image processing application. The same careful control achieved by a photographer using colored filters can be achieved by rendering a scene in full color, and then adjusting the brightness of the red, green, and blue channels of the rendering before converting to grayscale. By processing an image after it is rendered, you can make changes and adjustments without rerendering the scene. To create the superior black-and-white image shown on the right side of Figure 6.15, the intensity of the red channel was reduced, and the intensity of the blue channel was increased, before the conversion to monochrome.

On an RGB monitor, the red, green, and blue components do not each contribute equally to the brightness of a pixel. Instead, in a pure white light, the green contributes about 55% of the brightness, the red about 35%, and the blue about 15%. Many paint programs take this into account in converting to grayscale, and convert red, green, and blue into different shades of gray, as shown in Figure 6.16.

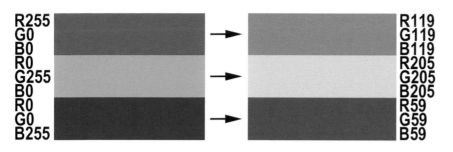

6.16 Red, green, and blue values are weighted differently in a conversion to grayscale in Adobe Photoshop.

6.2.5.1 TINTING BLACK-AND-WHITE IMAGES

Some black-and-white images can benefit from being tinted. You can produce a tinted black-and-white image in almost any paint or compositing program, by first removing any color or saturation, and then assigning a hue and saturation to the entire image.

Even before color film was invented, filmmakers recognized the emotional impact of color. Some early black-and-white movies have scenes tinted with colored dyes. For example, in the final print shown in a theater, the footage in which a building was on fire would be tinted with a dip in red dye, and then spliced back into the film.

Black-and-white photographs are also sometimes colored or tinted with oils, and very old photographs sometimes turn yellow with age, even without any intentional coloring. Figure 6.17 is made to appear more nostalgic by being tinted with a sepia tone.

6.3 COLOR BALANCE

If you want to accurately simulate the way a light source would appear if it were really photographed, then you need to start by understanding the idea of *color balance*.

6.17 After removing the color from this rendering, it was given a sepia tone.

Colors of light do not directly translate into the tints that are reproduced in a photograph. Instead, the colors that appear in a photograph are relative to the color balance of the film that was used.

The color balance of the film determines what color of light will appear to be white light, and which other colors of light will appear to be tinted. For example, film color balanced for indoor use would make objects lit by a regular light bulb look normally colored, but light coming through a window could be unnaturally tinted blue, as rendered in Figure 6.18.

On the other hand, using film color-balanced for outdoor use, objects lit by sunlight will appear normal, while objects lit by a household lamp will appear strangely yellow or orange tinted, as rendered in Figure 6.19.

Color balancing is not unique to photographic film. A similar adjustment, called *white balance*, is accomplished electronically on video

6.18 Film color-balanced for indoor use turns outdoor light blue.

6.19 Outdoor film makes daylight appear white, but tints indoor lamps orange.

cameras and digital still cameras. Even your own vision automatically adjusts to compensate for different lights.

In different environments or at different times of day, people sometimes see the world lit by a reddish sunrise, sometimes by a household light bulb, and sometimes by a blue light from the sky. People's vision adjusts to the dominant casts of color in each environment. Once you have grown accustomed to the light in an environment, you start to perceive the dominant color of light as though it were almost white, so that the objects around you seem normally colored.

Unlike a real camera, the camera in most 3D rendering programs does not have any controls to simulate different color balances. To simulate different color balances in your renderings, you need to mentally take color balance into account in adjusting the color of your individual lights. This means that two things need to be known before you can pick a realistic light color: the characteristic color of the type of light source you want to represent, and the color balance you want to simulate in your rendering.

The color of a light, and the color balance of photographic film, are both described by a *color temperature*, measured in degrees Kelvin. This is the standard system used by filmmakers and photographers to discuss colors of light. It is worth taking a few minutes to understand color temperature and photographic color balancing, so you can pick more realistic colors for the lights in your 3D scenes.

6.3.1 COLOR TEMPERATURE

Working in the late 1800s, the British physicist William Kelvin found that as he heated a block of carbon, it glowed in the heat, producing a range of different colors at different temperatures. The black cube first produced a dim red light, increasing to a brighter yellow as the temperature went up, and eventually produced a bright blue-white glow at the highest temperatures.

Color temperatures are measured in degrees Kelvin, which are a variation on Centigrade degrees. Instead of starting at the temperature water freezes, the Kelvin scale starts at *absolute zero*, which is −273 Centigrade. Add 273 to a Kelvin temperature, and you get the equivalent in Centigrade. However, the color temperatures attributed to different types of lights are correlated based on visible colors, and are not the actual temperature at which a filament burns.

Table 6.1 shows the color temperatures correlated with light sources that you might encounter in the real world. The low color temperature values (starting with the match and candle flame) appear a more reddish color, and the higher numbers appear more blue.

TABLE 6.1

COLOR TEMPERATURES OF DIFFERENT LIGHT SOURCES

Source	Degrees Kelvin
Match flame	1700–1800K
Candle flame	1850–1930K
Sun: At sunrise or sunset	2000–3000K
Household tungsten bulbs	2500–2900K
Tungsten lamp 500W–1k	3000K
Quartz lights	3200–3500K
Fluorescent lights	3200–7500K
Tungsten lamp 2k	3275K
Tungsten lamp 5k, 10k	3380K
Sun: Direct at noon	5000–5400K
Daylight (Sun + Sky)	5500–6500K
Sun: Through clouds/haze	5500–6500K
Sky: Overcast	6000–7500K
RGB monitor (White Pt.)	6500K
Outdoor shade areas	7000–8000K
Sky: Partly cloudy	8000–10000K

There is no fixed relationship between the color temperatures in Table 6.1, and the RGB values that you will choose for a light. The color temperatures can help you choose realistic colors for your lights, after first choosing a color balance. You could choose a conventional color balance such as 5500K to simulate daylight-balanced film, or 3200K to simulate tungsten-balanced film, or use some other color balance of your choosing. After you have chosen a color balance, then you can adjust the colors of your lights based on their relative color temperature compared to the color balance you have selected. The tints that you will give your lights based on this relationship are indicated in Figure 6.20.

After you have chosen a color balance for your scene, and decided what type of light you are trying to represent, you can use a tint from the

6.20 Colors for lights are all relative to your chosen color balance.

range of colors shown in Figure 6.20. Choose a color for your light as follows:

- If your light source has exactly the same color temperature as the color balance you have chosen for the scene, then it would appear to be white or gray, as shown near the center of Figure 6.20.

- Any lights with color temperature values lower than your color balance would be tinted yellow or red, using colors found to the left side of Figure 6.20.

- Any light source with a color temperature value higher than your color balance would be tinted blue, as shown on the right side of Figure 6.20.

Generally, the bigger the difference between the light's color temperature and the scene's color balance, the more saturated the color of light will appear. How far you go in saturating your lights, and the specific choice of RGB color values, is up to you. There is no mathematical equation determining the specific RGB color value you should use for a light.

If you ask two different photographers or cinematographers to shoot a scene, you are likely to see two different representations of the colors in that environment. Even in realistic, "accurate" photographs, there is enormous variety in how the hue (and saturation and brightness) of a light can be portrayed.

After understanding all the measurements and calculations that might go into a color choice, your final adjustments are still done by sight. Specific examples of outdoor, indoor, and mixed lighting will help to better illustrate the process.

6.3.1.1 OUTDOOR LIGHT COLORS

One of the most common types of film is *daylight* (also called *outdoor*) film, which is color balanced for 5500K.

Once you have picked 5500K as your color balance, then you know that any light source that was exactly 5500K would be white or gray. However, in real life, there is almost always a combination of light colors

> **NOTE**
>
> In an interesting twist of language, people use the opposite temperature associations when describing colors as "warm colors" or "cool colors" in common English. Red and yellow are called "warm" colors, perhaps because they are the colors of fire and the sun. Blues and greens are called "cool" colors, perhaps because of the color of the trees, sky, water, and ice.

in any environment. Daylight is a combination of different light colors, with some light coming directly from the sun, and other light coming from other parts of the sky.

In Table 6.1, direct sun is listed as between 5000K and 5400K—a lower color temperature value than the color balance of 5500K. This means that the color for a 5000K light source will appear to be yellowish, as shown in Figure 6.21. The light from the sky is generally a broader range from 7000K through 10000K, which would make light from the sky appear blue, as shown on the right side of Figure 6.21.

A light representing the sun will be given an RGB color to give it a yellow tint. Even with the aid of a color temperature chart, the specific shade of yellow (how bright a yellow, how saturated, and so on) is still subject to your own judgment, and might be different from one rendering to another. In Figure 6.22, the RGB values 222, 198, 175 were used for the key light representing the sun. (These RGB values are measured on a 0–255 scale; the same color would be 0.87, 0.78, 0.69 if your software uses a 0–1 scale.) The fill light representing the sky is given an RGB value of 72, 153, 210, tinted blue to reflect its higher color temperature.

6.21 Outdoor light colors are chosen relative to the film's color balance.

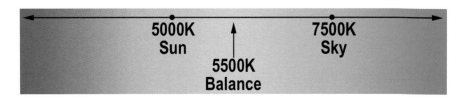

6.22 RGB values are assigned for the sunlight, sky light, and environment.

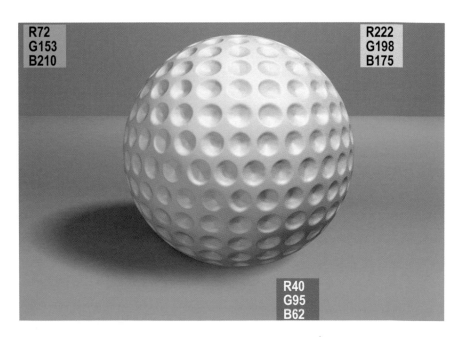

The colors of illumination in daylight don't stop with the colors from the light sources themselves. In real life, some of the light from the sun bounces around, and is reflected off other surfaces in the environment before it illuminates your subject. The effect of light being tinted when it is bounced off of other surfaces is sometimes called *color bleeding*. Whatever colors are predominant in your environment, such as the green in a green lawn, should also become a part of your lighting. A dim green light was added in Figure 6.22 to simulate light reflected up from the ground. The RGB values 40, 95, 62 were not directly based on the color of a light source, but instead came from one of the colors in the environment.

NOTE

See Chapter 9, "Materials and Rendering Algorithms," for a much more complete discussion of the ways light is bounced and transferred between objects in a scene.

6.3.1.2 INDOOR LIGHT COLORS

Film designed for indoor light is also called *tungsten-balanced* film, and is balanced for 3200K. Tungsten is the kind of filament used in ordinary household light bulbs, as well as several types of studio lighting equipment.

Refer to Table 6.1 for the color temperatures of different kinds of tungsten lamps. The notation 500W means a studio lamp that operates at 500 watts. A "1k" is a 1000 watt studio lamp, and a 2k is 2000 watts. One general pattern you can observe is that most man-made light sources are more red in tone, while light from the sun and sky uses more blue colors (except at sunrise and sunset).

An ordinary household light bulb (with a tungsten filament) is listed at 3000K. This is slightly lower than the film's color balance that you are simulating, so a lamp will appear slightly yellow, as shown in Figure 6.23. If a room is also lit by sunlight through a window, then find direct sun listed at between 5000K and 5400K—a higher color temperature value than the color balance of 3200K. This means that the color for a 5000K light source will appear blue-tinted, as shown in Figure 6.23.

In Figure 6.24, a slightly yellow color is used to represent the light from the lamp, while a blue tint is given to the sunlight coming through the window. Note that the sunlight with a 5000K color temperature was given a different RGB value in this indoor-balanced scene than in the outdoor-balanced example shown previously.

NOTE

Tungsten studio lighting equipment generally has very accurate, consistent color temperature, as long as the voltage is consistent. The reason that different wattage lighting instruments are used on a film set (1k, 2k, 5k, 10k), instead of simply brightening and dimming one kind of lamp by varying the voltage, is to avoid the shifts in color temperature that would occur with a lowered voltage.

**3000K
Lamp**　　**5000K
Sun**

**3200K
Balance**

6.23 Indoor light colors are chosen relative to the film's color balance.

6.24 RGB values are assigned for the sunlight, sky light, and environment.

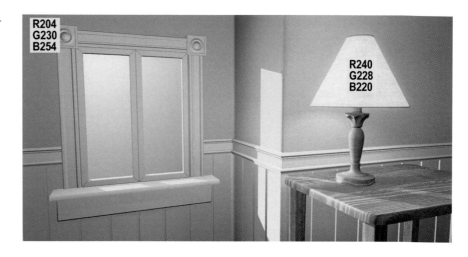

A real scene is usually illuminated by a variety of colors of light. Even if all of the light came from similar light bulbs, colors from the walls could still be added to your fill light to simulate color bleeding, and colors from tinted lampshades should also be mixed into the color you choose for indoor lights. There is no fixed equation for this, but you should look at each scene and think about the extent to which a colored lampshade or painted wall should influence the colors you see around it.

Another factor that can change indoor lighting is the use of fluorescent light. Fluorescent light is listed in Table 6.1 as 3200K through 7500K—a wide range of possible color temperatures. To make fluorescent lighting more pleasant and natural-looking, different brands of fluorescent tubes are tinted to different colors.

Color temperature listings don't tell you about the amount of green in a light; the color temperature generally only indicates the shift from red to blue. In many cases, a fluorescent light can appear greenish in comparison to other lights. Adding more green to the RGB value of any light helps make it look fluorescent, and even can make a whole environment look more artificially lit.

6.3.1.3 CHOOSING INDOOR OR OUTDOOR FILM

There are cases where "indoor" film is used outside, and "outdoor" film is used inside. If you are indoors, but the scene is lit mainly by daylight entering through a window or door, then you might want to use the same 5500K color balance as outdoors. Conversely, if you are outdoors, but a scene is lit mainly by artificial lights (especially at night), then you might want to use the same 3200K color balance as you would indoors. Despite the names "indoor" and "outdoor," it is the dominant light source, not the location, that determines your color balance.

NOTE

The color temperature correlated to a nonincandescent source, such as a fluorescent tube, is less meaningful than the color temperature of an incandescent source. Incandescent light is produced when an object is heated to become luminous, like the light source first examined by Kelvin. Standard light bulbs, candles, and even the sun, are incandescent sources. Apart from fluorescent tubes, another example of nonincandescent light is the glow from phosphors in a monitor or television set.

If you use an ordinary point-and-shoot 35mm camera, you may use the same roll of film for indoor and outdoor photographs, but not see any discoloration. Most film sold to consumers is daylight-balanced. To avoid discoloration when indoors, your camera's built-in flash adds daylight-tinted illumination to the room, so that the same film can be used outdoors, as long as you use the flash. Additionally, in a photo lab, a set of colored filters is automatically used when prints are made from negatives, to further correct the hues of a home snapshot.

6.3.1.4 OTHER COLOR BALANCES

Apart from choosing one of the two most popular color balances in film stock, filmmakers also have other tools available to them to control the colors in an image. Colored filters can be mounted on a camera to tint the image seen from the camera to almost any color. A change of filter can allow daylight film to be used indoors, or tint a scene for almost any stylized appearance or color desired for a particular shot.

Even after a film is shot, a process called *color timing* offers another chance to change a scene's color balance. Color timing is the adjustment of the exposure of red, green, and blue light used in making prints from a negative, and it makes the colors you see in a film differ from the colors of the lights on the set.

Film productions also use colored *gels* to tint light sources and match the colors of light in a scene. A gel is a piece of a tinted transparent material. A large gel can be mounted just outside of the window, to tint its color, as well as reducing the brightness of the direct sunlight. This allows the color of light seen through a window to match the colors of light used indoors, with no visible difference in tint.

Gels are designed to resist heat, so that they can also be mounted directly in front of lights, as shown in Figure 6.25. Instead of "gelling" the window, you could add gels to each of the indoor lights, to tint them closer to a daylight color. With different gels, a film lighting instrument can be made to match the characteristic colors of sunlight or lamplight, or almost any other color.

Color balance is used in film not just to ensure realistic color reproduction, but also as a cinematic tool to stylize and control the look of an image. Choosing a color balance for your scene can be a creative process, based on how you want your scene to appear. An "unnatural" tint to a scene can sometimes add to the quality of your production more than a realistic or conventional color balance. For example, there are times when a tinge of green can make a space look more stark or less natural, or connote sickness, or look cold and impersonal. All of

---

NOTE

For information on all types of light sources, filters, color temperatures, and an exhaustive collection of charts, tables, and related articles about film, cameras, and lights, see the industry-standard reference book, the *American Cinematographer Manual*, published by The American Society of Cinematographers.

these things were accomplished in Figure 6.26 by giving the lights a green tint.

Feel free to play with the colors of the lights in your 3D scene to achieve whatever looks you want in your final product. Just as live-action film frequently cheats and colors lights to appear different than they are in nature, you should be able to depart from the values suggested by a color temperature whenever you think you can improve your rendering by doing so.

6.25 A gel adjusts the color temperature of a light source.

6.26 Vaclav Cizkovski's rendering sets a mood with a green light.

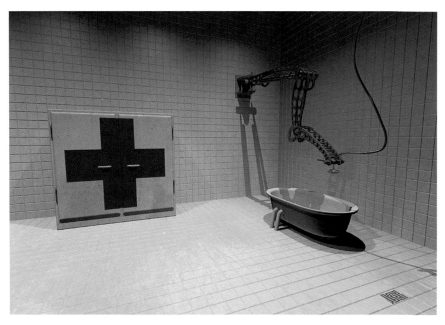

As a deliberate stylistic choice, you might sometimes want boldly colored lights to tint an image. For example, in Figure 6.27, the natural color temperature difference has been exaggerated, instead of reduced. This builds a stronger color contrast, and emphasizes the difference between the warm indoors and the cold-looking exterior.

6.3.1.5 SOFTWARE WITHOUT COLOR BALANCE

As mentioned previously, the cameras in most 3D graphics software do not support any kind of color balancing. Despite this, some developers have attempted to provide support for adjusting light colors via color temperatures, instead of directly controlling the light's RGB value. Some software lets you specify that a light has a color temperature of 3200K, but would not let you specify whether the film you were trying to match was color balanced for tungsten, daylight, or any other color temperature. The software would then need to assign an RGB value to the light for you. Without knowing the color balance, it might not do a good job.

The actual RGB colors assigned to lights via an interface that attempts to skip color balancing might not be as realistic or accurate as colors chosen via the process described previously. For example, if you want your key light to represent the direct sun, and your fill light to represent light from the sky, a solution that did not include color balancing might determine that both lights should be very similar shades of blue (because both have high color temperatures.) Using similar blue tones for both the sun and the sky would rob the scene of the richness and diversity of colors that can be captured with proper color balancing. The "Outdoor Light Colors" section earlier in the chapter, shows how you could

6.27 The different color temperatures inspire the tinting of the light sources.

choose more varied colors for the sun and the sky, based on their variation from a point of color balance.

A point of color balance must exist at some point on any spectrum of light colors. If some of your lights are going to appear blue, and some are going to appear red, then by necessity there is some color temperature in-between, at which lights have not been tinted more blue or more red. Quick-fix solutions that don't ask you for a color balance must actually have chosen some color temperature, internally, at which they arbitrarily center the spectrum, only they don't allow it to be adjusted by the user.

Just as proper exposure is necessary to capture the dark and light tones of a scene, proper color balancing is needed to capture the hues of light in a scene. Improper or poorly chosen color balance can limit your color reproduction, and you should steer clear of charts or plug-ins that would have you always use the same RGB color values for the same kind of light.

Don't assume that a plug-in that claims to select the "correct" color for a light for you is necessarily picking the best color for you. Your own visual sense, and understanding of natural color temperatures and color balances, might help you mix an RGB color yourself that looks better than the color selected for you by a plug-in. Even though different interface options are available to adjust the colors of a light, your renderer is actually storing and using an RGB color value internally during the rendering process. Understanding your 3D software's native RGB color is an important part of controlling the colors in a rendering process.

6.4 RGB Color

Rendering software calculates the way that light colors combine, filter through transparent surfaces, and are reflected by colored surfaces, based on the RGB color model. Because your renderer is working in RGB color, your color output will be more understandable and predictable once you understand RGB color.

6.4.1 The Spectrum

RGB color is a limited representation of the actual spectrum of colors that can exist in real life. In real life, a single source can emit more than one wavelength of light. The full spectrum of colors that make up a light can be plotted, as in Figure 6.28. The spectrum shows the *amplitude* (also called the brightness) of the light at each visible wavelength (the color).

Instead of being able to emit colors of all of these wavelengths, color televisions and computer monitors use light-emitting phosphors of only three colors: red, green, and blue. Your monitor varies the intensity of light in three areas of the spectrum, as shown in Figure 6.29, in order to represent color. No light of wavelengths between the colors of the monitor's red, green, and blue is controlled.

It may seem surprising that such a limited representation is perceived as "full color." The reason that RGB color works convincingly is that people's eyes only sample the intensity of three overlapping, general areas of the spectrum, and perceive colors based on the relative intensity of light within each range of wavelengths. Pigmented, light-sensitive cells in people's eyes called *cones* are responsible for detecting color. There are three kinds of cones: one type which is pigmented to filter light and responds most strongly to shorter wavelengths (in the area of the spectrum labeled "S" in Figure 6.30), one that best responds to medium wavelengths (labeled "M"), and one that responds to longer waves of light ("L"). Human perception of color is based on the relative strength of the responses from the three types of cones.

Because people only sense the relative intensities of three areas of the spectrum, RGB color's incomplete reproduction of the spectral distribution of light is adequate to represent most colors. Much of the information that is contained in a color of light is invisible to the naked eye.

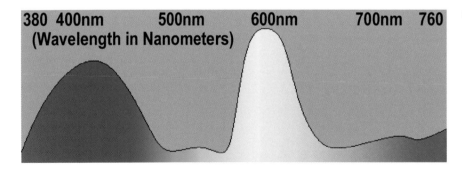

6.28 The spectral energy distribution of light can be a complex mixture of wavelengths.

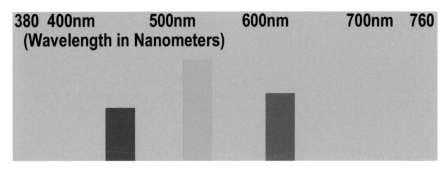

6.29 RGB color re-creates only a few frequencies of light.

6.30 Humans compare the intensity of light in three areas of the visible spectrum to perceive color.

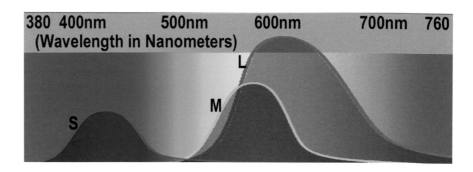

There can be cases where different light sources have very different color makeups, but appear identical to a viewer. Splitting the light with a prism would reveal that the sources consist of very different spectral energy distributions, but there would otherwise be no way to perceive the difference with the naked eye. If you refer to Figure 6.28, you see that the plotted spectral distribution of light consists of blue and yellow light, with very little green in between. People still would see the light that is plotted as being green light, and could not tell a difference with the naked eye between that light source and a light source with a continuous spectrum concentrated in pure green.

In music, you can hear the difference between a chord and a note played by itself. With colors, you are blind to the equivalent difference. When two colors of light are mixed, the resulting combination of wavelengths can look the same as a spectrally pure color of an intermediate wavelength. It is as if, when you played a "C" and an "E" at once on the piano keyboard, you could not tell that chord from a single "D" note being played. This might seem as though you are missing a lot of the information available in a color of light, but it also has its advantages: It is what makes possible RGB color and all other cases of "color mixing" to simulate intermediate colors with mixed paint, ink, or light.

6.4.2 SPECTRAL PURITY

Under most conditions a colored light is not *spectrally pure*, or consisting of all one wavelength. If you adjusted the color of a light in the computer to make it purely green, with no red or blue, then you would have created something that you would rarely encounter in real life. The left side of Figure 6.31 shows a white light illuminating several different color objects. The right frame shows exactly the same scene, lit by a pure green light. The result does not appear realistic. The objects that were a whole range of different colors, have now been rendered in groups of three identical green balls and three identical black balls.

6.31 RGB purity can produce unrealistic results.

This result shows a degree of purity and digital perfection that you would not encounter in a live action production. If the green light had any variety in its spectral distribution, then there would have been at least a small variation of the hue of the three balls that now appear the same shade of green. If the blue, magenta, and red balls had any dirt, dust, or imperfections on them, then they would have reflected at least some of the green light, instead of appearing pure black.

For a naturalistic scene, be sure to "pollute" any unrealistically pure RGB values, by adding at least a little bit of red, green, and blue, even to the most boldly colored lights. Examine the range of RGB values you find in a digitized photograph, and you'll be likely to find a diversity of red, green, and blue values, and not many pixels of any "pure" RGB color.

6.4.3 DIGITAL REPRESENTATIONS

Different 3D programs use different numeric ranges for RGB values: Some represent RGB values in a range from 0 to 255, some from 0.0 to 1.0, others from 0% to 100%. With any of these ranges, the result is the same: The 0 value still means black or none of a particular color value, and the top value still means the full amount of a particular color value. The range of 0 to 255 gives direct control over the range of color values used in most 3D programs, which only have 256 possible levels of intensity for the red, green, and blue components of a color. The other ranges are more flexible, and could be used to control your software even if different *bit-depths* of colors were used.

The bit-depth is the number of binary digits (bits) of information used per pixel of your rendering. The lowest possible bit-depth in computer graphics is 1-bit color, which creates a monochrome display. For each pixel of a 1-bit display, a single bit has a value of either 0 (off, usually set to black), or 1 (on, usually shown as white, green, or amber, depending on the color of phosphors in the monochrome monitor.)

As more bits of information are added per pixel, the number of possible colors increases. 2-bit color uses two binary digits per pixel, which leads to four possible color values, as shown:

- If the two digits are "00" then Color 0 is displayed.
- If the two digits are "01" then Color 1 is displayed.
- If the two digits are "10" then Color 2 is displayed.
- If the two digits are "11" then Color 3 is displayed.

With just two binary digits per pixel, four colors can be used in a color display. Each added bit doubles the number of possible colors, such that three bits creates eight possible colors, four bits creates 16 possible colors, and eight bits creates 256 possible colors (the number of colors equals 2 raised to the power of the bit-depth).

Displays that show 256 or fewer colors usually use a *Color Look-Up Table* (also called a *CLUT* or *Palette*) that describes what color should be shown for each possible numeric value. For example, a CLUT for a 2-bit color display could specify that Color 0 will be black, Color 1 will be red, Color 2 will be purple, and Color 3 will be yellow. The entire image would have to consist of one of the possible colors in the CLUT. This can mean that reduced-color images do not always have enough tones to create continuous shading, or include every color from a 3D rendering, as shown in Figure 6.32.

When you move above 8 bits per pixel, arbitrary palette selections are no longer required in order to represent colors. Instead, the three color values of red, green, and blue, are each considered to be *channels* of information in an image, and each get their own numeric value at each pixel. Most 3D renderings are output with 8 bits per channel of color information, which allows for 256 possible intensities of red, green, or blue. Figure 6.33 shows how the red, green, and blue of an image each

6.32 From left to right: An image displayed at 1 bit per pixel (2 colors), 2 bits per pixel (4 colors), 4 bits per pixel (16 colors), and 24 bits per pixel (16,777,216 colors).

can be viewed as a separate channel. With three channels using 8 bits per channel, this color representation is called *24-bit color*. 24-bit color allows for 16,777,216 possible colors within an image (256 × 256 × 256 = 16,777,216), and is the most popular format for output from 3D rendering software.

Sometimes renderings need to be created for distribution in less than 24-bit color, for use in interactive media, CD-ROMs, or GIF files on the World Wide Web. If you need to do this, the best approach is usually to render in 24-bit color from your 3D program, but stick to a well-controlled, limited color scheme, that will work well with a reduced palette of colors. Then, after your rendering is completed, use a paint or image-processing program to convert the 24-bit color images into the reduced-color format of your final product.

32-bit color includes the same number of visible colors, and the same RGB information, as 24-bit color. 32-bit color adds an extra 8-bit channel called an *alpha channel*, which can hold extra information such as each pixel's transparency, or masks used for compositing. Chapter 10, "Compositing," discusses the use and content of alpha channels in detail. The addition of this extra 8-bit channel creates a total of 32 bits per pixel, but the RGB display is exactly the same as with 24-bit color.

For some digital film applications, more than 8 bits per channel are sometimes used. 16 bits per channel is optionally output from some renderers, which allows for much greater precision in the intensities of red, green, and blue. With three color channels, plus a possible alpha channel, this adds up to 48 or 64 bits per pixel. 48-bit or 64-bit color is especially useful in making sure that images can be manipulated or color-corrected after rendering, with minimal degradation to the picture quality. Rendering in higher bit-depths does use more storage space for your rendered frames, but generally does not slow down the rendering process compared to 24-bit color. In fact, some renderers internally compute all the colors in your rendering at 16-bits per channel, and only clip or round down to 8-bits per channel when the image is actually output.

> **NOTE**
>
> There can be some confusion between the terminology used by computer graphic artists in the motion picture industry compared to artists developing multimedia content. In general, people working with film refer to bit-depth on a per-channel basis, such that when they say "16-bit color" they mean 16 bits per channel, with 48 or 64 bits per pixel. Multimedia developers refer to bit-depth in terms of the total number of bits per pixel, such that "16-bit color" would mean only 16 bits total per pixel.

6.33 Red, green, and blue channels (from left) combine to form a full-color image (right).

6.4.4 CONCLUSIONS

There are five main points to remember when choosing colors for a 3D scene:

- **Focus on creating a clearly defined color scheme for your scenes, instead of using colors at random on different objects.**

- **There is no one "true color" that will always appear for a type of light source.** Light colors are viewed in relation to a camera's color balance or to a dominant color cast to which your eyes are adjusted.

- **Even though specific colors might change from scene to scene, the relative tints of different types of sources maintain recognizable relationships based on their color temperatures.** No matter how a shot is color-balanced, a household lamp will appear more red than the noontime sun, and the fill from the sky will appear more blue than the sun itself.

- **Your scene becomes richer and more realistic if there is variety in the colors of light illuminating your subjects.** Differences in the color temperature are a good starting point for adding variety to your lighting.

- **Lights that pick up colors from the surrounding environment add more variety, and simulate the natural color bleeding in indirect light.**

There are very few rules limiting what you can do with color in your renderings. The most common sin is neglect—too often, users render without thinking about color, and miss the opportunity to take advantage of the principles covered in this chapter.

6.5 EXERCISES

1. Try loading a scene you have previously created, and rendering it with different colors of light. See if you can change the mood of the image, to make it more cheerful, more sad, or more frightening. See if you can make the scene look like it was set at night, or at sunrise. Show your re-colored scenes to your friends, and discuss how they respond to the different versions.

2. In a paint program, load a piece of your own work, and try removing the color. In many cases, people like some of their own renderings better in black and white, and with increased contrast. Also try

tinting the image to different colors. Can you identify a clear color scheme in your renderings?

3. You have been commissioned to render a logo for the Official Express courier service. What color would you use for the word "Official?" What color would you use for the word "Express?" Why?

4. On television, you watch a politician deliver a confession of a personal nature, and notice that the entire shot has a warm, yellowish tint. How could that footage have been given a different hue from other footage shot in the same room? Why would someone have wanted to give the scene that appearance?

5. Try lighting a scene with light from two different sources. When a viewer cannot see the light source in the shot, can you make the type of light clear from the colors you use?

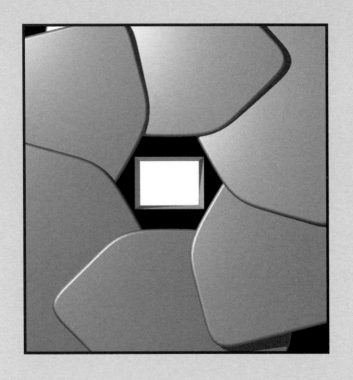

EXPOSURE

7

EXPOSURE

Exposure IS THE all-important moment when a camera's shutter opens and allows light to reach the film. A camera's exposure primarily controls the brightness and contrast of a shot, but can also influence an image's grain, focus, and the amount of motion recorded. When you work in 3D graphics, it is up to you to simulate the results of a real camera's exposure settings. This chapter will explain how to measure and control the functions in 3D graphics that relate to exposure, how exposure is controlled in a real camera, and how to simulate photographic exposure in a 3D scene.

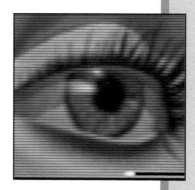

7.1 HISTOGRAMS AND COMMON EXPOSURE PROBLEMS

This section discusses a number of common problems related to exposure and contrast that can hurt the quality of your renderings if you don't identify and correct them. Your own visual inspection of test-renderings is always the most important way to monitor the tones used in your scene. However, a valuable tool called a histogram can help you double-check your scene's exposure.

A *histogram* is a chart plotted by the computer to show how frequently each possible tone appears in an image. To see a histogram of your rendering, load it into any paint, image processing, or compositing program that has a histogram function.

Figure 7.1 shows a typical histogram. For each of the 256 possible levels of brightness in the image (analyzing an image with 8 bits per channel), a vertical column is plotted. The height of each column is determined by the number of pixels in the image that use the tone corresponding to the column. The columns on the left show the number of pixels using black and dark values, the height of the columns in the center shows how many pixels use medium tones, and the height of the columns on the right shows how many pixels use brighter tones, up to pure white on the extreme right.

A histogram offers a useful window into your use of different shades in a 3D rendering. The following sections will show how a histogram can help you identify and correct various exposure-related problems, such as:

- Overexposure
- Underexposure
- Banding
- Low contrast
- High contrast
- Clipping

Each section discusses different problems that you can identify with a histogram. Checking a histogram to augment your own visual appraisal of a scene is a valuable skill that will help you maintain the quality of your work, and ensure that your renderings can survive the transition from your monitor to other monitors, film, television, or print output.

7.1.1 OVEREXPOSURE

A problem frequently seen in beginners' work is *overexposure*. Overexposed images use only light tones and do not take advantage of the darker side of the available palette.

7.1 A histogram plots the frequency of different numeric color values in a rendering. (Head model by Amy E. Medford, from the NURBANA Collection.)

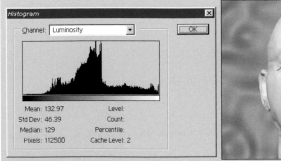

Without having taken full control over their lights, beginning users often allow too much light to spill everywhere, and end up overexposing every scene they render.

The histogram in Figure 7.2 indicates an image that is overexposed. The tallest columns are on the extreme right, indicating many bright pixels used in the rendering. The lowest columns of the histogram are on the left, indicating that few black or darker tones are used.

Unless your entire scene needs to be brightly lit for a specific reason, such as to show a flash of lightning within an animation, you generally should take advantage of the full palette, including dark tones as well as light ones. If your histograms reveal a lack of darker tones in your renderings, you can take several steps to improve your lighting:

- Be sure that you are not using too many light sources: Delete any lights in your scene that don't have a clear and specific purpose.

- Turn off global ambience, to be sure that no extra light is being added to all the surfaces in your scene.

- Restrict the scope or spread of your lights by limiting the falloff range of lights to a specific area or limiting the cone angle of spotlights.

- Be sure that shadows are being fully rendered and that you don't have a lighter tone selected for your shadow color or umbra intensity. After adjusting your scene, make a new rendering, and check the histogram again to ensure you are using a full range of tones from dark to light.

If your renderings are overexposed according to a histogram but don't look overexposed on your computer's monitor, be sure there isn't too much glare hitting your monitor or too much light reflecting off the screen, and be sure your display is bright enough to show a full range of tones.

7.2 A histogram shows overexposure as a concentration on the right side of the graph.

Overexposure is usually an easy problem to fix. Within a few weeks or months, most students learn not to overexpose all their scenes. Sadly, right around the time students start paying attention to their lights, they often trap themselves into making the opposite mistake: *underexposure*.

7.1.2 UNDEREXPOSURE

The histogram in Figure 7.3 reveals an underexposed image. The columns of the histogram appear on the left side only, indicating that only the dimmest shades of the palette are being used in this rendering.

If a histogram reveals that your renderings are underexposed, check your 3D scene for some possible causes of underexposure:

- Your lights might have too low an intensity, and some need to be made brighter.

- Your lights may be set to attenuate or decay before they reach your subjects, so you may need to increase the fall-off distance or reduce the attenuation.

- Be sure that any reflective surfaces have something to reflect, and that there is something to see when you look through any transparent surface. If a surface is surrounded by blackness, then being reflective or transparent would only make it darker.

- Lights can sometimes be accidentally shadowed, such as by the light-fixture models that surround them. If one of your lights doesn't seem to be brightening your scene the way it should, check to see if the surrounding geometry needs to be excluded.

- Check any global settings, such as depth fading or fog effects, which can sometimes darken a scene no matter how bright your lights appear.

After you have fixed underexposure problems in a scene, you should render it again, and be sure that the histogram shows a full use of the palette, instead of only the dimmest shades.

7.3 A histogram shows underexposure as a concentration on the left side of the graph.

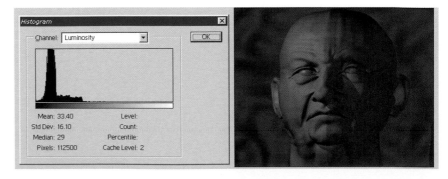

7.1.2.1 STUDENT MURK

Many students who are struggling to make more realistic or subtle 3D renderings discover that darkness is a convenient way to hide their mistakes. Almost any problem that can appear in a rendering, whether due to a badly adjusted material, a seam or glitch in the geometry, a misplaced shadow, or an unattractive highlight, can be hidden if the scene is dark enough. As a result, some student renderings suffer from *student murk* or the chronic underexposure of scenes.

The student murk problem in computer graphics courses is similar to a grade-school student's habit of covering up bad spelling with illegible handwriting. In both cases, students are really obscuring the entirety of their work, not just the mistakes they intended to hide. Underexposing a scene is a mistake that can catch up to you when your rendering is printed, projected, or viewed on video. Instead of sinking in the murk, strive to fix your scene's underlying problems.

7.1.2.2 OPTICAL EFFECTS AND UNDEREXPOSURE

A particularly deadly combination occurs when an optical effect, such as a light glow or lens flare, is used in an otherwise underexposed scene. Bright optical effects can make a scene appear to be fully exposed in a histogram, even if the objects themselves are all underlit. Figure 7.4 shows an example.

Bright optical effects in a shot make objects that were already murky even harder to see. If you need to add optical effects in a scene, start by making test renderings without the effects to determine if your subject is properly exposed.

7.1.3 BANDING

A problem closely related to underexposure is *banding*, also called *posterization* or *contouring*. An image with banding problems appears to have distinct steps or bands of color instead of continuous shading. Potential

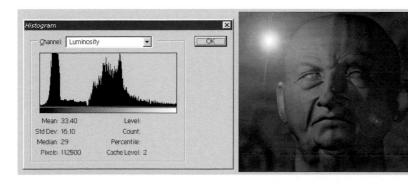

7.4 A badly underexposed subject can have a deceptive histogram if it contains glows or optical effects.

banding problems can be indicated by gaps between the columns within the histogram, as shown in Figure 7.5.

Banding is often caused by performing excessive manipulation or image processing on an image. This problem commonly appears when you try to correct a dimly lit rendering by brightening the image in a paint or image-processing program. The gaps in the histogram appear because the small number of adjacent shades used in the original image spread out across the palette when you brighten the image. Similar banding artifacts are sometimes caused if an image has been represented with a reduced bit-depth or in an indexed color mode, and then converted back into full color.

You can fix or avoid banding problems in several ways:

- Be sure that your scene is fully lit, not underexposed.

- Consider adding texture maps to any untextured surfaces. Sometimes even a small amount of color or bump mapping gets rid of banding artifacts.

- If you are digitizing images or texture maps with a flatbed scanner, try to adjust the brightness and contrast to your satisfaction within the scanner's control panel, instead of adjusting the image after digitizing.

- Give lights a realistic tint, rather than using pure white lights. Staggering the red, green, and blue channels reduces any banding or stepping to one third.

- Activate a small amount of dithering, if it is still needed, to avoid any remaining banding artifacts.

Not every gap in your histogram is necessarily a problem. Natural variation in an image sometimes makes more of one tone appear than another. Even if you are not worried about banding, however, the guidelines to prevent banding are good general work habits, and do not take much extra effort to follow.

> **NOTE**
>
> A monitor display needs to be set for "true color" (also called "millions of colors," "24-bit," or "32-bit") in its control panel in order to evaluate the fine points of a rendering. Otherwise, your display could make any image you view appear banded, even if nothing was wrong with the file.

7.5 Banding artifacts are shown in a histogram as gaps between the columns, and are especially noticeable on the man's cheek in the rendering.

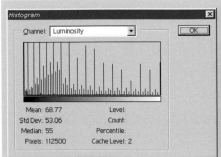

7.1.4 LOW CONTRAST

A histogram that appears concentrated entirely in one area of the palette, as shown in Figure 7.6, reveals a low-contrast image. When an image uses only tones towards the middle of the palette, without taking advantage of more extreme dark or light tones, the scene can appear faded, or as if you are viewing it through a fog.

Technically, both overexposure and underexposure (as described previously) are types of low-contrast images. An overexposed image is a low-contrast image that uses only the brightest available tones, and an underexposed image is a low-contrast image that uses the darkest available tones. This means that you should start fixing any low-contrast scene by reviewing the overexposure and underexposure checklists earlier in this chapter.

If your renderings are suffering from low contrast, also be sure that you have clearly defined the source and direction of one key light, and that any fill lights in your scene do not add up to rival or overpower the brightness of your key light. (Review Chapter 3, "Three-Point Lighting," for more information on key-to-fill ratios.)

Low contrast is only a problem if it is unwanted, or inappropriate to your scene. There could be times when you want to intentionally create low-contrast scenes, for example:

- Low contrast can help simulate an atmosphere filled with fog, dust, or snow.

- Low contrast images can look nostalgic, such as a faded yellow photograph.

- Low contrast scenes can appear softer, as with photographs of models shot through gauze.

- Low contrast renderings can serve as neutral backgrounds, such as design elements that will be layered behind text in a title sequence.

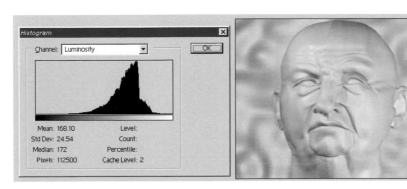

7.6 A low-contrast scene is shown in a histogram as a concentration all into one narrow area.

If you find a low-contrast rendering appropriate for your needs, then you don't always need to consider limited contrast to be a problem. In fact, too high a level of contrast can also be a problem in some scenes.

7.1.5 HIGH CONTRAST

A histogram that is divided into separate columns of dark and light tones, with very few medium tones in between, indicates a very high-contrast rendering. The histogram in Figure 7.7 shows the image has almost no shading, only a flat area of white, and a flat area of black.

High-contrast images can be used for dramatic effect. A bold, high-contrast image will often help grab a viewer's attention more than a low-contrast image. While maintaining adequate contrast is essential to making a viewable image, too much contrast can mean that portions of the image are hidden in darkness or overexposure, and that shading between the extremes of dark and light is not being used as fully as it could to model the form of your subject. Focus on controlling your level of contrast to create the level of definition you need in a scene, without losing all of the intermediate tones required for full shading.

You can manipulate several factors if you want a high-contrast image.

- To achieve high contrast, choose spotlights, instead of omnidirectional lights, to focus your light in concentrated areas.

- Be sure your shadows are being rendered with a dark enough shadow color for high contrast, and choose raytraced shadows if you also want a starker edge.

- Lights that are set to attenuate rapidly with distance or that use an inverse square falloff pattern, generally contribute to a high-contrast scene.

- To raise the contrast, turn off any global ambience in your scene, and use low or moderate amounts of fill lighting.

7.7 A high contrast scene creates a histogram with discontinuous concentrations of both bright and dark pixels.

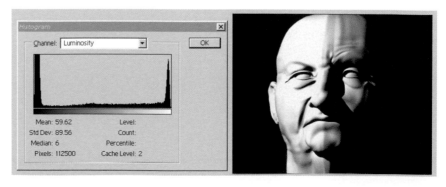

Be sure to check your image itself if you are verifying the level of contrast, instead of relying solely on a histogram. The histogram will show the use of tones from all over your image, while contrast is most visible where bright and dark tones are placed near each other, with a sharper transition between them.

7.1.6 CLIPPING

An annoying problem with digital images is *clipping*. A digital palette reaches the maximum level of brightness it can represent at pure white, and a minimum level at pure black. Sometimes, in areas of extreme highlight or shadow, the shading of your scene crashes into these limits, beyond which the variation of tones cannot continue. For example, if an area of your rendering is already pure white, then no matter how much extra light you add, the area will not get any lighter. Any extra light or shading above pure white is clipped down to the brightest displayable value. Figure 7.8 shows a scene where the white level has been clipped—the histogram builds up to its highest column on the extreme right.

If you want to take advantage of the full palette, including bright and dark tones, then you can't completely avoid all clipping. At times, having areas of your scene touch pure black and pure white can be desirable, and won't necessarily be a visible problem in your rendering.

Clipping can become very visible, however, if you brighten or darken an image after it is rendered with clipping. For example, Figure 7.9 shows what the image from Figure 7.8 would look like if it were darkened in an image-processing program. The area that was previously blown out to pure white has darkened into a uniformly gray area that is unnaturally flat and lacks shading. The problem is that clipping gave all the pixels in overexposed areas an identical pure white value, with no shading or variation. If image processing is used to darken the clipped image file, it can reduce all of the pure white pixels to a uniform gray tone, but it

> **NOTE**
>
> Some programs keep track of the areas of your scene that are "whiter than white" so that visual effects such as glows can be applied around them, but the final output image will still be clipped to the limits of the image file. The option to render and process an image with more than the standard 8-bits per channel can significantly reduce clipping artifacts with some software.

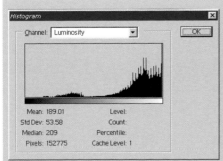

7.8 Clipping is represented in a histogram with a sharp "cliff" on the side of the value range.

NOTE

Photographic film also has limits to how bright or dim part of an image can appear. The range of brightness that is possible in a particular film stock is called its *exposure latitude*. However, the exposure latitude of analog film does not end with an abrupt, absolute cutoff point as in digital systems, so clipping is mainly a digital problem.

cannot show any of the shading and variation that was clipped away in the original rendering. The same flat, clipped appearance could also result from an area that had been underexposed or pure black in the rendering, then brightened through image processing.

Pay attention to the level of clipping if you are planning to adjust the brightness of your images after they are rendered. You don't want to tie your hands by blowing out areas you might want to darken later or by completely underexposing areas you might want to lighten. Chapter 10, "Compositing," discusses a special case of darkening images: If you will need to add a shadow to an image, be sure that surface receiving the shadow isn't blown-out to pure white.

7.1.7 GAMMA CORRECTION

Every output device has a *gamma* value that describes the relationship between the signal sent to the device, and the device's final output. A video monitor's gamma describes how different video signal levels correspond to the actual brightness on the screen. A printer has a gamma that describes the relationship between the levels of shading in an image file, and the darkness of the ink it actually applies to the paper.

Once black ink is added to white paper, the paper can start getting dark very quickly. A color value that appears to be halfway between white and black on your monitor might produce a much darker tone on a printed page. If you have developed your renderings by viewing them on a computer monitor, and then want to print them out, *gamma correction* will usually be necessary. Gamma correction is an image-processing function that adjusts an image to compensate for the gamma of different devices. Gamma correction can be viewed as a curve, plotting a relationship between the original tones of the image and the output tones, as shown in Figure 7.10. A straight line (as shown on the left side of 7.10) would indicate no change to the image, with every output tone being identical to every input tone. The curve on the right would increase the image's gamma, making the midtones of the original image brighter.

7.9 Digitally adjusting the brightness of an image after it is rendered can transform any clipped areas into unrealistically flat regions of the picture.

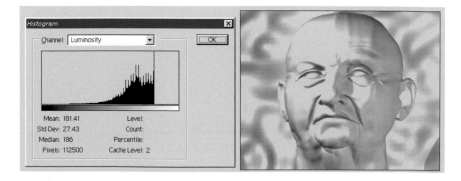

Changing the gamma can appear to change the brightness of an image. However, it does not necessarily move the black level (the darkest tones used in an image) or the white point (the brightest tones used in an image). The gamma controls the speed of the transition in between the dark and light. Figure 7.11 shows an image before and after gamma correction for print. Notice how portions of the histogram have been expanded where the gamma curve became steeper, and compressed where the curve had less of a slope.

If you make good use of the available palette when initially designing and rendering a scene, then your rendering should be able to survive whatever image processing is applied (either manually or automatically) to output the rendering to more than one medium.

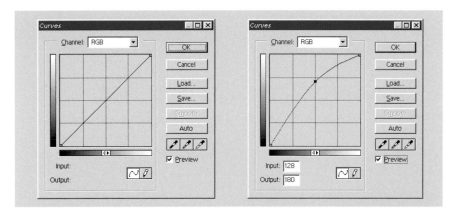

7.10 Gamma correcting for print changes the transition from dark to light using a relationship that can be viewed as a curve.

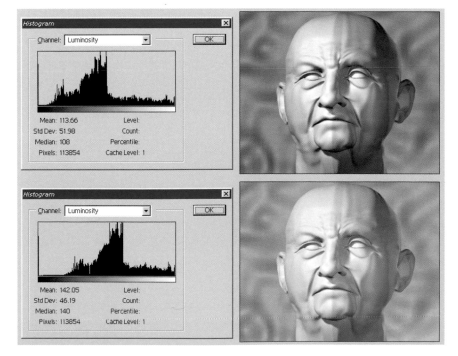

7.11 Histograms before gamma correction (top) and after (bottom) show a shift in the brightness of midtones.

It is a good idea to check your histogram after any image processing change, especially a gamma correction. It is normal to see at least a few gaps appearing in your histogram, from any areas that have been stretched by a gamma correction. This effect should remain relatively minor if you have properly exposed your original image. However, if you have been underexposing your scenes, then you could develop serious banding problems when you gamma-correct for print.

Checking work during image-processing operations is actually the most common use of histograms. In everyday 3D production work, most professionals do not check a histogram very often while lighting a scene. However, any time you are not sure about your overall use of dark and light tones, checking a histogram is a good idea. As you practice realistic 3D lighting, checking each project with a histogram will provide you with an objective "second opinion" to confirm that the tones you see on your monitor are really what is going into your file.

7.2 SIMULATING REAL-LIFE CAMERAS

Working in 3D, you control the brightness and contrast of your renderings by adjusting the lights and surfaces in your 3D scene. In shooting live-action scenes, on the other hand, the brightness of a shot is controlled by adjustments made to the camera.

This section explains how photographers measure available light with light meters, and then adjust the f-stop and shutter speed of a camera to control its sensitivity to light. Other factors, including the film speed, also affect the brightness of the image that gets recorded.

Most 3D programs lack any direct simulation of these exposure settings on their virtual cameras. Even so, understanding them will help you simulate their results in 3D, as well as improving communication and integration with live-action productions.

7.2.1 METERING

Histograms give you an objective way to measure the brightness of a 3D scene. Out in the real world, photographers and cinematographers use *light meters* to measure levels of illumination. Light meters come in various shapes and sizes: Some are separate hand-held devices as in Figure 7.12, others are built into a camera.

There are two ways that a light meter can be used. An *incident* light reading measures the amount of light reaching the subject, taken with the meter at the subject's position, pointing toward the light. A *reflected* light

7.12 A white plastic hood slides sideways to adapt a meter for incident light readings.

meter reading measures how much light is reflected off the subject, and is measured from the position of the camera. Often light meters have a translucent hood (as shown in Figure 7.12), that slides over the sensor during an incident reading, to receive illumination from a range of angles.

In essence, histograms of your test renderings are a kind of reflected light reading. They indicate the tones of light that actually reached the camera, after a subject was illuminated by the light. This means that the color and brightness of the surfaces visible in the rendering will influence the histogram just as much as the color and brightness of the lights.

After reading the light meter, a photographer can gauge an appropriate setting for the camera's aperture and shutter speed, based on the amount of light in the scene.

7.2.2 APERTURE

One of the most important exposure controls on a real camera is the *aperture*, the opening through which light passes to expose the film. In most cameras, the size of the aperture can be adjusted larger or smaller, so that different amounts of light can reach the film during the exposure.

The aperture size varies via an arrangement of metal flaps, which can give the aperture a hexagonal or octagonal shape, as shown in Figure 7.13. The shape of the aperture is sometimes seen as a feature of some lens flares.

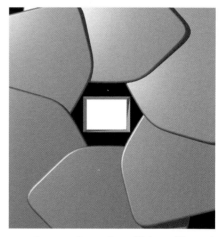

7.13 A camera's aperture dilates with a set of metal flaps.

7.2.2.1 F-STOPS

The size of the aperture is measured in *f-stops*. A higher f-stop number, such as f64, indicates a narrow aperture, which allows in very little light. A lower f-stop number, such as f1.4, specifies a wider aperture opening, which would allow in more light.

The series of f-stop values available on a camera, as in Figure 7.14, may look complex and arbitrary, but they are actually calibrated so that each increase in f-stop cuts the light in half. Different lenses may have different maximums and minimums, but often include the f-stops 1.4, 2, 2.8, 4, 5.6, 8, 11, 16, 22, 32, 45, and 64.

7.2.2.2 DEPTH OF FIELD

Your choice of f-stop has side effects beyond simply changing the brightness of the scene. The biggest side effect is the depth of field in the scene. *Depth of field* is the measurement of how near or far from the camera a subject can be while still appearing to be in focus.

7.14 The aperture widens at lower f-stop numbers, and narrows at higher numbers.

While technically a lens is focused to one specific distance, the depth of field shows the range in which objects remain acceptably in-focus, so that they are not noticeably blurred. A higher f-stop number, such as f64, creates a large depth of field, which is sometimes called *deep focus*. Deep focus throws everything in focus at once, from objects very close to the camera, to the distant background, as shown on the left side of Figure 7.15.

A lower f-stop number, such as f1.2, creates a shallow depth of field. A shallow depth of field could mean that only a few objects could be in focus, as shown on the right side of Figure 7.15. Any subject that stepped closer to the camera, or stood further back, would quickly fall out of focus.

Deep focus requires a large amount of light. In a dim environment, the aperture would need to open wide to get enough light, and this would reduce the depth of field. The first film to make extensive use of deep focus shots, Orson Welles' 1941 masterpiece *Citizen Kane* required huge banks of flood lights to keep the camera on a suitable f-stop.

Depth-of-field effects in 3D programs sometimes ask for an f-stop value to simulate depth of field. As shown in Figure 7.16, you could choose a low value such as f1.2 if you wanted a very limited depth of field, or a high number such as f64 if you wanted deep focus.

When a 3D program asks you for an f-stop setting to control the depth of field, it is only to simulate the depth of field associated with the f-stop. The f-stop you specify will not influence the brightness of the shot, even though that is the primary function of f-stop adjustment on a real camera. In some software, the depth of field controls even skip the f-stop designation altogether, and simply allow you to specify a starting and stopping distance for your focus, which can be easier to control.

7.15 A smaller aperture gives a larger depth of field (left), while a larger aperture produces a more shallow depth of field (right).

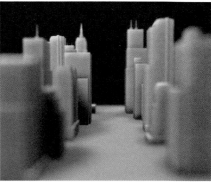

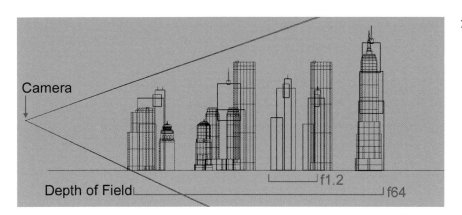

7.16 Adjusting your depth of field may be specified via simulated f-stops.

7.2.3 FILM SPEED

Another way that cinematographers can influence a camera's exposure is by choosing different kinds of film. Some film stocks are more sensitive to light than others. A designated *film speed* measures how quickly a particular film stock responds to light.

As with all other exposure-related decisions, there are trade-offs involved in choosing a film speed:

- A *high-speed film* is highly sensitive to light, allowing a smaller aperture or a higher shutter speed in ordinary lighting conditions. This could provide a picture with a deep focus or crisp reproduction of rapidly moving subjects. However, the disadvantage of high-speed film stocks is that they often have more grain and provide less contrast than slower film stocks.

- A *low-speed film* often offers the sharpest film stock, with the finest grain and best reproduction of color and contrast. Because lower speed film is less sensitive to light, it has the disadvantages of sometimes requiring a slower shutter speed (which can increase motion blur) or a wider aperture (which can limit depth of field).

When bright light is available, such as if you are shooting on a sunny day, then a low-speed film can be used for crisp, accurate images. In lower light conditions, high-speed film is often more useful.

Because they don't require film, video cameras obviously don't depend on a choice of film stocks. However, video cameras do have an extra factor in their exposure called *gain*. Gain is the electronic amplification of the signal received from the video camera's light-sensitive chip or picture tube. The result of gain is similar to the side-effects of film speed described previously: If a video camera is used in a darker environment, the gain can make the image grainy, and reduce resolution, in much the same way that some higher-speed film stocks affect a filmed image.

7.2.4 MOTION AND FRAME RATE

Video and motion picture cameras have a *frame rate*, which is usually measured in frames per second (or *FPS*), and specifies how many individual frames or images are exposed per second of moving film or video.

Motion picture film is usually shot at 24FPS. 24FPS is called *sound speed*, because it is the standard speed for film with a synchronized soundtrack.

Different television standards around the world have different frame rates. The *NTSC* standard, common throughout North America and much of the Pacific Rim, uses a frame rate of just less than 30FPS. Two of the world's other major standards, *PAL* and *SECAM*, use 25FPS.

7.2.4.1 SHUTTER SPEED

Closely related to frame rate is the *shutter speed* of a camera. The shutter speed is a measurement of how long a camera's shutter opens to allow light to expose the film and is usually expressed as a fraction of a second. A common shutter speed in live-action film is 1/48 of a second, which results from the shutter being opened and closed at even intervals in filming 24FPS.

The longer the shutter is open, the more light is allowed to reach the film. A shutter speed of 1/4 second would allow twice as much light to reach the film as a speed of 1/8 second. Doubling the duration the shutter stays open makes a light in the scene appear twice as bright.

Instead of a fraction of a second, another notation indicating shutter speed that you may see is called the *shutter angle*. The shutter of most motion picture cameras is a revolving disc. The disc rotates 360 degrees for each frame that is exposed. A window in the disc allows light through to the film when the shutter is in the "open" position. On the other side of the shutter, opaque metal blocks light. The shutter angle controls the angle of the opening in the shutter, which can be made narrower by the position of a small metal flap, as represented in Figure 7.17.

The most common shutter angle of 180° means that the shutter was opened half of the time, and closed half of the time. At a 180° shutter angle, the shutter speed would be equal to half of the frame rate. For example, at film's standard frame rate of 24FPS, with a shutter angle of 180°, the shutter speed would be 1/48 of a second.

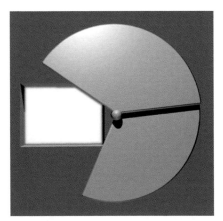

7.17 An opening in a revolving shutter creates the shutter angle.

The shutter angle divided by 360 will tell you what portion of the frame rate is actually being used as the shutter speed for an exposure. For example, if the shutter angle was 90°, then the shutter would be open 1/4 of the time. A 90° shutter at 24FPS would therefore be equivalent to a shutter speed of 1/(4 × 24) or 1/96 of a second.

7.2.4.2 MOTION BLUR

Besides changing the amount of exposure, a shutter speed has a very visible side effect in controlling the amount of *motion blur* in a shot. Motion blur is the amount of movement or change within a scene captured during the exposure of one frame, as in Figure 7.18.

Many rendering programs have an option to adjust the simulated shutter speed used to render motion blur. Often, this shutter speed is measured by a number running from 0 to 1, or sometimes 0% to 100%. If you have a logged shutter angle from live-action footage, divide the shutter angle by 360 to get the value for your 3D program. For example, if a scene were shot with a 180° shutter, enter 0.5 (or 50%), which would produce results as seen in Figure 7.18.

As a rule of thumb, keep your motion blur between 0.5 and 0.75 for the most natural, realistic results. Too low a level of motion blur could make the action seem jerky or unnatural. On the other hand, a full value of 1 (or 100%) for your software's motion blur would simulate a 360° shutter. A 360° shutter angle would mean that the shutter never shut, and there was no time allowed to advance the film to the next frame, making this setting technically impossible in a real motion-picture camera. Too high a number can appear to create an after-image or trail behind objects as they move, instead of resembling natural motion blur.

To simulate the most photo-realistic possible motion blur, you might also take into account the fact that slower shutter speeds are commonly required to let in enough light in darker environments, and very high shutter speeds are only possible in brightly lit environments. Dark scenes might appear more natural with more motion blur, to simulate a slower shutter speed. You can use less motion blur if a scene is very bright, to simulate a higher shutter speed.

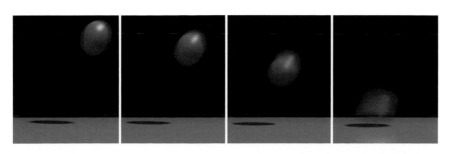

7.18 A motion blur of 0.5 simulates a 180° shutter angle.

7.2.4.3 VIDEO FIELDS

In most video cameras, frames are actually created through two separate exposures per frame, called video fields. A *field* is one half of a video frame, split by alternate scanlines, as shown in Figure 7.19. (*Scanlines* are the horizontal lines of image information that make up a video frame, corresponding to one row of pixels running across your rendering.)

The odd-numbered scanlines are displayed first, then another field is displayed showing all the even-numbered scanlines. When the two fields are interlaced a full-resolution frame is created on the screen, taking advantage of all of the scanlines from both fields to reproduce the picture.

The advantage of splitting the frame into two fields is that moving subjects are effectively sampled at twice the frame rate, for a smoother, more accurate reproduction of motion. Instead of having the shutter open only 25 or 30 times a second, it opens and captures a field 50 or 60 times a second. This means that any moving subjects are scanned twice as frequently.

Most 3D rendering programs have an option to render field-rate video. When activated, the renderer will output twice as many image files, rendered at each frame as well as at each half frame, so that the two field images can be interlaced to show different points in time. This essentially simulates how motion would have been recorded by an ordinary video camera.

By cutting in half the shutter speed, the amount of motion blur is also cut in half by using field-rate video. Some 3D artists even turn off motion blur when rendering field-rate video output, although the complete lack of motion blur could sometimes look unrealistic. The renderings of an animated object in Figure 7.20 illustrate your different rendering choices for fields and motion blur—you can see that the motion blur matters less when rendering on fields.

Figure 7.21 illustrates the *wagon wheel effect*, the confusion sometimes caused by actions that repeat at a pace similar to the frame rate. The wagon wheel effect got its name from chase scenes in Western movies, which often featured speeding wagons. The rotating wheels often

> **NOTE**
>
> An alternative to interlaced fields is *progressive scan*, which describes a type of display that does not split each frame into fields, and instead scans directly through all the scanlines of each frame, in order. Progressive scan is used by computer monitors, some advanced television and high-definition television systems, and optionally by some digital camcorders.

7.19 Two fields are interlaced on a television screen to form a frame.

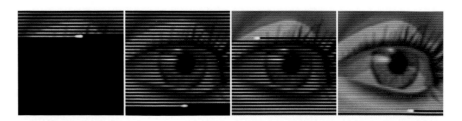

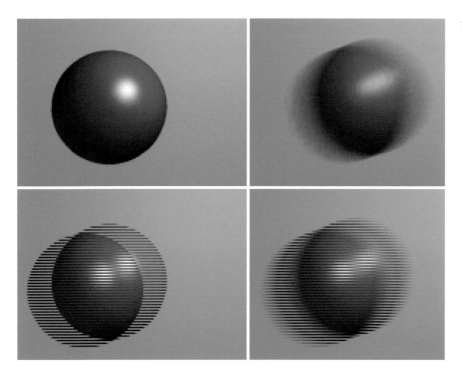

7.20 An animated object with no motion blur or field-rate rendering (upper left) appears static. Motion blur is added to the right, and field-rate motion is added to the lower renderings.

7.21 Looking at these frames, it might be difficult to tell which direction the wheel is turning.

appeared to spin at the wrong speed, or rotate backward, when viewed on film. The problem was caused because similar-looking spokes change places while the shutter was closed, making it difficult to follow their motion between frames. The wagon wheel effect can be reduced by adding motion blur, increasing the frame rate if possible, or activating field-rate rendering in cases where field-rate rendering is appropriate.

Rendering 3D on fields is only recommended for some 3D animations, and not others. Here are some of the situations you might want to render at field-rate.

- Field-rate rendering should be used for graphics in video or television productions where you want the smoothest motion possible.

- 3D elements that will be combined with interlaced footage shot with a video camera can appear best integrated if rendered at field-rate.

- Field-rate rendering can be used when you want to render with little or no motion blur, but still want smooth motion.

- Field-rate computer graphics are a staple of corporate video production, "flying logo" style animated graphic designs, and elements involving moving titles.

However, some judgment is needed before choosing to activate field-rate rendering for a project. Here are some times when you would not want to render on fields.

- Field-rate rendering should only by used for products output and displayed on interlaced video, not for any graphics going to film or progressive-scan computer screens.

- Character animation generally shouldn't be rendered on fields, even when output to video. The intermediate interpolated poses added by field-rate rendering hurt, rather than help, the quality of keyframed animation.

- Renderings that will be output to several different television standards, for international release, can maintain more quality through the conversion if not rendered on fields.

- When used in television projects in which the live-action footage is shot on film or progressive-scan systems, 3D elements should not be rendered on fields, and should instead be rendered at the frame rate of the live-action footage.

- 3D elements that will be manually retouched, resized, rotated, blurred, or otherwise manipulated after rendering generally shouldn't be rendered at field-rate.

For any video productions where you still aren't sure if you want field-rate rendering, the appearance of your final footage is the most meaningful test. Output test sequences to video, with or without field-rate rendering, and with any level of motion blur that you will use, and see for yourself which setting best improves the quality of your shot.

7.2.5 OTHER EXPOSURE CONTROLS

Besides the aperture, shutter speed, and film speed, there are other factors that can influence a real camera's exposure.

- A *Neutral Density* (or *ND*) filter, when it is mounted in front of a camera's lens, limits exposure without degrading the image or changing other factors.

■ When film is processed, different processing techniques can increase the exposure of the film by the equivalent of several f-stops, usually changing the grain and color reproduction in the process.

■ When photographic prints are made from negatives, or when projectable motion picture film is printed from the negative, various controls allow further manipulation to the brightness and colors of the images.

■ When film is digitized in a *telecine* (a system for real-time conversion to video) or a *film scanner* (high-resolution digitizer), the equipment can be adjusted in many ways to fine-tune the brightness and contrast.

In short, by the time you see most images on film, on video, or in print, they have been through a lot! Many decisions and processes lead up to the final choice of tones used to represent any part of a photographic image.

The most important conclusion you can draw from studying a real camera's exposure controls is that brightness in the real world does not directly translate into the tones of an image. A photograph or filmed image is not an objective record—not something just "taken" from real life—but is one photographer's subjective depiction of a scene.

7.3 EXERCISES

1. Load some of your own 3D scenes into a paint or image-processing program, and examine them in a histogram. Do you see any of the problems or issues identified in this chapter? Going back to the 3D scene, are there any changes that you would make?

2. Examine individual surfaces in your 3D scenes, and see if any stand out as if they were not a part of the same environment. How bright is the darkest part of the surface? How bright is the brightest part of the surface? How similar is the surface to other objects illuminated by the same light source?

3. In a rented movie, stop and examine some scenes filmed at night or in a dark environment. How deep is the depth of field? Is there a lot of motion blur when a subject moves rapidly? What trade-offs do you think the cinematographer made in filming the scene? Also ask yourself the same questions about a scene shot outdoors in the sun.

COMPOSITION AND STAGING

THIS CHAPTER DISCUSSES issues essential to the layout of your rendering as a whole, not just to your lighting. Where should each object appear within your rendering? Where should the camera be positioned to create the best image? What kind of shots will you use to render an animation? Answering these questions can produce more artistic, more professional work. To help you answer them, this chapter covers *composition*, the layout of your entire rendering, and *staging*, how you arrange the objects and characters in your shot. The artistic rules and cinematic conventions discussed in this chapter depend more on your camera than on your lights, but understanding these rules is a vital step in creating a compelling shot or a beautiful final rendering.

8.1 TYPES OF SHOTS

The language of film involves a certain number of basic shots. It is important to learn to recognize and describe shots in the terms that filmmakers use, so you can plan and discuss your digital productions, or adopt cinematic techniques to tell a story.

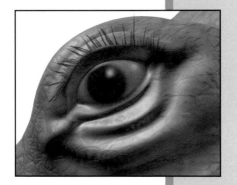

8.1.1 SHOT SIZES

One of the major distinctions between types of shots is the *shot size*. The shot size identifies how large an area will be visible within the frame. In order from showing the smallest area to the largest, here are the five most common shot sizes:

- **Extreme close-up (ECU).** Makes a very small detail fill the screen. A shot showing only part of a character's face would be an extreme close-up.

- **Close-up (CU).** Framed tightly on a specific area, such as a character's face.

- **Medium close-up (MCU).** Between a close-up and a *medium shot* in size, frequently showing a character's head and shoulders.

- **Medium shot (MS).** Shows a broader area than a close-up. Often a medium shot shows a character's upper-body, arms, and head.

- **Wide shot (WS or WIDE).** Shows a broad view of an entire location, subject, or action. Often a wide shot will show an entire character from head to toe, or whole groups of characters.

The yellow boxes in Figure 8.1 show the areas of a character typically covered by these shot sizes. These are only general guidelines—actual shot sizes are relative to the size of the subject or environment you are portraying. For example, in an animation of a football game, a wide shot

8.1 An ECU (extreme close-up), CU (close-up), MCU (medium close-up), MS (medium shot), and WIDE (wide shot) are common shot sizes you could choose to render a character.

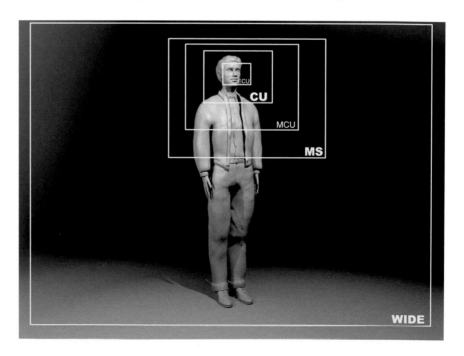

might show the full stadium, and a shot showing one individual player could be called a close-up. In an animation starring animated insects, a wide shot might only cover a few inches of space.

Using a variety of shot sizes, as shown in Figure 8.2, can make your renderings and animations more interesting and cinematic. Explore your 3D scenes for interesting areas that could produce close-ups or extreme close-ups of your character or environment.

Wider shots can show whole environments, capture broader actions, or show the positions of multiple characters at once. Before moving in to show close-up detail, you can give your audience an idea of the overall scene with an *establishing shot*. An establishing shot is a wider shot that functions to set up the scene for the rest of the shots and shows the surroundings that might not be shown in each close-up. Sometimes, before beginning a scene set inside of a building, an establishing shot is included that shows the exterior of the building, to establish the full location of the room.

Medium shots and close-ups help draw the audience into the scene, and reveal details or facial expressions. Close-ups are especially important in renderings made for television or smaller screen displays.

A *reaction shot* is a shot that shows a character's response as he or she watches or reacts to some other event, usually using a close-up of the character to show the reaction. Making reaction shots is one of the most important uses for close-ups—don't forget to include reaction shots in every action sequence you create, if you want to keep your audience engaged in the human side of a story. Even if you are animating an enormous scope of events, with wide shots of spaceship battles and city-smashing lizards, your audience will care more about what is happening on the screen if you also show the individual people being affected by all the action.

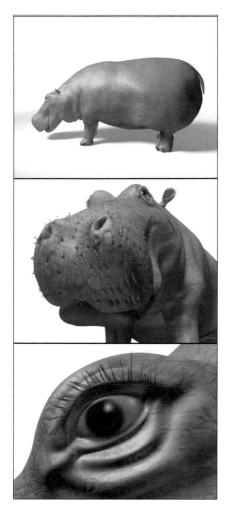

8.2 A wide establishing shot (top) helps orient the audience, a medium shot (middle) covers the action, and an extreme close-up (lower) reveals more detail.

8.1.2 Z-AXIS BLOCKING

In a three-dimensional scene, a shot doesn't always have to be just a close-up or just a wide-shot, but can have different objects or characters at different distances from the camera.

Staging your scene with different subjects at different distances from the camera is called *Z-axis blocking*. An example of Z-axis blocking would be when one character walks toward the camera, making that character appear in close-up, while another character remains at a greater distance in the background, as shown in Figure 8.3.

8.3 Z-axis blocking combines a close-up of one character with a wide shot of other characters in this scene staged by Jorge R. Gutierrez.

NOTE

Z-axis blocking may sound as if it is a computer graphics term, but in reality the phrase has been used by cinematographers since before the advent of 3D rendering.

Take advantage of the 3D space available when staging your scene, instead of lining up all of your characters the same distance from the camera!

8.1.3 SHOT/COUNTER-SHOT

Specific types of shots can be put together to help you stage a conversation, interview, or other scenes in which two characters are facing each other.

8.1.3.1 THE TWO-SHOT

A *two-shot* is simply a shot showing two characters, as in Figure 8.4. While a two-shot is a convenient, straightforward way to show both characters, it can look flat and uninteresting. A smarter way to cover a scene between two characters can be to start with a two-shot as an establishing shot, then cut in to close-ups and over-the-shoulder shots.

8.1.3.2 THE OVER-THE-SHOULDER SHOT

An *over-the-shoulder shot* (abbreviated *OSS*) is a type of close or medium shot showing one of the characters, shot with a portion of the other character's back in the foreground, as shown in Figure 8.5. An OSS focuses on one of the characters, while showing just enough of the other character to indicate his position. Even though you can't see the face of the character whose back appears in the foreground, his or her presence serves to frame the shot and establish the spatial relationship between characters.

Rendering an over-the-shoulder shot simply involves positioning the camera to look over the shoulder of one character, as shown in Figure 8.6, to frame the medium or close-up shot of another. Using a depth-of-field effect can help separate the foreground from the background, but is not mandatory. An OSS as shown here could be set up to render the scene from over the shoulder of either character.

8.4 A two-shot simply shows both characters.

8.5 An OSS (over-the-shoulder shot) shows one character, with the back of the other character included for reference.

8.6 An OSS is named because the camera is positioned looking over the shoulder of one character to frame the shot of another.

A series of shots that alternate between an OSS of each character, sometimes also including close-ups of the characters, is called *shot/counter-shot* coverage of your scene. This is a common and effective way to capture almost any kind of interaction between two characters. Whether characters are exchanging words, bullets, kisses, or punches, you will see shot/counter-shot coverage used over and over in movies and television programs once you start looking for it.

If you render OSS shots of each character, and adopt shot/counter-shot instead of rendering a fixed two-shot for the full scene, it can create a more engaging, cinematic look for your animation, and do more to draw your audience into the action of the scene. Rendering an OSS instead of a two-shot through a dialog scene has an added bonus that you can skip some of the facial animation on one of the characters during that shot, while watching the other character react to what is said.

8.2 CAMERA ANGLES

You can change the appearance and function of your shot by where you place the camera to render your scene. Your camera angles come from the positions you choose for the camera.

8.2.1 THE LINE OF ACTION

If you are rendering a scene from several different camera angles, and plan to edit the different shots into a seamless sequence, then a vital rule to follow is to make all of your camera angles come from camera positions on the same side of a line of action. A *line of action* is the path along which your subjects are looking or traveling, or an imaginary line between two characters who are interacting. For example, in the view of the scene in Figure 8.7, the line of action is the line between the two characters.

You would not want to cut to any angle on the characters filmed from the other side, because that would reverse the direction that the characters appeared to be facing. For example, if a character had been facing toward the right side of the screen, you should not choose a camera angle that suddenly makes him appear to be facing to the left in the next shot, because he will appear to have turned around.

For a character who is traveling or in a chase, if he was running toward the right side of the screen in one shot, then he should continue to appear running toward the right side of the screen in every shot, unless the character is forced to turn around. No change of camera angles should be used that would reverse his screen direction.

Football fans are familiar with this concept from the way football games are televised: All the cameras are normally put on the same side of the stadium. On occasion, a camera will be used on the opposite side, to capture action that would not have been visible otherwise. To avoid confusion, the words "Reverse Angle" are superimposed on the television screen whenever they cut to the camera from the opposite side of the line of action.

If your camera shoots from one side of the line of action, then your lighting should also be guided by it. Generally, you will position your

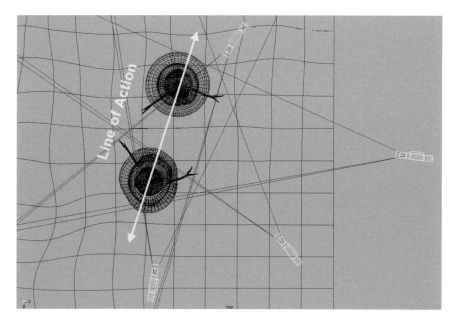

8.7 This top view shows how camera angles all come from the same side of an imaginary line of action (drawn in yellow) between the characters.

key and most of your fill lights on the same side of the line of action as your camera. In most scenes, only back lights and lights illuminating the set need to be on the other side of the line.

8.2.2 HIGH-ANGLE AND LOW-ANGLE SHOTS

The most normal looking shots of most subjects will be the ones taken with the camera at the height of an average person's eye-level, or with the camera at the same altitude as the eyes of the characters in the scene. Moving the camera to different heights can create other camera angles that are sometimes more interesting or dramatically useful.

To render a *low-angle shot*, the camera is positioned below your subject, looking upward, as seen on the left side of Figure 8.8. The low angle can serve to make a character look bigger, stronger, or more noble, and low-angle shots can also exaggerate the size of environments and architectural spaces.

For a *high-angle shot*, the camera is positioned above the subject, looking downward, as seen on the right side of Figure 8.8. A high-angle shot can make a character look smaller, younger, weak, confused, or cuter and more childlike.

8.2.3 PERSPECTIVE

Another important distinction in how you render a shot is the *perspective*. When the camera is in a different position, it shows the scene from a different perspective.

Your scenes will look different if the camera is positioned far from your subject, even if you zoom the camera in to a very narrow field of view to compensate for the shot size. Figure 8.9 shows three different perspectives on the exact same scene, rendered from three different camera positions.

NOTE

Flip back to Chapter 6 and notice how the dramatic low angle in Figure 6.13 makes the doors look even bigger and more difficult to open.

8.8 Even with the character in the same pose, a low-angle shot (left) makes her appear larger, while a high-angle shot (right) makes her appear smaller and more helpless.

In the top frame of Figure 8.9, the camera was close to the subjects, using a wide, 80-degree field of view to capture the whole scene. In the center frame, the camera was further away, using an average, 40-degree field of view. In the lower frame, the camera was very far away, using a narrow, 20-degree field of view. Notice how the perspective changes the apparent length of the hallway, and changes the perceived amount of space between the red balls. The nearby camera produces a greater sense of depth, and would also exaggerate any motion toward or away from the camera in an animation.

When the camera is moved near to an object, there is a broader view of the background behind the character, and the space seems larger. Rendering with the camera near a character can also make a character's actions or animation seem to be moving more quickly or covering a greater distance. This is especially true for any motion directed toward or away from the camera.

Rendering a close-up from a distance seems to compress the scene and reduce the sense of size and depth in the room. The sense of "flattened space," as shown in the bottom frame of Figure 8.9, could be useful if you wanted a room to appear cramped or a character to appear lost in a crowd, but could reduce the impact of other animated shots.

NOTE

A disturbing effect, sometimes used in horror movies, is possible if a camera's position and field of view are both animated at once, in opposite directions. For example, if the series of shots shown in Figure 8.9 were frames in an animation, simultaneously moving the camera away from the subject while zooming in to compensate, the perspective would shift oddly during the shot.

8.9 The change of perspective makes the same hallway look very long in the top frame, and short in the bottom frame.

If you want to choose a natural-looking perspective, a good rule of thumb is to think about where a person might be standing within the 3D space to watch your scene, and position the camera at the same distance. For example, if a scene takes place indoors, the camera should not be much further back than the size of a real room would naturally allow.

It is important to note that your perspective on a scene only changes when the camera is moved to a new position. Perspective is not changed by the camera's zoom (or focal-distance or field-of-view) control when the camera is left in the same position. For example, Figure 8.10 shows two different shot sizes, rendered from the exact same camera position. The perspective on the word "perspective" in the left frame is exactly the same as the perspective in the zoomed-in frame. If you enlarged the word as seen in the left frame, it would exactly match the image on the right.

8.10 Focal length changes by themselves do not change the camera's perspective.

In choosing a perspective, photographers generally consider pictures taken from a distance across a room to be more flattering than pictures taken with the camera very near to a person's face. Telephoto lenses with a narrow field of view (that allows close-up shots to be taken from across a room) are sometimes called *portrait lenses*, and they are used to take natural-looking, undistorted pictures of people. Taking a picture with a wide-angle lens positioned very close to a person's face can distort the shape of his or her face and be less flattering.

8.2.4 POV Shots

Another popular choice of camera angles is a *point-of-view shot (POV shot)*. A POV shot positions the camera to shoot the scene exactly as one character would see it.

POV shots are easy to set up in 3D: You just position the camera right between a character's eyes, as shown in Figure 8.11. If a character is moving, group or constrain the camera to follow any character motion, or animate the camera to simulate the motion of the character. Usually, you will want to hide the character whose POV is being shown, unless some body parts such as her hands become visible in the shot.

Here are some ideas for how POV shots could be useful in your animations:

- **Seeing a scene from a character's point-of-view can help an audience better identify with a character or sympathize with his position in a scene.** For example, if something is going to jump out and surprise a character, it might be animated to appear suddenly and leap toward the camera, surprising the audience.

- **A POV shot can create a dynamic way to capture an action or event.** For example, if a character were falling down a hole, the camera could be animated to move through space just where his head would be.

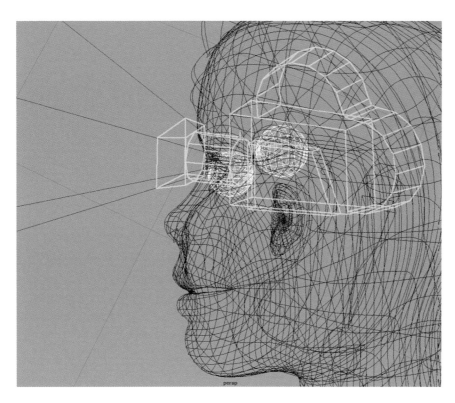

8.11 Constraining a camera between a character's eyes makes for a quick POV shot setup.

- **POV shots can be used for comic effect in some animations, by animating the camera with an attribute of a character.** For example, an animated camera might imitate the motion of a staggering drunk or a bounding dog.

- **POV shots can show a character's view when she looks through a gunsight, telescope, or keyhole.** Often POV shots such as these are processed after rendering to imitate the shape of the telescope or keyhole or to simulate the distortion or focus of a viewing device.

- **A POV shot can be a convenient "shortcut" to rendering some scenes.** Because you don't see the character himself while you are watching through his eyes, you don't have to animate or render him in that shot.

- **A convention from horror and suspense films is to show the POV of a killer or monster as it stalks and hunts for its next victim.** The use of the POV shot prevents the audience from seeing the actual killer; they only see the killer's-eye-view of the unwitting victim.

Have fun using POV shots when they are appropriate to your animations. The one concern you should weigh before using a POV shot is that they can be very noticeable, and sometimes even distracting, if overused.

8.2.5 CAMERA MOVES

Animating the position of the camera is one of the most overused techniques in 3D animation, and can also distract an audience when it is not used properly. Unnatural camera moves can call attention to the camera and remind the audience that they are watching computer graphics. If you want to animate more realistic and natural camera moves, it helps to study the most popular types of moves possible with a real camera.

- **Pan.** The camera rotates from side to side, so that it aims more to the left or right. The camera does not need to change location during a pan, it only needs to face a different direction.

- **Tilt.** The camera rotates to aim upward or downward, without changing the position where the camera is mounted.

- **Zoom.** The camera's lens is adjusted to increase or decrease the camera's field of view, magnifying a portion of the scene without moving the camera. A *zoom in* will narrow the field of view to create more of a close up. A *zoom out* will widen the field of view.

- **Dolly.** The camera's actual position changes, such as to move alongside a moving subject or to travel closer to a character during a scene. A *dolly in* moves the camera physically closer to your subject, to create more of a close up. A *dolly out* backs the camera away from your subject.

- **Rack Focus.** A camera's focal distance changes during a shot, so that subjects at a different distance from the camera come into or fall out of focus, as shown in Figure 8.12.

Note that most of these common types of camera "moves" do not involve actually changing the position of the camera. When the camera pans, tilts, zooms, or rack focuses, it can remain mounted in the same place on a tripod, and only the aiming direction or the lens is adjusted.

A camera move should be used only when it is motivated by an action or event in the story. Here are some times when a camera move might be motivated:

- When a character or vehicle is moving, sometimes you can pan or dolly the camera to follow the character's motion. Be sure to let the character start moving before the camera moves, so that the camera follows the character, instead of appearing the other way around!

- POV shots from moving characters and vehicles will require a moving camera.

8.12 A rack focus adjusts the focus of the camera to reveal another subject without moving the camera.

- A moving camera can dolly into an environment as a way to explore the space, especially for sweeping establishing shots when an environment is first seen.

- For dramatic effect, sometimes a camera can move slowly toward a character to emphasize certain actions or dialog.

You don't need to animate the position of the camera if alternatives such as panning to follow your animation, or simply cutting to a new shot, will do just as well. If a camera animation is not motivated, it could distract the audience, instead of helping you tell a story.

When animating any camera move, it is a good idea to make it begin with a well-composed static shot before easing into the move. During the course of a camera move, the framing will often be compromised, but upon completing the move, the camera should come to rest at another well-composed static shot. This way, whoever is editing your footage will not be forced to cut in or out from the middle of a moving camera shot.

8.3 FRAMING

Framing is the art of how you position your subjects within the images you render. How you frame your scenes determines what objects will be visible in your rendering, and how the space within the image will be divided.

Placing a subject dead-center in a frame does not look very natural or interesting, and generally produces a bad composition. Your rendering will look better composed if you place your subject off-center to a certain extent.

8.3.1 THE RULE OF THIRDS

A useful guideline when composing a shot is to picture the frame divided into thirds, both horizontally and vertically, as shown in Figure 8.13. To make use of these imaginary lines, position your subject along one of the lines (shown in black), or position an area of interest where two lines intersect (shown in red).

If there is a horizon line in the scene, putting the horizon one third or two thirds of the way up the frame can look much better than placing the horizon in the center, which could appear to split the rendering in half.

WARNING

Some technically minded users of 3D software have attempted to "automate" the process of framing shots, by constraining the camera to aim at the center of an animated object or character. This is a bad idea. Not only does it weaken the composition of the shot, but it hides the overall motion of the subject, by unnaturally pinning it in the center of the rendered frames. Even a quick job of aiming the camera yourself can look much better than letting the camera automatically center your subject.

8.13 The "Rule of Thirds" helps position your subject in a well-composed shot.

8.3.2 POSITIVE AND NEGATIVE SPACE

Most images can be said to consist of both *positive space* and *negative space*. Positive space is the part of your frame showing your main subject or foreground objects. Negative space includes the parts of your rendering that can be considered the background, or surrounding area around your subject. Your composition is a balance between the positive and negative space. The left side of Figure 8.14 shows the negative space in black, and the positive space in white.

8.14 The shapes created by the negative space in your composition (shown in black) can be just as important as the positive space.

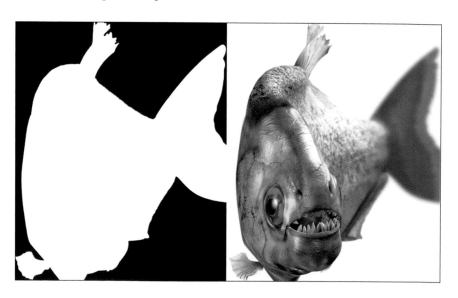

Sometimes, extra empty space is required in a shot to create a greater sense of balance or closure. For example, in a close-up or medium shot, a character's face or eyes looking to one side creates a powerful vector that directs the audience's attention to one side of the frame. To balance your composition, you usually want to leave negative space in front of your character, in the direction that he or she is looking. Camera operators sometimes call the extra space left in front of a person *look space* or *nose room*. The top image in Figure 8.15 is a balanced, complete rendering with negative space giving you room to follow the direction of the character's gaze.

Without look space, or with the negative spaces distributed elsewhere, viewers cannot follow the direction a character is looking, and the composition will seem cropped, unbalanced, or incomplete. In Figure 8.15, a viewer could even interpret the character's pose differently based on the negative space—in the unbalanced lower frame, the woman appears to be deliberately turning away, and isolating herself from her surroundings. With no change to her pose, the character is given a more sullen, introspective appearance in the lower frame solely by the change of composition.

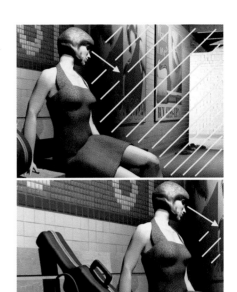

8.15 A balanced composition (top) leaves look space for a character (shown in yellow). An unbalanced composition (bottom) can trap your eye on the side of the frame.

8.3.3 GRAPHIC WEIGHT

Everything that appears in your rendering has a graphic weight. The *graphic weight* of an area or object is the amount that it attracts attention or dominates the composition. Items with a bold color, or a brightness with contrast against the surrounding scene, have the greatest graphic weight. Larger items have a bigger graphic weight than smaller details. Areas near the edge of the frame also can have a greater graphic weight.

Simply put, there is graphic weight in anything that catches your eye. To judge which objects in your scene have the most graphic weight, just glance at the whole rendering, and see on which areas you find yourself focusing. The eye-catching objects are the ones with a high graphic weight, and they need to be arranged carefully in your frame to achieve a balanced composition.

The red shovel added to Figure 8.16 has a high graphic weight, and could unbalance the composition, especially because it is near the edge of the frame. Looking at the left picture in Figure 8.16, your eye is drawn to the shovel and the area around the shovel, to the exclusion of the rest of the frame. Balance is restored on the right side of Figure 8.16, where another colorful object is added to the opposite side of the rendering, and the shovel is also moved away from the edge.

8.16 The graphic weight of the shovel unbalances the composition (left), but the scene can be balanced with a few adjustments (right).

Your lighting can increase or decrease the graphic weight of different parts of your scene. Areas of your rendering that are dimly lit, washed-out, or lacking contrast will have less graphic weight, while areas with more shading, contrast, or color can stand out with higher graphic weight. Sometimes adding colored light, or extra highlights and contrast, can increase the graphic weight of some part of your scene. For example, the top image in Figure 8.17 is unbalanced, with all areas of interest on the right. In the lower image, a blue back light makes the hills more colorful and eye-catching, drawing the eye back into the rest of the scene.

8.3.4 FRAMING FOR FILM AND VIDEO

Framing your work is not just an art, it is also a science. As you produce work for different media, you need to understand a few things about different film and television formats.

8.3.4.1 FORMATS AND ASPECT RATIOS

The actual frames in which you arrange your scene can have different proportions, depending on the format of film or television for which you are rendering your graphics. The proportion of the width to the height of an image is called its *aspect ratio*. For example, if the width of an image were exactly twice its height, it would have an aspect ratio of 2:1.

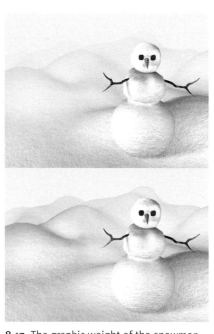

8.17 The graphic weight of the snowman on the right unbalances the composition (top), but a lighting adjustment adds punch to the left side of the frame (bottom).

Another notation used to write aspect ratios is to write only one number, the result of dividing the width by the height. For example, in this notation, 2:1 could also be written as a 2.0 aspect ratio. A higher number means a wider screen, and a lower number means a taller screen.

In professional rendering for film and television, you could be asked to frame your shots for a number of different aspect ratios.

■ **1.33.** Standard television sets have a 1.33 aspect ratio (speaking out loud, say "one three three"). Even though television broadcasts in different countries around the world are encoded with different systems that have different resolutions, all standard televisions use the same 1.33 aspect ratio.

■ **1.78.** HDTV and other wide-screen television systems have a 1.78 aspect ratio, which is more commonly referred to as 16:9 (say "sixteen by nine"). This allows viewers at home to see an aspect ratio closer to some of the most popular wide-screen presentations in movie theaters.

■ **1.85.** The world's most popular aspect ratio for motion pictures is 1.85 (say "one eight five"). Sometimes a filmmaker will refer to the format being shot as "Academy Aperture," meaning that it fills the part of the film negative standardized by the Academy of Motion Picture Arts and Sciences.

■ **2.35.** The second most popular aspect ratio for feature films in the United States is 2.35 (say "two three five"). This aspect ratio is sometimes called *Cinemascope* or *Panavision*, which are trademarks for specific formats using a 2.35 aspect ratio.

■ **1.66.** Less popular in the United States, but a popular format in some parts of the world is the 1.66 aspect ratio (say "one six six"). Being closer in shape to the format of a television screen allows 1.66 films a greater consistency between the composition shown in theaters, and the appearance of the film when adapted for television.

The shapes of these different aspect ratios are all shown in Figure 8.18.

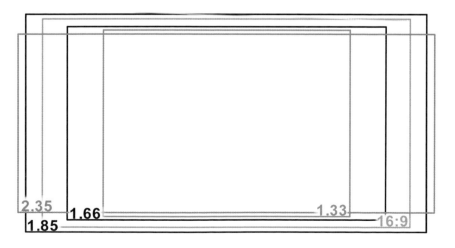

8.18 The five most common aspect ratios for film and television production are 1.33, 1.66, 1.78 (or 16:9), 1.85, and 2.35.

Some film formats actually expose a larger frame than the 1.85 aspect ratio intended to be shown in theaters, so that audiences in theaters see an image that has been cropped from the center of what was actually shot on the negative. For the purpose of visual effects, the entire film frame is often digitized *full gate* (including the negative area beyond the 1.85 rectangle) for use in visual effects work. This can mean that larger renderings need to be created, especially if the film's producers are preserving the option to convert the full frame of some of the shots to the home video version of the film. On the bright side, this practice can also give you greater flexibility in visual effects creation, because different portions of a larger background plate can sometimes be used to shift the framing of a 1.85 shot to use parts of the image recorded above or below it on the negative.

A popular aspect ratio for films shot outdoors with sweeping panoramas is 2.35. It is sometimes used in bigger-budget films and regarded as a high-quality format. Usually 2.35 film is shot and projected with an *anamorphic* lens, which is a lens designed to squeeze the image horizontally to fit onto the 35mm film. The anamorphic lens fits the image to the space on the negative more efficiently than standard 1.85. This can give films shot in 2.35 a higher-quality picture. 2.35 also gives directors more options in lighting scenes, because the ceiling is more likely to be cropped off compared to a scene shot with a taller frame, making more room to position overhead lights in a studio.

While 2.35 has advantages, modern movie theaters are commonly being divided into many smaller screens to show different films at once, and the width of the screen cannot be greatly increased to show 2.35 format films. The result is that 2.35 films are often projected as a smaller frame, so that the width of the screen is still used, but the image is less tall. If film publicists were honest, most screenings of 2.35 format films would be advertised as "short-screen presentations" instead of "wide-screen presentations," because the only change to screen size is the reduced height of the frame.

8.3.4.2 ADAPTATION TO TELEVISION

When films or other wide-screen programming are adapted for standard television or home video, the 1.85 or 2.35 aspect ratios need to be converted for display on 1.33 screens.

The technique of *letterboxing* is one approach to adapting wide-screen images to standard video. A letterboxed image consists of the original wide-screen composition shown in its entirety, with a black area above and below the image to fill the rest of the taller-screen format. The left

side of Figure 8.19 shows a full 1.85 image, as it would appear when letterboxed in a 1.33 television frame. Letterboxing is a faithful way to preserve the composition of a wide-screen film, but many home viewers
don't like to lose inches off their television picture size, with the top and
bottom of their screen showing solid black areas.

To fill a full TV screen with a picture, another technique, called *pan and
scan*, is commonly used to adapt wide-screen footage to standard television. The pan and scan process involves going through a movie and
selectively cropping off portions of the left and right of each shot, usually showing only the center of an image in the final shot on television.
The right side of Figure 8.19 shows the cropped 1.33 composition that
would result. Recalling the previous discussion about the importance to
a film of the full composition and spacing of a shot, this practice is seen
by some as an unnecessary modification of a filmmaker's original work.

The pan and scan process also can involve animating the area that gets
cropped from each frame. For example, a shot on video might virtually
pan across the original film frame, starting by showing the left side of
what was filmed, and ending by showing the right side of what was
filmed. This is supposed to appear similar to the results of the original
film camera having panned, but appears more as if you were scrolling
across the image. When watching movies on video (which are not letterboxed), see if you can spot the small horizontal pans added occasionally
in the process of converting wide-screen films to video.

8.3.4.3 VIDEO OVERSCAN

Unfortunately, you can't expect audiences watching your work on television to see all the way to the edges of your rendered frames. A portion
of a video signal may be cropped off of the screen by a process called
overscanning. A television picture tube overscans an image by projecting a
slightly larger picture than the size of the actual screen. Overscanning
was designed into early televisions to hide fluctuations of picture size
that could result from variations in the electrical current powering the

8.19 A 1.85 frame can be converted to 1.33 by letterboxing (left) or pan and scan (right). (I rendered all the subway scenes at the Art Center College of Design; Lisa Tate worked with me in modeling the human figures.)

television receiver. The amount of overscanning, and the centering of the image, varies greatly between televisions, depending on their age, model, and how they are adjusted, so different people viewing your work might see it cropped differently on different televisions.

There are suggested guidelines, as shown in Figure 8.20, that help you take overscanning into account when framing scenes that will be output to video or shown on television. If you are putting any text onto television that your viewer needs to read, it is especially important that no letters be lost in a television's overscan area. Text should be kept in the center 80% of the screen, within a guideline called the *Title Safe Area*.

To ensure that no one in your viewing audience misses an important action, make sure that vitally important parts of your scene fall within the central 90% of your frame, within a guideline called the *Action Safe Area*.

As you approach the outer edge of the frame, parts of your scene outside of the *Picture Safe Area* (sometimes called the *Safe Projection Area*) are likely to be cropped off by the majority of television receivers.

8.20 Keep important elements within the Title Safe, Action Safe, and Picture Safe areas to avoid losing them to video overscan.

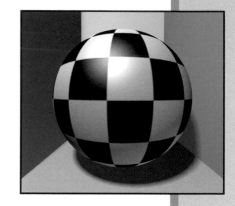

CHAPTER] 9

MATERIALS AND RENDERING ALGORITHMS

THIS CHAPTER FOLLOWS your rendering software through the main stages of shading, texturing, and rendering your scene, and suggests how to get the best quality and software performance along the way. The rendering process starts by setting up how your surfaces will respond to light to achieve properly shaded surfaces. Texture mapping adds variation and realism to your materials, and raytracing effects allow objects to accurately shadow and reflect each other. Finally, you will learn some advanced global illumination techniques for illuminating objects with bounced or indirect light.

9.1 SHADING SURFACES

Creative lighting doesn't stop when you have positioned your light sources. How light bounces off or is absorbed by a surface matters just as much to your rendering as where you position the lights. To get the best results, you need to understand how 3D surfaces respond to light, and how to adjust your materials or shaders for the most realistic shading.

9.1.1 DIFFUSE AND SPECULAR LIGHT TRANSMISSION

Shading algorithms used in 3D graphics have their origin in the physics of real light. There are several different ways that light can reflect off a surface in real life. On a shiny surface, *specular* reflection (also called regular reflection) could occur, as shown on the upper left of Figure 9.1.

9.1 Specular reflection propagates light without scattering it, glossy surfaces scatter rays concentrated around one angle, diffuse reflection scatters light uniformly in all possible directions, and mixed specular and diffuse reflection scatters light with a concentrated highlight in the specular area.

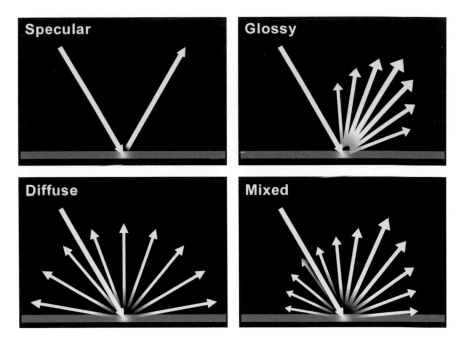

With specular reflection, the light remains focused and reflects off the surface without scattering. A perfectly specular surface would reflect all light exactly at the same angle, with absolutely no scattering of light or blurring of reflections. However, when specularity is simulated in a computer, this is not exactly what happens.

Most common types of light in a 3D scene radiate from an infinitely small point in space (except for area lights, which originate from a scalable area). A true specular reflection of an infinitely small point light would produce a tiny specular highlight too small to see. As a workaround to this problem, shading algorithms in 3D graphics provide control over *highlight size* on your material, which arbitrarily enlarges the highlights. Specular highlights are designed to simulate the reflection of a spherical area light, even when the light source is just a regular point or spot. When specular highlights are larger and softer, they are a better simulation of glossy light reflection than of true specular reflection.

Glossy reflection, as shown on the upper right of Figure 9.1, is a reflection of light that is concentrated in one direction, but slightly scattered or diffused.

If a surface is more rough or less shiny, then *diffuse* reflection could occur, as shown in the lower left of Figure 9.1, which scatters the light in all possible directions.

In theory, a perfectly diffuse surface would scatter light uniformly in all directions. However, in real life, no surface is perfectly diffuse, and no surface is perfectly specular. Instead, real surfaces mix the results of scattered and focused reflection. With a mixed surface, as shown on the lower right of Figure 9.1, light is scattered in different directions, but an increased amount of light is focused at the angle of specular reflection.

The mixed light reflectance of real-life surfaces is best imitated in 3D graphics by adding together diffuse and specular shading. As shown in Figure 9.2, diffuse shading simulates the light that becomes scattered (or diffused) uniformly in all possible angles. Specular shading simulates light that reflects all in the same direction, without scattering (although the highlight size control simulates an amount of glossiness). Combining both diffuse and specular shading, in appropriate proportions, produces more realistic renderings than purely diffuse shading alone. Even if you don't want big, visible highlights, adding at least a small amount of specularity leads to more realistic shading than a purely diffuse surface.

9.1.2 VIEW DEPENDENCE

A common misconception is that specular highlights are centered in the brightest point of the diffuse shading. In reality, the positioning of the specular highlights is derived separately from the diffuse shading. The diffuse shading is based on the position of a surface and its angle relative to the light. Specular shading, on the other hand, can only be calculated from a specific camera angle, and is based on the angle between the light, the surface, and the camera.

Specularity is one example of view-dependent shading. *View-dependent shading* is any effect that varies depending on the camera angle. (Shading effects that can be computed without regard for the camera angle, such as diffuse shading, are called *non-view-dependent*.)

Figure 9.3 shows four angles on a scene, with only the camera moving between frames. (The texture-mapped grid and dots help pinpoint fixed locations on the geometry.) Look at the point on the sphere marked by a red dot. From any camera angle, the fall-off of the diffuse shading stays fixed at the red dot. The edge of a shadow also stays in place, as marked by the yellow dot in each frame. Because they do not change with the camera angle, you can see that diffuse shading and shadows are non-view-dependent.

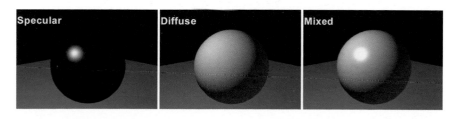

9.2 3D surfaces can be shaded with specular shading, diffuse shading, or a mixture of both.

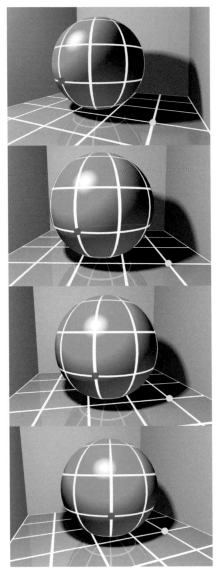

9.3 View-dependent shading effects, including specularity and reflections, appear in different places when viewed from different camera angles, whereas diffuse shading and shadows remain in position regardless of camera angle.

In Figure 9.3, watch how the specular highlights, and the reflection on the floor, travel to different positions from each camera angle. From this observation, you can tell that specular highlights and raytraced reflections are view-dependent shading techniques.

> **NOTE**
>
> To preview view-dependent shading when you test render your models, make a turn-table test instead of just a still image. A *turn-table test* is an animation of your object spinning around 360 degrees in front of the camera. This test shows your highlights traveling over all the surfaces of your model.

To set up a comparison of view-dependent specular shading and non-view-dependent diffuse shading, Figure 9.4 shows a simple scene consisting of an omnidirectional point light in the exact center of a sphere. The sphere is cut in half, to render the shading on the interior. If the sphere is rendered with only diffuse shading and no specularity, then the result will be unrealistic: The sphere will appear completely flat, with no variation of shading at all, as shown on the left side of Figure 9.5.

Adding specular shading to the sphere will restore the shading, as shown on the right side of Figure 9.5, with the shading appearing brightest where the surface reflects the light directly back to the camera. The left side of Figure 9.5 looks unrealistic because it does not exhibit any specularity.

In real life, there are no perfectly diffuse surfaces. Adjusting your specularity appropriately for each surface is a vital part of realistic rendering. Be careful, however, not to use too much specularity, which is also a serious mistake.

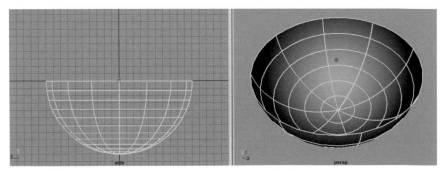

9.4 A point light positioned at the exact center of a sphere will illuminate the diffuse shading uniformly at all points.

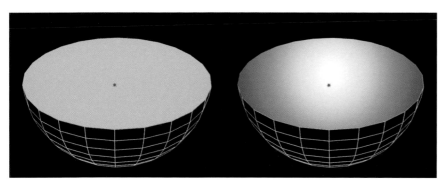

9.5 The sphere interior appears flat and unrealistic rendered without specularity (left, using a Lambert shader, which renders perfectly diffuse surfaces). Adding specularity (right, using a Blinn shader with specular shading) provides an additional source of variation to the shading.

9.1.3　REALISTIC SPECULARITY

Big, bright, airbrushed-looking specular highlights are one of the most conspicuous clichés of 3D graphics. Some people call specularity "a cheat," or a "fake" way of simulating the reflection of a light source. Specular highlights appear fake in many renderings because they are often misused or poorly adjusted. However, almost all surfaces in the real world exhibit some degree of specularity, and using it appropriately can add realism to your renderings.

You can improve the quality of your shading if you give your specular highlights an appropriate size, color, shape, and position. Your best bet when adjusting your specular highlights is to find a real-world example of the material you are trying to simulate, and study how it responds to light. For the best results, always adjust your specular highlights based on real-world observations, instead of preconceived notions or software presets.

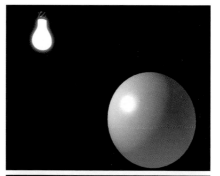

9.1.3.1　HIGHLIGHT SIZE

The size of your specular highlight should appear plausible considering the size and position of the light source. If the light source is small, or far away, then the highlight should be small, as shown on the top of Figure 9.6. If you are simulating a larger light source, and it is close to the object, then you would expect a large specular highlight, as shown on the bottom of Figure 9.6. This correlation may sound like common sense, but you can't always expect your 3D software to make this determination for you. To make the highlight size match the size and distance of the light source, adjust the highlight size of your surface shaders or materials. Test render your scene to make sure that the highlights appear to be reflections of the light source.

Apart from matching the light source, your highlight size should also be appropriate for the type of material you are representing. For example, metals, glass, and other hard surfaces have the smallest, tightest specular

9.6 The size of a highlight should be adjusted until it visually matches the size and distance of the light source.

highlights. Materials such as paper and painted wood often have a softer, more diffuse appearance with a larger (although less intense) specular highlight. The best way to check your highlights is to study a real-world example of your material.

The property of a surface that causes a specular highlight to spread out is called *roughness*. Roughness does not always appear as big, visible bumps. Microscopic roughness in a surface's structure can make a surface appear smooth, while still diffusing reflected light. For example, the surface of a rubber pencil eraser diffuses light due to a microscopic roughness to its structure, even though it looks and feels smooth. In this sense, any surface with a matte finish instead of a glossy finish can be said to be rough.

9.1.3.2 SPECULAR COLOR

The color of your specular shading is adjustable, but in most cases it should be left as a shade of white or gray.

A white or gray specular color means that the color added for specular shading will be based on the color of the light source, which is usually the most natural source of color for a specular highlight. With a middle-gray specular color, the highlights will be a mix of the object color and the light color, as shown in Figure 9.7.

9.7 A neutral gray specular color allows the highlight to reflect colors from the lights and blend naturally with the diffuse surface color.

You may sometimes give your specular color a value brighter than pure white (sometimes called *super-white*), by typing a higher number than would be allowed on color sliders. This will give you brighter, more visible highlights. In some cases, especially for highlights on transparent surfaces, super-white specular values are necessary before your highlights will even be visible.

You don't need to make the specular color match the diffuse color for it to blend in. If you want your highlights to be more subtle, simply reducing the brightness or using a darker shade of gray will do the trick. For materials that are not made of metal, shades of gray allow the specular shading to naturally blend into the diffuse shading, and pick up the color of the light source. A saturated color specularity would also respond more strongly to lights of a similar color, and filter out different colored lights, as shown in Figure 9.8. Using a gray specular color allows all colors of light to be reflected by the surface.

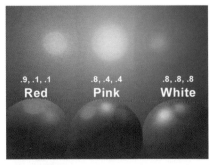

9.8 Saturated specular colors (such as the red specular color used on the left sphere) reflect similar colored lights most brightly, whereas less saturated (middle) and desaturated (right) specular colors will reflect lights of different colors.

In the case of metals, a metallic shader will use the color of the material as the color of the specular highlight. For example, if you were rendering gold, it would have a golden specular highlight color. Sometimes metals even have a dark diffuse color and receive most of their color and shading from the colored specularity.

9.1.3.3 ANISOTROPIC HIGHLIGHTS

The microscopic roughness that is responsible for diffusing light is not always randomly distributed, and doesn't always scatter all light randomly in all directions. Some surfaces have small grooves or grain in their structure instead of random bumpiness. Brushed steel, human hair, phonograph records, compact discs, and wooden objects are examples of surfaces with grooves or grain that affect their shading. Reflections and highlights are stretched in a direction that runs along with the grain or grooves in the surface, for a result called *anisotropic shading*. Surfaces that spread reflected light evenly in all directions are called *isotropic*. You can see the difference in Figure 9.9.

9.1.3.4 THE FRESNEL EFFECT

The French physicist Augustin-Jean Fresnel (1788–1827) advanced the wave theory of light through a study of how light was transmitted and propagated by different objects. One of his observations is now known in computer graphics as the *Fresnel effect*.

The Fresnel effect is the observation that the amount of light you see reflected from a surface depends on the viewing angle. As shown in Figure 9.10, if you look straight down from above at a pool of water, you will not see very much reflected light on the surface of the pool, and you can see down through the surface to the bottom of the pool. At a glancing angle (looking with your eye level with the water, from the edge of the water surface), you will see much more specularity and reflections on the water surface, and might not be able to see what's under the water at all.

A shader that allows you to vary the specularity and other parameters according to the viewing angle of the surface is often called a Fresnel shader. A Fresnel shader lets you specify a specular color to be seen on parts of a surface directly facing the camera, and another specular color to be seen on parts of a surface that are perpendicular to the camera.

NOTE

Augustin-Jean Fresnel is also known as the inventor of the Fresnel lens, which he designed to project beams of light from lighthouses. Still popular today, Fresnel lenses are built into the front of film and television lighting equipment, and filmmakers call this type of focusable lighting instrument a *Fresnel*.

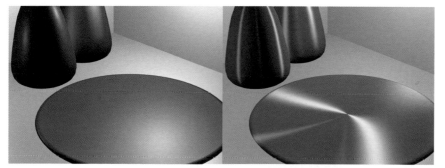

9.9 Isotropic shading (left) spreads specular highlights uniformly in all directions, whereas anisotropic shading (right) causes specular highlights to elongate.

9.10 The Fresnel effect increases reflection and specularity on surfaces viewed at a glancing angle (right).

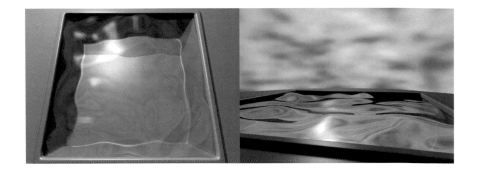

Besides the usual specular highlights and reflectivity, some Fresnel shaders can also control parameters such as the color or transparency.

Not every program uses the name "Fresnel" for setting up the effect. Sometimes a parameter can be set differently for the center and edge of a surface, which allows for the same kind of variation. Another way the Fresnel effect can be created is by linking the surface angle of an object to the shader attribute that needs to change, such as the specular brightness, as shown in Figure 9.11.

9.1.3.5 MULTIPLE HIGHLIGHTS

Some objects have different kinds of highlights layered over each other. In real life, some surfaces consist of more than one layer, especially surfaces coated with varnish, shellac, wax, or liquids. In a multilayered

9.11 In Maya's Hypershade window, the Facing Ratio attribute of a surface is linked through a ramp into the surface's specularity. The intermediate ramp allows the center-to-edge specularity to be edited as a gradient.

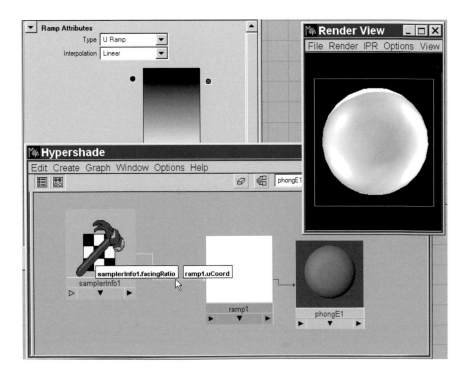

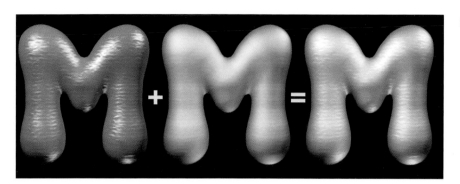

surface, the upper transparent layer might exhibit one kind of specular reflection, while the base surface has different specular properties. Layering multiple highlights, as shown in Figure 9.12, can be especially useful if you want tighter highlights to be layered on top of broad, soft highlights.

There are several ways to set-up multiple highlights on a 3D surface.

- Some programs have shaders specifically designed for multiple highlights, that allow for several highlight descriptions to be separately edited.

- Some programs have the capability to layer shaders, with each shader having different specular settings.

- With almost any program, you should be able to create a second, outer copy of a surface that can be transparent except for the secondary highlights.

- You always have the option to render your object twice, with two different specularity settings, and composite together both renderings.

Of the preceding four choices, a shader specifically designed for multiple highlights is likely to be the most efficient, if it is available, but the other options have the advantage of allowing different bump mapping to be applied to the different highlight layers.

9.1.4 SURFACE NORMALS

A renderer calculates shading based on the surface normals of the object being rendered. A *surface normal* is a vector that runs perpendicular to each point on a surface. (A *vector* means a specific angle or direction, and being *perpendicular* to a surface means it sticks straight out from the surface.) Most 3D programs have a function that allows you to view a surface's normals, which are represented by small lines in your viewport, as shown in Figure 9.13.

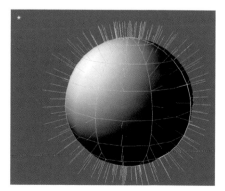

9.13 Visible surface normals (shown as green lines) indicate the orientation of each polygon in an object.

The surface normal is usually the most important factor in determining diffuse shading. The angle of the surface normal is used as follows:

- Where the surface normal points directly toward the light, diffuse illumination is brightest.

- The further from the light the surface normal points, the less diffuse illumination is contributed by the light.

- Where the surface normal aims at least 90 degrees away from the light, the light adds no illumination to the surface. The line where the diffuse illumination cuts off is called the *terminator*.

- Surface normals also tell a renderer whether a surface's faces are oriented to the front or back of a scene. To efficiently render single-sided surfaces, a renderer will skip polygons whose normals face away from the camera.

On a sphere, there is a gradual transition between the angles of adjacent surface normals, producing smooth gradients in shading. On other objects, such as a primitive cube, there can be sudden jumps or discontinuities between the angles of adjacent surface normals, which produce sharp edges in the shading.

9.1.4.1 **BEVELS**

When two surfaces intersect at a right angle, with no bevel or transition between them, then the surface normals of adjacent polygons jump suddenly by 90 degrees, without any normals ever being aimed diagonally. You can see this in the primitive cube on the left side of Figure 9.14. The lack of surface normals in intermediate directions means that the surface's shading will ignore or skip illumination coming from any of the intermediate directions. This can create unnatural looking shading, because in real life a light coming at a diagonal should still be able to illuminate the corner of an object.

Instead of modeling with perfect right angles, take a more realistic approach and bevel or round the edges of all your objects. Bevels create intermediate surface normal angles, and more realistically catch light from all directions, as with the beveled cube on the right of Figure 9.14. Bevels may appear to be a small detail, but they make a big difference in the way your objects respond to light.

Of course, not every bevel is a perfectly uniform, round transition between surfaces. Study the shape, size, and angle of the transitions between real surfaces, and you will see a variety of welds, moldings, grout, stitching, and other attachments—the only kind of transition

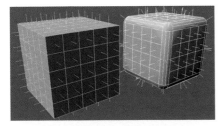

9.14 The non-beveled cube (left) lacks diagonal surface normals. More complete and realistic shading is created with the beveled object (right).

you won't find in the real world is the perfect, razor-sharp angle used in a primitive cube.

9.1.4.2 THE TERMINATOR

The line where the diffuse shading from a light ceases to illuminate the surface is called the *terminator*. Increasing the brightness of a light (or increasing the *diffuse* setting of a shader) can make the terminator into a more visible and abrupt transition, as seen on the right side of Figure 9.15.

Representing a terminator as a high-contrast line can lead to interesting renderings, as shown in Figure 9.16, in which the entire image is rendered in pure black and pure white, without the use of gray tones. However, if you want to render with a softer look, the terminator should usually be more subtle or invisible.

No matter how bright the light is, it will not extend beyond the terminator. The position of the terminator is fixed where your surface normals aim 90 degrees away from the light source. This is consistent with how light behaves when illuminating hard, solid objects, such as a metal ball. However, real-world observation shows that a light can have an influence on more than half of an object, if the object is surrounded by any kind of dust, fuzz, or atmosphere, or if the surface is multilayered or internally translucent. In computer graphics, there are only a few cases in which a light can wrap around more than half of a spherical form.

■ Using an array of several light sources instead of a single light is usually the easiest solution to extending your illumination around an object.

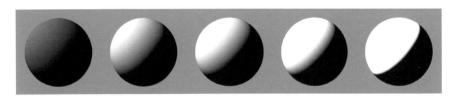

9.15 As a light source gets brighter, the terminator where the illumination ends becomes more visible.

9.16 Still from Project BW (see www. projectbw.com for credits), which used a shading remapping technique to achieve a high-contrast terminator.

- Large area lights located near an object can sometimes wrap around more than 180 degrees, because each part of the area light functions as its own light source.

- If your software supports environmental illumination through High Dynamic Range Images, these can reproduce natural illumination wrapping all the way around a model and should be considered as a replacement for fill lights.

- Bump mapping can cause a light to show up around more than half of a sphere, because it causes new values to be used in place of the geometry's surface normals.

If future lighting models allow for a light's terminator to be directly adjustable beyond 180 degrees around an object, they will facilitate a greater range of shading effects.

9.2 TEXTURE

Texture mapping is the art of adding variation and detail to a surface that goes beyond the level of detail modeled into the geometry. This section will discuss the types of textures you can create, different ways to create textures, and how to align textures with your models.

9.2.1 COMMON MAPPING TECHNIQUES

Textures can be used to control many different attributes of a surface, to produce different effects in your rendering. Seven of the most common mapping techniques are:

- Color mapping
- Specular mapping
- Luminosity mapping
- Transparency mapping
- Clip mapping
- Bump mapping
- Displacement mapping

9.2.1.1 COLOR MAPPING

Color mapping (sometimes called *diffuse mapping*) replaces the main surface color of your model with a texture. A black-and-white grid is applied as a color map in Figure 9.17.

9.17 As a color map, a grid replaces the diffuse value of a model.

Your color map sets the amount of diffuse light reflectance by a surface. In some renderers, color mapping and diffuse mapping are listed as two different kinds of maps. In this case, the tones of the color map are multiplied by the tones of the diffuse mapping (when normalized to a scale of 0 to 1). For example, adding a 50% gray in a diffuse map would be the same as using half as bright a color in the color map.

If your object is going to be illuminated and shaded by the light sources in your 3D scene, then you do not want illumination, shading, or highlights to be "built-in" to the color map. For example, notice the very flat appearance of the color map in Figure 9.18. The map for a realistic face indicates the color variation and detail of the skin surface, but does not include any of the shading, highlights, or shadows that you would see in a photograph of a face.

Sometimes, you may "cheat" on this issue, and paint some highlights and shadows into your color map to help simulate small details without using bump or displacement mapping. If you do this, be careful that your mapped highlights and shadows match in tone and position with the highlights and shadows added by the illumination and rendering process.

9.18 In order to respond realistically to your lighting, a good color map has a flat appearance. This map was derived from photographs, but manipulated to avoid built-in illumination artifacts such as highlights and shadows, which are not desirable in a color map.

Color mapping replaces the object color used in diffuse illumination, but does not override your lighting and shading. If you want to entirely pre-light an object (with all the illumination and shadows coming from the texture maps, instead of the 3D scene's lighting) then constant or luminosity maps (as described later in this section) could be a more appropriate mapping technique, because they are exempt from the influence of lights and shadows in your scene.

In a realistic rendering, object colors usually should not include pure black or pure white, and should avoid completely saturated red, green, or blue colors. A 100% brightness white color would mean that 100% of the light hitting the surface was diffusely reflected, which is not something found in the real world. Similarly, a pure black surface would show no diffuse light reflectance, which is also unrealistic. In most cases, it's a good idea to keep the red, green, and blue color values in your texture between 15% and 85% values, preferably toward the low side of that range.

Even with a color map that looks flat and has a limited tonal range, you can still have vivid, high-contrast renderings. Your lighting and shadows shade your map, and other effects are added on top of the diffuse shading, such as specular highlights. The flat color map from Figure 9.18 is applied to the head model in Figure 9.19.

9.2.1.2 SPECULAR MAPPING

Specular mapping varies the brightness and color of the specular highlights on different parts of an object's surface. A checkered pattern is applied as a specular map around the entire object in Figure 9.20, but its influence is only seen in the area of the specular highlight.

9.19 The basic shading of a model (left) is based on the modeling of the face and the lighting of the scene. Adding the color map (right) preserves the shading, because of the map's flat appearance.

Your specular map will *not* create specular highlights by itself—highlights still need to come from light sources. Your specular map can tint the highlights, change their brightness, or even block them completely, but the effects of specular mapping will only be visible in places where a specular highlight would have appeared anyway.

Bright areas in your specular map make highlights brighter, creating a glossier or shinier area on your object. Dark tones of a specular map make highlights less visible, and pure black in a specular map completely prevents highlights from showing up on the corresponding parts of your model. For example, a specular map for a man's face is shown in Figure 9.21. White areas of the map produce a shiny forehead and nose, while dark areas prevent highlights on the stubble of his chin and cheeks. (This specular map was used in the rendering in Figure 9.19, where you can see the specular highlights only hitting the parts of his face with a bright specular color.)

Because the effect of a specular map is only seen in highlight areas, specular maps are sometimes difficult to pin down and adjust. If you are having trouble with a specular map, try to isolate the effect. Be sure the surface has no reflectivity (which could be confused with specularity)

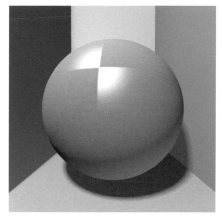

9.20 A specular map is only visible in the highlight areas, and can change the specular color or limit the specular brightness on a surface.

9.21 This specular map makes the man's forehead shinier than his chin, and modulates where highlights can appear.

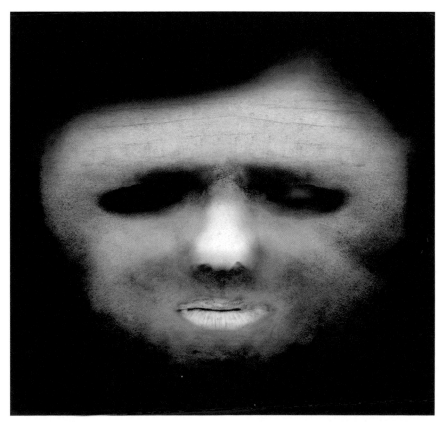

and is not being blended or mixed with other textures, and then render a turn-table test to inspect the highlights. You can reactivate the reflectivity and other effects after you have test-rendered the specular map. If alignment is an issue, you might initially create the specularity map as a color map, and only change it into the specular map once you are sure it is applied correctly.

9.2.1.3 LUMINOSITY MAPPING

Luminosity mapping (also called *incandescence, ambience,* or *constant mapping*) uses a texture map to simulate self-illuminating properties of an object, and applies the map's colors without regard for your lighting. As shown in Figure 9.22, luminosity maps are visible on a surface even in shadow areas, without needing a light source to illuminate them.

Luminosity maps are perfect for tasks such as adding illuminated lights to the side of a building or ship, adding the glowing picture to a television or monitor, or texturing the surface of a light bulb as in Figure 9.23. Luminosity maps are also handy if you want to combine two-dimensional pictures with your 3D renderings, and have the pictures keep their own lighting (often this would be done in conjunction with *clip* mapping, discussed later). Luminosity maps can also be used as a way to cheat an object brighter, reducing contrast and brightening the object beyond the illumination it receives from ordinary light sources.

If a luminosity map is applied to an object that has no specularity (pure black specular color) and no diffuse shading (pure black diffuse color), then it can produce a flat area of color, with the exact shades and tones from the source map being output in the rendering of the object. In Figure 9.24, the rendered black-and-white tones on the sphere are the exact same RGB values as in the original texture map. Some renderers have a separate option to render with a *constant* or *lightsource* material, which produces this same effect, although a constant or lightsource material may not be as easy to blend with other shading effects as a luminosity map.

Ambience mapping is actually a slight variation on luminosity mapping. Even though it can be used to achieve the same effects, ambience mapping can be modulated by a level of ambience in a scene. Ambience is a parameter that may be set by a global ambience value. Ambience maps are at full brightness (identical to a standard luminosity/incandescence map) at a global ambience setting of 1, and completely disappear when global ambience is at 0. In other programs, dedicated ambient lights exist to control the ambience in different parts of a scene, and these also limit the intensity of your ambience map.

9.22 A luminosity map adds its colors to all parts of an object, in both light and shadow areas.

9.23 A luminosity map is perfect for texturing the surface of a light bulb, which does not require illumination from other light sources to be visible. (Image by Jacques Isaac.)

9.24 When applied to an object with no diffuse or specular shading, a luminosity map's original shades and colors are used directly in the final output, with no influence from your lighting.

9.2.1.4 TRANSPARENCY MAPPING

Transparency mapping is a technique with several useful functions. The simplest function of a transparency map would be to create a pattern in a surface's transparency, such as a stained glass window. (If you flip back to Chapter 5, the window in Figure 5.21 gets its color from a colored transparency map.) Dark areas of a transparency map will make a surface less transparent, and light areas of a transparency map will make other parts of the surface more clear, as shown in Figure 9.25. For example, if a window were dirty, the dirt on the window could be represented by darker areas in the window's transparency map.

9.25 A transparency map makes areas of a surface more or less opaque.

Besides transparent patterns, transparency maps are often used as a way to create a hidden transition between surfaces. Figure 9.26 shows how multiple surfaces are softly and subtly blended together with transparency maps. Creating surface continuity with transparency maps is not the most "proper" way to work, but people sometimes get away with it. The effect causes problems when shadows of overlapping transparent edges are cast onto the base surface, and the effect works only if you make the color maps match perfectly. This technique is rarely needed if you work with polygons only, but can be handy with other kinds of patch and NURBS geometry.

The hippo in Figure 9.26 also has eyelashes and ear hairs created as transparency mapped surfaces. The eyelash texture map (shown in Figure 9.27) creates the illusion of separate lashes or hairs by hiding parts of the eyelash surface in stripes of transparency. The same technique could be used to make a row of grass stick up from a lawn, the bangs of a character's hair, or a distant tree line on a hillside.

To add color and transparency with a single map, the texture map in Figure 9.27 has an *alpha channel*, an extra byte of information per pixel that can be used to store transparency information. Most 3D programs

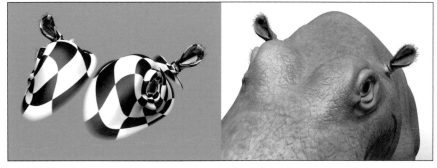

9.26 Transparency maps give surfaces soft edges (left) so that they can blend seamlessly with a base object (right).

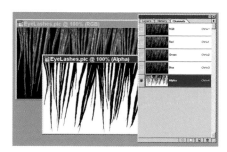

9.27 An alpha channel can embed transparency information into the same file as a color map.

9.28 A clip map makes areas of a surface completely invisible. One difference between this and Figure 9.25 is that that here the specular highlight is hidden in the clip-mapped areas.

can use a texture map's alpha channel to determine the level of transparency (or other designated effects) in a textured surface. One image file contains color information in the red, green, and blue channels (which can be applied as a color map), and also contains transparency information in its alpha channel. The information in the alpha channel can be interpreted in the same way as the shading in an ordinary transparency map, and produces the same results as a monochromatic transparency map from a separate file.

Areas of a transparency map that are pure black will make the corresponding part of an object solid and opaque. Pure white in the map will make the corresponding parts of the object completely transparent. However, even a 100% transparent area of a surface (created via a pure white area of a transparency map) will not necessarily be completely invisible; reflections, refraction, and other effects can be visible on a transparent surface. If you want to be sure transparent parts of your surface are completely invisible, many programs support a mapping technique called clip mapping.

9.2.1.5 CLIP MAPPING

Clip mapping (sometimes called *visibility mapping*) is a special variation on transparency mapping, used to create the appearance of holes being cut into an object. A completely white area of a clip map will hide the corresponding part of an object, even hiding specular highlights, refraction, or reflections. As shown in Figure 9.28, a clip map creates the illusion that the pattern has been cut out from the surface of the geometry.

If your software does not have clip mapping, you can usually use transparency mapping for similar results. Just check for specularity or reflectivity that might be visible in transparent areas, and either disable those effects or map them with the clip map as well. If you are raytracing, you may need to set your material's index of refraction to 1.

Used in conjunction with a color map, a clip map can cut holes into a pattern. For example, the window screen texture in Figure 9.29 consists of a color map and a matching clip map. Together, they create the impression of a screen with holes between the wires.

Replacing a complex 3D object with a clip-mapped flat surface is sometimes called *bill-boarding*. Bill-boarding of a 3D object is achieved by rendering the object that needs to be replaced, and then applying the rendered image as a color map on a flat surface with the rendered alpha channel as your clip map. This kind of technique can sometimes save a lot of memory and rendering time, especially for more distant objects.

9.29 Simple geometry (left) can be textured to represent a complex surface (right) when patterns are trimmed away through clip mapping.

9.2.1.6 **BUMP MAPPING**

Bump mapping is a mapping technique that perturbs the surface normals of an object, making them deviate from being perfectly perpendicular to a surface. The modified normals are used to add variation and simulate ridges, depressions, and small surface details in an object's shading. Figure 9.30 shows the influence of a grid as a bump map.

A slope is derived from the difference in brightness between adjacent pixels in the bump map, which contributes to the angles of the surface normals used to calculate shading. Bright tones of a bump map are portrayed as being raised up from the surface, and dark tones of map as being lowered into the surface. Sometimes, small changes to a bump map, such as blurring or gamma correcting the map, will make a big difference in the rendered appearance of the bump mapping effect, because they can affect the slopes calculated between pixels of the map. Areas of a bump map that are a constant color, with no variation in shading, will have no effect on a surface, because the slope between adjacent pixels is flat.

Bump mapping does not actually change the shape of your geometry. A bump map can render more quickly than a displacement-mapped model, but bump mapping is not a perfect simulation. There are five main effects, that can be accurately simulated by a bump map.

- Diffuse illumination and shading are varied as if the bumps really existed in the surface.

- Specular highlights are broken up and scattered by bump maps. Tiny highlights can even appear on individual bumps caused by a bright pixel in a bump map, although this can cause jittering problems in animation.

- Reflections (raytraced or reflection mapped) are distorted and scattered by bump maps.

- Refraction (the view through transparent, raytraced surfaces) is correctly modified and distorted by bump maps.

9.30 A bump map perturbs the shading of a surface, without actually changing its shape.

- Caustic effects (see the "Caustics" section later in this chapter) can be redirected or differently focused by a bump map, when you use software that supports this.

There are also five drawbacks that can prevent bump maps from achieving their illusion.

- The outline or silhouette of an object is not changed by a bump map, and remains smooth or straight, even if the map simulates a very rough surface. For example, a sphere with a bump map still has a perfectly circular outline.

- Shadows cast by a bump-mapped object still have their original shapes.

- Shadows received on a bump-mapped surface remain straight, and not distorted as if they really landed on rough ground.

- Unlike modeled or displaced details, details added to a surface via a bump map do not cast attached shadows onto the surface.

- The line where a bump-mapped object intersects with another object is not changed by a bump map, and can give away the real shapes of the objects.

These five limitations of bump mapping are all corrected with *displacement mapping*, because displacement mapping truly provides the change to a surface's shape that a bump map only simulates.

9.2.1.7 DISPLACEMENT MAPPING

The brightness of a displacement map is used to change the shape of a surface, as shown in Figure 9.31. A brighter tone in a displacement map moves the corresponding point on a surface outward along its normal, and a darker tone moves the surface inward. Unlike a bump map, this changes your object's profile and shadow and can even change how different surfaces intersect.

In many programs, a detailed displacement map will require that a surface be tessellated (subdivided into many small polygons) during the rendering, using a much higher polygon count than would be used without a displacement map. This can add to the memory and time required to complete your rendering, but can be required if you want a more detailed displacement map. In renderers that require tessellation, using too little subdivision on a displacement mapped surface can result in a blocky, jagged, or poorly defined displacement, as shown in Figure 9.32.

> **NOTE**
>
> Standard displacement mapping that moves surface points in or out along the normals is called *scalar displacement*. Pixar's Renderman also supports *vector displacement*, which allows surface points to be displaced in other directions, such as for thorns that protrude at an angle, or scales that bend back over other parts of a surface.

If a displacement map were very smooth or low-resolution, as if you only wanted to add a gentle wave or undulation to the surface of a waving flag, then additional tessellation might not be necessary. Softer displacement maps that don't require additional tessellation aren't necessarily any more computationally expensive than other deformation approaches you might take to reshape a surface.

9.2.1.8 OTHER MAPPING TECHNIQUES

The seven common mapping techniques listed previously are by no means a complete list. In fact, the number of effects that can be governed by texture maps is virtually unlimited. Specific maps may be used to control almost any kind of visual effect possible in your software. For example, some programs use a specific type of map to control the shape and color of a lens flare or the surface appearance of a particle. Even a plug-in might use its own type of texture maps for special purposes, such as determining the length, direction, and curliness of hairs emitted from a surface.

No matter which effects you want to create, or what aspect of your scene you want to control, similar processes can be used to create your texture maps. Maps need to be painted from scratch in a paint program, digitized from a real-world source, or created procedurally.

9.2.2 PAINTING MAPS

One way to create original texture maps is to paint them in a paint program. This approach is especially useful if you have experience drawing and painting in traditional media. While hand-painted maps may be created in almost any visual style, they are especially important for nonrealistic, fanciful, and illustrative renderings. Figure 9.33 was textured with hand-painted maps created in a 2D paint program.

The models underneath some texture maps may be simple, as with the buildings in Figure 9.34. The texture maps will be painted to add richness to the scene.

Figure 9.35 shows one of the texture maps being applied to the awning of a building. The map matches the shape of the geometry, and adds appropriate colors and ornamental details to the awning. Colors in the map are carefully chosen to integrate with the color scheme of the scene, using the same purple, yellow, and orange tones as are picked up in many other surfaces.

9.31 A displacement map changes the shape of a surface.

9.32 A displacement map on an insufficiently tessellated surface is blocky and poorly defined.

9.33 Hand-painted texture maps maintain the illustrative style of a fanciful scene. Eni Oken (www.oken3d.com) created "Little Village Far, Far Away" using 3D Studio MAX, with Cebas Professional Optic Suite for distance blur, smoke, nebula, flares, and glows.

9.34 Without texture maps, the buildings look crude and simple.

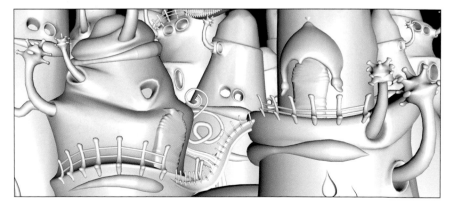

Light and shadows are often painted into a hand-painted map, to re-inforce the lighting in the scene or simulate details and dimensionality that never existed in the underlying geometry. Note how the door texture map in Figure 9.36 already contains shading and shadows. In the final rendering, these are added together with the shading and shadows of the geometry.

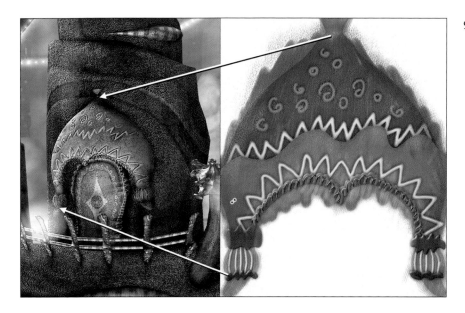

9.35 An ornamental texture map is applied as a color and bump map to the awning.

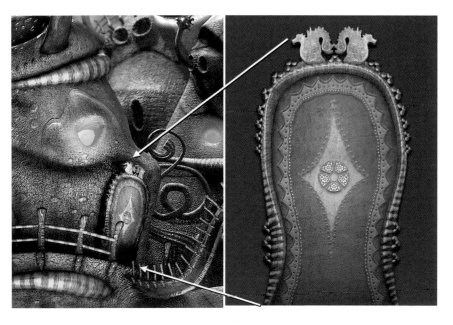

9.36 Color maps for the stylized rendering already contain shading and shadows.

9.2.2.1 ALIGNING WITH PLANAR PROJECTIONS

If you are painting a map that will appear on a flat object, like the door in Figure 9.36, or onto one side of an object, then the simplest kind of alignment to create is a *planar projection*. (Planar projection types are sometimes listed by axis, such as *XY projection* and *YZ projection*, or by viewing angle, such as *Side projection* and *Top projection*.) A planar projection casts each pixel of your texture in a straight, parallel ray that can match the Top, Side, or Front views in your 3D program.

To create a precisely aligned texture map for use in planar projection, capture an image of the screen in your 3D program, showing your model in Front, Side, or Top view (depending on which side of the object will receive the projected map). Bring this view into a paint program, and use it as the background layer while you paint or composite your texture map on top of it. You then can apply the texture map in planar projection to the model to match the alignment you saw in the paint program.

Planar projections are perfect for texturing flat walls, or sides of boxes, but produce streaking artifacts on surfaces that run parallel to the direction of the projection, as you can see in the left panel of Figure 9.37. To solve this problem, you could use multiple planar projections for different sides on your model, or switch to another projection type.

9.2.2.2 ALIGNING WITH NON-PLANAR PROJECTIONS

Planar projections may be the easiest to paint, but provide good coverage only to areas of your model that directly face the projection. Parts of a surface that run sideways from the planar projection display streaking artifacts or stretched textures. To more uniformly wrap a texture around an object, you will often need to switch to cylindrical or spherical projection, as shown in Figure 9.37.

9.37 A planar projection (left) becomes stretched at the top and sides when projected from the front of the object. Cylindrical projection (center) wraps around the front, back, and sides, but stretches the grid near the top. Spherical projection (right) wraps around all sides of this object more uniformly.

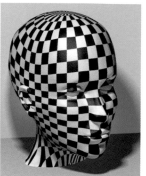

When you are working with texture projections that don't match any of your 3D views, this makes texture alignment more difficult. The approach of capturing a modeling window as a reference to use in a paint program is no longer an option. However, there are several other ways that you can create a texture map with features precisely aligned in non-planar projection.

- Many programs feature an unwrap function or plug-in, which is most commonly used with polygon meshes when applying cylindrical or spherical projections. An unwrapped object will show you the location of all the parts of your model, running all the way around the model. After performing an unwrap function, take a screen-grab of the unwrapped object into your paint program for reference.

- A 3D paint program can be used to create your final texture map, by painting directly onto your model.

- A 3D paint program can be used to create a *reference map*, a temporary map in which you have made marks tracing the key contours only and color-coding the features and areas of your model. The reference map can then be used as a background layer for painting and compositing a precisely registered final texture in a 2D paint program. (The advantage of this is that all your favorite 2D tools and processes can be used in creating the final texture map.)

- You can apply a *pattern map* as shown in Figure 9.38 using the chosen projection technique, and make note of where each distinctive part of pattern falls on the model. The pattern map can then serve as a guide for painting your final texture, which will be applied with the same projection as the test pattern.

- For a complex model, you can make the pattern-map approach more accurate by viewing the initial rendering of the pattern map, and painting reference marks onto the pattern map that attempt to mark or trace each of the features. Test-render the model with the new map version to see how close your marks fall to the actual features, and make a modified version of the map if there are areas where your marks need refinement. Once you have all the positions right, use the marked-up pattern map as the guide for creating your final texture.

All these approaches to aligning textures with non-planar projections will also be valid if you are using UV maps, but there are a few noteworthy differences between UV maps and projections.

9.38 A pattern map (left) makes each part of a surface recognizable, so that you can tell which part of a texture projection corresponds to each part of your model in a test rendering (right). This map is one of many that is downloadable from the assistant library at www.aliaswavefront.com.

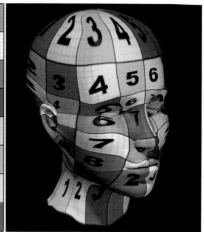

9.2.3　UV MAPS

UV maps are the most popular way to texture NURBS surfaces, and are growing almost as popular in texturing polygon meshes. A *UV map* is an alternative to projecting textures through space. A UV map is positioned based on the *UV coordinates* of a surface. The UV coordinates could be the *implicit* UV coordinates based on the structure of a NURBS surface, or *explicit* UV coordinates assigned to a polygon mesh.

9.2.3.1　IMPLICIT UV COORDINATES

NURBS surfaces, and some kinds of patches, have implicit (or "built-in") UV coordinates. From the moment a NURBS surface is created, it has implicit UV coordinates at each point.

The built-in UV coordinates are made possible by the structure of a NURBS surface, which is always a grid. A NURBS surface is a grid made up of a set of curves running in a direction called U, intersecting a set of curves running in the other direction, called V. Each point has its own UV coordinate value describing its position within the grid structure of the surface. Even though the surface can be bent and reshaped flexibly, it will always remain a grid. To preserve the grid structure, NURBS modeling software does not allow individual points to be deleted; the entire row or column of points would need to be deleted at once. A UV map applied to a NURBS surface will follow these coordinates, usually with the X (horizontal) dimension of the texture map running along the U direction, and the Y (vertical) dimension of the texture map running along the V direction.

The way you construct a NURBS surface will determine how your UV coordinates are distributed on your model. Figure 9.39 shows a head built with the U curves running around the head, and the V curves running vertically. A UV map follows these curves predictably, bending in the directions of each curve.

If a head were constructed differently, the UV mapping would create a different texture alignment. Figure 9.40 shows a head built with curves radiating out from the mouth. The UV map applied here follows the radial pattern, wrapping the bottom edge of the map around the mouth and stretching the upper areas of the map around the rest of the head. Half of the map is upside down, and the scale varies widely from one part of the head to another. This alignment would make it difficult to paint a texture in a 2D paint program. If you need to create a UV map like this, either use a 3D paint program, or initially create the texture as a planar or cylindrical projection, and then convert the texture into a UV map later on.

NOTE

The Convert Solid Texture function in Alias Studio and Maya plot out a map for use in UV alignment, based on any existing projection or 3D procedural texture. (In Alias terminology, a solid texture is any projection or 3D procedural, as opposed to a *surface* texture, which is in UV alignment.) The Rendermap function in Softimage can be used similarly.

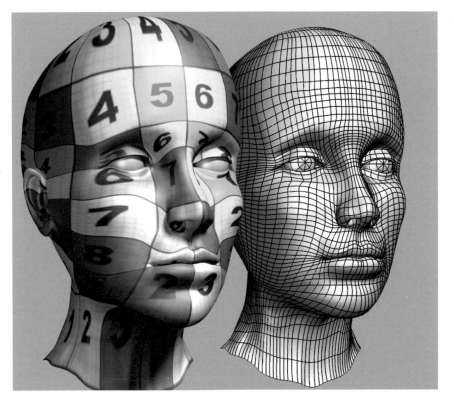

9.39 UV texture mapping will flow along the U and V curves that make up a NURBS surface.

9.40 A mouth-centered model creates a confusing radial assignment for UV maps.

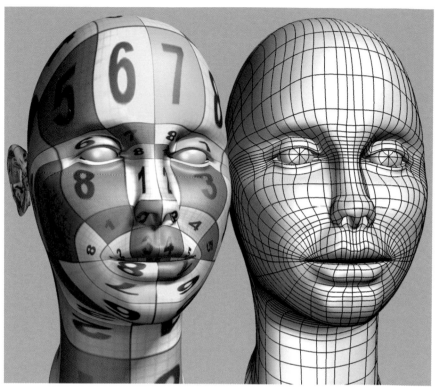

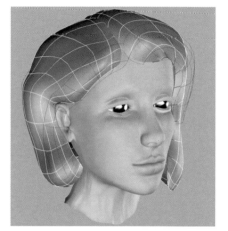

9.41 Curves of the hair surface are modeled in the direction of the hairs, in preparation to receive a UV map.

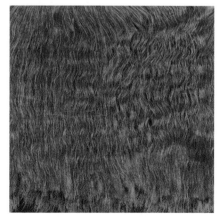

9.42 The hair in the texture runs vertically, which will correspond to the V direction of the surface when applied. (I created this texture by laying a hairpiece rented from a costume shop directly onto a flatbed scanner and combing the hair in one direction.)

There are also times when UV alignment makes it much easier to create a texture. For example, the effect of the texture flowing along the curves of a surface could be exactly what you needed if you were making a texture for a vine or plant stalk. With a little preplanning, you can sometimes model an object with curves designed to flow in the direction of the texture you want. For example, the model in Figure 9.41 shows a woman's hair modeled with the V-direction curves running in the direction that the hair should flow. This simplifies the mapping process, because the texture map (shown in Figure 9.42) can be made with the hair simply running vertically, up and down the map.

When the map is applied to the hair surface, the vertical dimension of the texture flows naturally along the V direction curves of the surface, making the hair grow naturally out of the head, as shown in Figure 9.43. Texturing hair on a head would be substantially more difficult if you didn't have implicit UV coordinates.

Implicit UV mapping also avoids another problem that is common with projections. When a texture map is projected through space, often a part of the map will appear in more than one place on your object. Planar projections cut all the way through the front and back of your model. Even a spherical projection will shoot the same texture point through

9.43 Hairs flow along curves of the geometry as a UV map.

the exterior of a character's nose as the inside of a nostril, making it difficult to choose a color that is appropriate in both places. UV mapping, on the other hand, creates a 1:1 relationship between UV coordinates of a surface and XY positions in your texture map, to guarantee you random access to the color of any point on your model.

9.2.3.2 EXPLICIT UV COORDINATES

Polygon meshes have a free-form geometric structure that does not have to be a grid and does not necessarily consist of four-sided polygons. Because there is no grid structure implicit in their geometry, polygon meshes do not have implicit UV coordinates like NURBS. Instead, polygon meshes use *explicit* (or "assigned") UV coordinates. Subdivision surfaces that are smoothed starting with a polygonal control mesh also use explicit coordinates, usually based on the coordinates assigned to the control mesh.

Functions for managing explicit UV coordinates vary between software brands and versions. Some programs will create UV coordinates when you first create a primitive polygon mesh, or will preserve the implicit UV coordinates of a NURBS surface when it is converted to polygons.

In other approaches, you first create a projection through space to texture a polygon mesh, then convert the mapping to explicit UV coordinates, with the software assigning UV coordinates to each vertex based on its position in the original texture projection.

The improving mapping tools in today's 3D programs are making the distinction between implicit and explicit textures less of an issue than it used to be. Even when texturing NURBS surfaces, which have implicit UV coordinates, some systems allow users to explicitly redefine or edit the UV values of a point.

Explicit UV coordinates are used extensively in developing video game characters and other content for real-time display. For real-time content development, the more modest polygon counts make it practical to edit the individual UV coordinates at each point on a mesh, and the strict memory demands of real-time systems require a focused optimization of the area covered by each pixel of a texture map.

9.2.4 ACQUIRING MAPS FROM REAL SURFACES

When you don't want to paint maps from scratch, a useful way to create realistic textures is to derive your texture maps from photographs or scans of real-world surfaces. You can save a lot of time, and improve the level of realism to your work, if you find a real-world object or location that has similar textures to what you want to create.

If you are making renderings for a work of fiction, then you may need to be creative in choosing what to digitize. For example, you might texture the hull of a UFO with maps derived from panels of a city bus, or take close-ups of leftovers from a seafood restaurant to texture an alien creature. Even if the real-world subjects you find are just analogous to what you will create in 3D, there is a richness to real life that is worth going out to capture.

9.2.4.1 SHOOTING TIPS

Not every photograph will be equally useful in making texture maps. Try to follow these seven tips when going out with your camera to collect textures.

- **Shoot on a cloudy day or in the shade.** You want to capture the color-variation from a surface itself, without having the lighting built-in to the texture map. If a texture map already included shading, shadows, and reflections, then these might not match the shading, shadows, and reflections added in the rendering process.

- **Go telephoto.** You get the flattest, least distorted images from a longer lens. When you have a choice, try to shoot pictures from a distance and zoom in, rather than standing close to your subject with a wider angle lens. Usually, the lens should be at least 60 mm (based on standard 35 mm cameras) for shooting flat surfaces.

- **Go close-up.** Even though this may seem to contradict the previous item, another favorite tool in collecting textures is a close-up lens. When choosing cameras or lenses for texture acquisition, look for the best *macro* (extreme close-up) capabilities you can find, to acquire images as in Figure 9.44. Extreme close-ups reveal a whole other world of textures and patterns for you to explore.

- **Note the scale.** Try to keep track of the scale of everything that will appear in your texture maps. For example, if you make a brick texture map, you will need to decide later how many bricks run top to bottom and left to right in a 3D wall. Either take measurements of what you photograph, or at minimum shoot an extra reference shot showing the bricks in context, or showing how many bricks high the whole wall is. Mismatched texture scales are one of the most common flaws in 3D renderings.

- **Note the edges.** Textures often change when you get near the edge of a surface, as shown in the base of the map in Figure 9.45. In addition to shooting the center of a surface, be sure to observe and shoot how the surface appears near the edges, such as photographing the wall near the ground or near a corner with another wall, or focusing on any area where two materials meet or intersect. You may find later that some of these areas need their own maps.

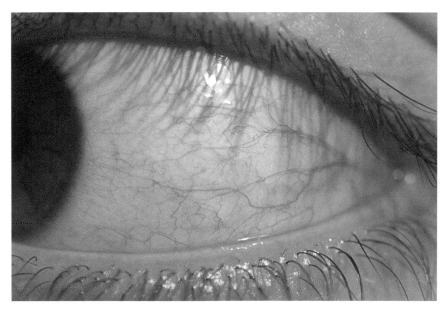

9.44 Go close-up to your subjects to grab a greater variety of photographic textures. This close-up was shot with a set of extension tubes (adapters that move the lens further from the film) behind a standard 50mm lens.

9.45 Note the edges of a surface. Here, a cinderblock wall is reinforced with a cement base. To include the different edge material, this map was made to tile horizontally, but not vertically.

- **Be specific.** Try to find maps that are specific, not generic. Bland, over-generalized patterns may seem technically easier to make into tiling maps, but sap your renderings of richness and diversity. If you need to texture an older brick building, try to capture all the decorative brickwork that's appropriate to the architectural style, and all the different ways the bricks could have been damaged and repaired over the years.

- **Collect families.** Collect texture maps in whole *families*, or groups of related textures taken from the same location. For example, if you need oak leaves, collect several different leaves from the same tree, so that your oak tree can have a natural variety in its foliage.

- **If it's flat, scan it.** If a material is flat and portable, such as a fern leaf or a wallpaper sample, then try to take the material back to your flatbed scanner to scan, instead of using a photograph.

Take the time to make maps you are proud of. When you first create a texture map, you may have no idea for how many other projects it might be reused.

If you shoot your texture photographs on film, then your next step is to digitize what you have shot.

SCANNING TEXTURES

There are a number of approaches bringing texture images into the computer.

- A flatbed scanner is a popular peripheral for scanning photographic prints, as well as pictures from books. Many studios already have flatbed scanners for scanning other kinds of art and documents. Samples of original materials can also be placed directly on the scanner to produce high resolution, evenly lit, undistorted digital files.

- Desktop slide and negative scanners are specially made for digitizing from your negatives and transparencies, which can capture high resolution and more dynamic range than scanning from a photographic print.

- Photo processing services can digitize your pictures for you after developing your film. This approach does not involve buying any computer hardware, and high-quality professional scanners are used to digitize directly from your negatives.

- Digital cameras can photograph textures from three-dimensional objects and digitize them instantly. A digital camera can also be used on a copy stand, to digitize other kinds of pictures or artwork.

One of your key concerns in digitizing images is to maintain enough image resolution to create high-quality textures. Here are a few tips on managing texture resolutions.

- **Start high-resolution, scale down.** Acquire images at a resolution that exceeds your needs, so that you can crop and manipulate the raw image when making a texture. When portions of a bitmap are rotated, distorted, and manipulated, the quality is slightly degraded. Keep your map at a high resolution until you get to a final version, then use a scaled-down copy as your actual texture map in production. For example, if you were producing texture maps at 512×512 final resolution, you might start with a 1600×1200-pixel scan, crop and manipulate it into a 1024×1024 map, then scale the final map down to 512×512 as your last step.

- **Look for pixels, not DPI.** The image size in pixels matters when you are digitizing, not the DPI. If your scanner resolution needs to be set through DPI, adjust the DPI until you get the number of

NOTE

DPI, or *dots per inch*, indicates how big a file should appear when it is printed, measured by how many pixels appear per inch across the paper. DPI and other sizing information is stored in some image file formats, but not others, and generally does not affect anything in 3D programs.

pixels you need. For example, if you want to acquire a map that is 1200 pixels across, you might need to scan at 100 DPI for a 12-inch wide original, or at 600 DPI for a 2-inch wide original, to get the 1200 pixel size.

- **Remember the memory.** A map of 1024 pixels by 1024 pixels is exactly 3 megabytes (at 24-bit color), and goes to 4 megabytes if there is an alpha channel. A 512×512 map is one-quarter as big (only 1 megabyte with an alpha channel). If you can't see the difference, don't use too high a resolution!

- **Don't be afraid of low-resolution.** At times very small maps, which consume very little memory, are sufficient for achieving the looks you want, even in creating high-resolution output. For example, if a map only appears on small objects, particles, or brush strokes, then a resolution of 64×64 might be more than enough. If your 3D program interpolates maps by smoothing them (instead of showing blocky pixels) then you might get away with using lo-res maps even when covering large areas, such as a map layered onto a surface to provide overall color variation.

A scanned image is usually just a starting point in creating a texture. After you have acquired a high-quality image file, your next step may be to retouch or color-correct it, to make it better match your scene or your other maps.

All the alignment techniques discussed in the "Painting Maps" section also apply to aligning photographic textures. For example, to match a planar projection, you could capture a front view of your object and bring it into a background layer of a 2D paint program as reference. You can also create reference maps from marks made in a 3D paint program, or from unwrapped views of your model. On top of your reference images, you can composite together and manipulate sections of your digitized texture, to achieve precise alignment with specific parts of your model.

Some texture maps need to be designed to fit a specific object, but others don't. A map of a person's face would need to be custom-fitted to your head model, to ensure that each facial feature is aligned with the correct positions on the model. But a map of a brick wall can be created as a general pattern, and then applied to many different brick surfaces that were built later. If you are making tiling maps that will repeat across a surface, or decals that will be superimposed over different areas of your material, you may create your texture maps without reference to a specific model, and then assign the maps to models later in your production. The next two sections discuss tiling maps and decals.

9.2.5 TILING MAPS

A *tiling map* is a texture map designed so that it can be repeated multiple times on a surface. Each repetition fits seamlessly with the adjacent copies, like a pattern printed on wallpaper. The left edge of a tiling map lines up seamlessly with its right edge, and its top aligns with its bottom so that you can't tell where one repetition ends and another one starts, as shown in Figure 9.46. Naturally, not every map needs to tile both horizontally and vertically. Depending on your needs, you might only need to make a map to repeat in one direction.

After you have attempted to remove the seams and match up your map's edges in a paint program, test your tiling map to make sure that multiple copies are truly seamless. As a test, you could scale the map down to a smaller size, and define it as a repeating pattern to fill the background of a new image file. Alternatively, sometimes the fastest way to preview a tiling map is to open your computer's display settings and paste the map into a "wallpaper" pattern that fills the background of your operating system's workspace.

Study the preview of your tiling map to see if there are any brightness or color shifts, such as the center of the map being brighter than the edges, or the bottom of a map being more blue in color than the top. Even if you have made the edges of your map seamless, these shifts can become a visible artifact if the map is repeated several times. Overall brightness and color shifts can usually be corrected by mixing your map with an inverted and heavily blurred copy of itself, which can cancel out any variation in the map that is larger than your chosen blur radius.

Be especially careful to study your tiling map to check for any distinctive features that repeat too often, which could make a visible grid out of the repetitions. If you want to add a distinctive and unique feature to your textured surface, without having it repeat many times along with a tiling pattern, then leave it out from your tiling map and apply the feature as a decal, layered on top of the tiling pattern.

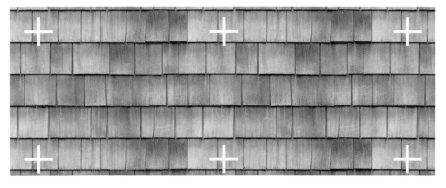

9.46 The white crosses indicate the four corners of the repeating shingle texture. A photograph of shingles was manipulated in Adobe Photoshop using the Filter ⋯⟩ Other ⋯⟩ Offset command, set to wrap around to make the edges seamless; then the Clone tool was used to hide the seam crossing the center of the image.

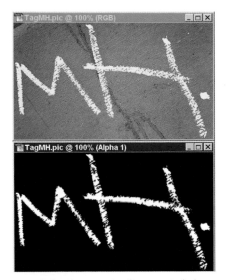

9.47 A decal texture is often created along with an alpha channel, which will control which parts of the map will be visible when it is layered on top of other textures.

9.2.6 DECALS AND DIRT

In texturing a detailed or realistic object, you will usually need to layer together more than one texture map. Some of the maps will be assigned to different attributes, such as your color map, your bump map, and so on. Some of the maps will be applied to different regions of your model, such as if you use multiple projections from different angles, or separate maps near edges of a surface. If you want to add a unique detail to a specific position of an object, even in a region where you already have other textures applied to the same attribute, then you may want to create a decal.

A *decal* (sometimes called a *stencil* or *label map*) is a texture map that has been masked-out for layering on top of other materials or textures, to add a unique detail to a specific position on an object. Creating a decal usually requires both a color image and a mask, as shown in Figure 9.47. The color image contains the texture of the decal area, and the mask contains white areas where the decal image should appear and black where the background material should be visible. The mask is usually stored in the alpha channel of the color map or might be a separate image file. Using alpha channel layering, many decal maps can be layered on top of one another, building up more detailed scenes as shown in Figure 9.48.

Bump and displacement maps sometimes behave differently from other attributes when masked-out into a decal area. If you want a decal to affect bump or displacement in a limited area, it's a good idea to fill the edges and unused color area of the decal map with a flat gray color.

9.48 Blue arrows indicate some of the locations where the map from Figure 9.47 is reused throughout the scene.

> **NOTE**
>
> In Alias|Wavefront Studio and Maya software, there are two different systems that can be used for layering and mixing maps. Using stencils and connections within the hypershade or multilister, you can already assemble as many decals or other textures as you want onto any mappable attributes of a shader. The second system is the option to use *layered shaders*, which render and combine two entire shaders (full material definitions), almost as if the surface had been rendered twice.
>
> Do not use layered shaders for your everyday texture layering, because they require far more rendering time than combining textures within a single shader. Layered shaders should be used only when you need to combine different shading models, different indices of refraction, or other special effects that are impossible within a single shader.

One of the most useful purposes for decals is adding dirt to your models. You can make maps that represent dirt, smudges, and other surface imperfections, and layer them on top of other textures.

Use dirt to add "signal," not "noise." When you need to make something dirty, avoid the common practice of superimposing random noise on it. Instead, choose dirt maps that add specific, motivated detail to your objects. Think through the story behind all the stains and imperfections on a surface—something has to cause any dirt, scratches, or stains that you would see. Here are few examples of motivations that would influence your design and position of dirt maps:

- Scratches don't appear randomly on a floor; they are more likely to appear in an area that gets scraped when a door opens.

- Carpets are most worn-out in the path where people walk.

- Mildew grows darkest near cracks and corners.

- Water leaves stains in the path where it drips down a surface, or where its surface reaches a high-water mark.

This kind of thinking is especially important in a fantasy world or imaginary environment—you need to imagine the whole history of what has happened in an environment to invent convincing dirt for it.

Dirt isn't all dark. Dirtying up your surface doesn't just mean darkening it, or just making it less saturated. Some kinds of dirt make your surface lighter in color, such as dust, scratches, water stains, and bird droppings. Rust, rot, and fungus can even add richness and color to an aging surface.

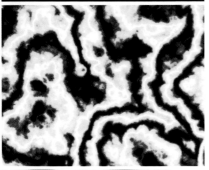

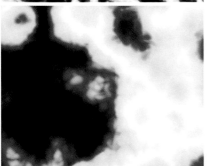

9.49 Each frame is a closer view of the center area of the previous frame, showing the resolution independence of this procedural texture.

9.2.7 PROCEDURAL TEXTURES

You have two choices for how to add a colored pattern to a 3D surface. Creating a texture map is one choice, but your other choice is to use a *procedural texture*, an algorithm in the computer that can generate a colored pattern based on input parameters, without needing to load any image file.

Procedural textures have some advantages, and some disadvantages, compared to texture maps.

9.2.7.1 RESOLUTION INDEPENDENCE

A texture map, based on an image with a fixed number of pixels, has a finite resolution. If you zoom in to an extreme close-up on a texture map, or use it in an extremely high-resolution rendering, eventually you will go beyond the pixel resolution of the bitmap, so that it could appear blurred or show visible pixels.

Procedural textures, on the other hand, are *resolution independent*. When you make a higher resolution rendering, or zoom in to an extreme close-up, a procedural texture can reveal more and more detail, as shown in Figure 9.49. Most procedural patterns can be mathematically derived at any scale, although some have a setting for the number of iterations or levels of detail to be computed.

Due to their resolution independence, procedural textures are well-suited for covering broad areas of a scene, such as when you need to add color to a landscape or terrain. A procedural texture could cover an infinitely large ground surface without ever repeating.

However, the resolution independence of procedural textures is not a guarantee that the close-up appearance of a texture will meet your needs or expectations. No matter which kind of texturing you use, designing a 3D scene to appear realistic and detailed in extreme close-ups requires a study of how your subject appears at close range, followed by test-rendering and development of appropriately detailed textures.

9.2.7.2 SOLID TEXTURES

Some procedural textures are *solid textures* (also called *3D textures*). Instead of being two-dimensional like a texture map, a solid texture is a procedure that produces a pattern based on a three-dimensional position in space. You can model any shape object, and a solid texture will always be applied evenly to every part of it. For example, the marble texture in Figure 9.50 wraps seamlessly from one side of the cube to another, and even into holes cutting through the object. This would require effort to setup if each surface were textured with a texture map, but happens automatically with solid textures.

A solid texture basically textures the full three-dimensional space in which an object exists, and the object's color at each point is a result of where it passes through the solid texture. This is terrific for creating the impression that an object was carved out of the texture's material (although it does not distort the texture at all to make it follow a modeled shape, making it unsuitable for jobs like the hair in Figure 9.43).

Many programs also support procedural textures that are two dimensional, so that they can be projected or applied to UV coordinates, just like a texture map. This can be convenient for times when you want the advantages of a UV map conforming to the curvature of a surface. If your 3D software only supports 3D procedurals, you can always convert it into a 2D image and apply it as a regular texture map.

9.50 A solid texture uniformly textures all surfaces as they pass through the texture space.

9.2.7.3 CONVERTING TO MAPS

It is possible to turn a procedural texture into a texture map. The most universal way to do this is to apply the procedural texture to a flat surface and make a rendering of the surface. The rendered texture can then be applied as a map on different objects.

Many programs have a function or plug-in specifically designed to convert solid textures into texture maps, or to render texture maps based on how a procedural texture intersects with a particular model.

> **TIP**
>
> If you want to convert a nonrepeating solid texture into a tiling map, apply your solid texture to a primitive torus, and convert the texture on the torus to a UV map. Because a torus is closed and continuous in both U and V, the edges of the converted map will tile perfectly. This technique also works with cylinders for maps that only need to tile in U.

9.2.7.4 SHADER TREES

Procedural textures really shine when used within a shader tree interface. A *shader tree* is a display in which materials, shaders, and textures are linked to share or inherit parameters. Both procedural textures and mapped textures can be combined and enhanced through-shader tree.

Because the appearance of procedural textures is based on user-selected colors and parameters, procedural textures benefit most from the hierarchical sharing and linking of parameters in a shader tree. For example, a procedural texture that creates a checkerboard pattern would have two

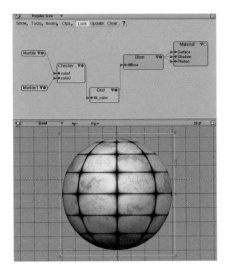

9.51 A shader tree interface (top) allows procedural textures to be combined in creative ways. Here, the two colors of squares in a procedural checkerboard pattern are replaced with two marble textures.

user-adjustable colors to adjust the colors of the squares. In a shader tree, these two coloror colors' parameters could themselves each be replaced by other textures, such as different marble textures, as shown in Figure 9.51. By using the output of one texture to control specific parameters of other textures, complex procedural output can be synthesized by a network of simpler procedural textures.

The essential function of a shader tree is that it is an interactive interface that allows the end-user to create new procedural looks and effects, without programming.

- Nodes inserted into a shader tree can perform image-processing functions, such as blurring, color-correcting, or increasing the contrast in a texture, even if you have started with a texture map from a file.

- Many shader trees also support switches or branches to define different appearances for a shader based on whether the front or back of the surface is being rendered, the surface's distance from the camera, or the viewing angle of the surface. For an example, refer to Figure 9.11 where the Fresnel effect was simulated by connecting the output of a node measuring surface angle into the surface's specularity.

- Shader trees also allow for more control by isolating different attributes of an object's rendering. For example, different shaders and settings can be used to define an object's shadow rather than its appearance when rendered directly, or a separate photon shader can control the color of indirect light reflected off the surface.

As with all software features, shader trees vary between applications, so each of these examples might not be possible in every program.

9.2.7.5 RENDERING EFFICIENCY

There is no blanket rule stating that either procedural textures or texture maps are more efficient. It is possible for a procedure to be simple or complex, and for a texture map to be large or small.

- When rendering with motion blur, solid textures can take a long time to sample, and switching to texture maps can greatly speed up rendering.

- Complex procedures, such as fractal noise with many levels of detail, can slow down your rendering. Converting a complex procedure to a texture map is like creating a look-up table in place of complex calculations, and can speed up the rendering.

- Procedural textures can be animated by varying some of their parameters over time. The procedure produces new textures at each frame based on only a few bytes of data. Accomplishing similar animation through texture maps would require a sequence of multiple texture maps, filling a directory on your hard disk with images.

- High-resolution texture maps use a lot of memory in your computer. A 1024×1024 map uses 3 megabytes, or 4 megabytes with an alpha channel. A 2048×2048 map with an alpha channel uses 16 megabytes of memory. These can quickly add up to something that slows down your rendering.

Both procedural and bitmap textures have their places in production. Texture maps may be more popular because they offer additional control and random access to coloring specific points on an object, but you should never overlook the possibility that a procedural texture might be the best tool for a particular job.

9.3 RAYTRACING

Even after your objects have been lit and textured, they are not each rendered independently. In real life, light bounces between objects in an environment, and all of the objects can cast shadows and create reflections onto other objects. An optional part of the rendering process called *raytracing* simulates the natural reflection, refraction, and shadowing of light by 3D surfaces.

The process of raytracing seems "backward" in comparison to real life, in that the rays begin at the camera. In real life, a ray of light begins at a light source, bounces off objects, and eventually reaches the camera. In raytracing, rays are projected from the camera to sample the objects in the scene.

To begin a raytracing process, the renderer divides the camera's field of view into an array of pixels, based on the resolution of the image being rendered. For each pixel, a ray is projected from the camera, sampling one point from any objects that it intersects, as shown in Figure 9.52. With antialiasing, more than one point may be sampled per pixel, further multiplying the amount of work your raytracer needs to do.

When the ray hits an object, the object is checked to see if it is reflective or refractive, or may be receiving shadows, which need to be computed by sampling other rays. If the object were reflective, for example, then after computing the diffuse and specular shading of the point on the surface, an additional ray would be traced bouncing off the object into 3D space, checking to see whether any other object's reflection would appear at the point being rendered.

9.52 In raytracing, a ray (shown in yellow) starts at the camera, then bounces off visible objects.

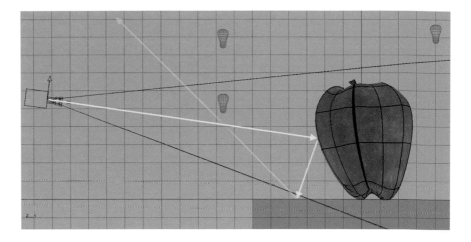

If another reflective object were encountered, then another ray would be cast from that object, further extending the amount of rendering work done for that pixel.

9.3.1 RAYTRACED REFLECTIONS

Raytraced reflections serve a similar role to specular shading. Raytraced reflections are specular reflections of other objects in the scene, while specular shading is a specular reflection of a light source.

Often a raytraced reflection makes a better highlight than specularity does by itself, because you can better control the shape of a raytraced reflection. Figure 9.53 shows a comparison of an apple with only a specular highlight and an apple with a raytraced reflection of a window. To add a reflection, just build a simple model in the shape you want, and position in near a light source. The model built to appear in the reflection could be just one polygon, and could be given any texture map. As long as it is bright enough, and the rendered surface is reflective, your custom shape will show up in your rendering.

Often you'll want to keep your specular highlights and your raytraced reflections both visible on a surface. The key is to make sure that the brightness and position of both reflections and highlights work together, so that they look like part of the same effect.

9.3.1.1 THE SURROUNDING ENVIRONMENT

The most common beginner's mistake with raytraced reflections is failing to surround reflective objects with other objects to reflect. Do not make any object reflective if there are no other objects in the scene. If a reflective object were surrounded by empty black space, no reflection would appear, and the object would simply get darker.

9.53 An object can show reflected light with a specular highlight (left), a raytraced reflection (middle), or both (right).

Carefully check the environment around any reflective object, to be sure that there are no gaps in the modeling that could be given away in the reflection. For example, many 3D artists are in the habit of building rooms with only three walls, and leaving the fourth side opened, so that the camera can look through the opening. A reflective object in such a three-walled room would have a black square missing from its reflection, as shown in Figure 9.54.

Making the fourth wall single-sided, so that the camera can look through it with back face culling, would be a better solution than omitting a wall entirely. Another solution available in some renders is to make the fourth wall a reflect only or secondary rays object, so that it would not appear in the camera's view except in reflections.

9.54 A tell-tale reflection gives away the lack of a fourth wall in a 3D room.

You don't need a heavily subdivided surface to add a wall. A flat wall doesn't necessarily need more than one polygon. It is the quantity of polygons, not the area they cover, that has the greater influence on your rendering time. Feel free to build complete objects and environments for your raytracing, including all the sides of a scene that might appear in a reflection, and all the sides of an object that might affect a shadow. To maintain efficiency, reduce the amount of detail and subdivision in the surfaces where it is not visible or needed.

9.3.1.2 SOFT REFLECTIONS

Standard raytraced reflections produce perfectly specular reflections of other objects. Often, the reflections can appear too perfect, because real surfaces blur and distort reflections of other objects.

A soft raytraced reflection is an option in some raytracers that scatters or randomizes reflected rays to produce a naturally blurred reflection. The reflected image seen within a raytraced soft reflection varies naturally between crisply reflecting nearby objects and a more diffused reflection of distant objects. Notice in Figure 9.55 how the right apple is reflected clearly, while the upper parts of the right apple are heavily blurred.

The same light-reflection types that apply to basic shading (as seen in Figure 9.1 at the beginning of this chapter) still apply in raytracing reflections of other objects. A soft raytraced reflection is *glossy*, while a standard raytraced reflection is purely *specular*. (To complete the analogy to all four reflection types in Figure 9.1, a "diffuse" or "mixed" reflection from other objects will require a global illumination algorithm, as described in the final section of this chapter.)

Soft raytracing effects can greatly increase the realism of a raytraced rendering, but can come at a price of greatly increased rendering time. The scattered rays use the same kind of stochastic (randomized) over-sampling that is used in 3D motion blur, raytraced depth-of-field, and area light shadows, and involves a similar amount of computational over-head. Many people avoid this effect because of its speed, and prefer to render reflections separately to blur them in post (see Chapter 10, "Compositing," for more info), or distort their raytraced reflections with a bump map on the reflective surface.

9.3.2 SHADOWS

Another major function of raytracing is rendering shadows. Chapter 4, "Shadows," described how raytraced shadows differ from *shadow-mapped* (also called *depth-mapped*) shadows. Here is a summary of the main differences:

- Shadow-mapped shadows render more quickly than raytraced shadows.

- Lower resolution shadow maps produce soft-edged shadows. Getting consistently crisp results from shadow maps can require very high shadow map resolutions, which can use extra memory and rendering time.

TIP

If you're looking for a quick alternative to soft raytraced reflections, adding a fine bump map will distort the reflections seen on a surface, and even warp the view through a refractive, transparent surface.

9.55 The reflections in the table are split between standard (left) and soft (right) reflections. The soft reflections becomes more diffused with distance and create more natural looking wood.

- Transparent and transparency-mapped objects can cast transparent shadows with raytracing. Most implementations of shadow maps ignore the level of transparency in an object. Most (but not all) raytracers even allow raytraced shadows to pick up colors from colored transparency maps.

- Small details are reproduced more accurately in raytraced shadows.

- Raytraced shadows are extremely crisp and sharp-edged by default.

- When raytraced shadows are made soft (usually by using an area light as a light source), they become diffused in a realistic way, but at a substantial cost in rendering time.

Refer to Chapter 4 if you want to read more about shadows.

9.3.3 TRANSPARENCY AND REFRACTION

When making an object transparent, you have the same concern as with raytraced reflections—the object's surroundings will affect the shading. A transparent surface left in limbo in an all-black environment will only appear darker as it becomes more transparent. Be sure that there is another object or background behind the transparent object that you will be able to see once the object becomes transparent.

Refraction is a raytracing effect that adds a lens-like distortion to the image seen through a transparent surface. You control the refraction through a surface with a number called the *index of refraction*. Figure 9.56 shows an object rendered with several different index of refraction values. A value of 1 gives you no refraction, allowing rays to pass straight through the object. As you set values above or below 1, the amount of refraction increases. For a convex surface, such as a sphere, values above 1 will make it enlarge the refracted image, like a magnifying glass, while values below 1 will make the refracted image shrink.

Table 9.1 lists some common materials and their indices of refraction. Refraction happens when light leaves one kind of material and enters another, such as leaving air and entering glass, or leaving water and entering air. Because of this, index of refraction values are all relative to two materials. The values in Table 9.1 are based on the listed material surrounded by air, with one exception. The listing of "Air (from under water)" might be used at a water surface when looking up at air, or on bubbles of air seen under water.

9.56 From left to right, vases are rendered with an index of refraction of 1.0 (no refraction), 1.04, 1.15, and 1.44 (glass). There is no difference in the transparency of the vases—the black edges appearing on the right are purely a function of refraction from the environment.

TABLE 9.1

USEFUL INDEX OF REFRACTION (IOR) SETTINGS FOR MATERIALS

Material	IOR
Air (from under water)	0.75
Air/Neutral	1.00
Smoke	1.02
Ice	1.30
Water	1.33
Glass	1.44
Quartz	1.55
Ruby	1.77
Crystal	2.00
Diamond	2.42

Table 9.1 lists numbers that can be useful starting points, but you will probably make most adjustments based on sight. You need to see the refractive settings on your own model before you can be sure that the index of refraction gives you the look you want.

Just like an optical lens, your 3D models will focus rays differently depending on their shape and proportions. The models in Figure 9.57 all share the same index of refraction (1.44) but focus rays differently due to their different shapes. How concave or convex a model is, and whether you look through a single surface or both a front and back surface, will produce completely different refractions.

9.3.4 RAYTRACE DEPTH

In a scene where there are many reflective or refractive surfaces, there is a risk that a raytracer could get caught in an infinite loop, forever tracing

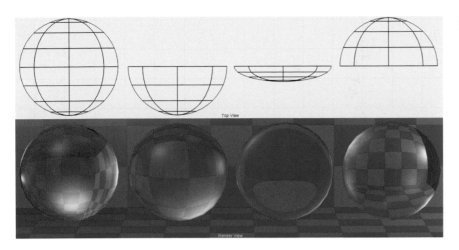

9.57 Even though all use an IOR of 1.44, differently shaped models produce different refraction effects.

a ray from one surface to another surface. Figure 9.58 shows a situation where mirrors on each wall of a room reflect one another. To render the mirror on the right, the raytracer must include the reflection of the left mirror, which in turn requires a calculation of the left mirror's reflection of the right mirror, which again reflects the left mirror, and so on. As the rays of light seem to bounce infinitely between mirrors, the scene could take an infinite amount of time to raytrace.

To complete raytracing in a finite amount of time, you need to limit the *raytrace depth* (called *ray depth*, *trace depth*, or *ray recursion* in different programs), which limits the number of bounces a ray can take between surfaces. In addition to reflections, raytrace depth also caps the calculation of transparency and sometimes shadows. At a raytrace depth of 1, you cannot see reflections within reflections, and cannot see through more than one transparent surface. Higher levels are needed (especially for

9.58 Mirrors facing each other could create an infinite loop in raytracing.

transparency) based on the number of surfaces you need to look through. Figure 9.59 shows the effect of different raytrace depths on ray-traced transparency and refraction.

Different brands of software vary in the amount of control they offer over raytrace depth. Many programs allow different numbers to be specified for the number of reflections and for the number of refractions. Some raytracers allow the depth to be set locally for each shader, as well as globally for the entire rendering. Shadow depth, governing shadows seen through transparency and in reflections, is sometimes set separately on a light source or shader. Despite the differences in the controls, there are some common tips for adjusting your raytrace depth:

- If you are raytracing a scene with many reflective or transparent surfaces, turning down the raytrace depth could significantly speed your rendering.

- If you can count a number of transparent surfaces through which a ray of light needs to be transmitted in a rendering, then set your raytrace depth to at least one higher than that number.

- Objects that are made of glass or crystal are often slightly reflective, but you don't need to let two sides of a glass reflect back and forth too many times. Keep the raytrace depth for reflections down to 1 or 2 on self-reflective transparent surfaces.

- If you see any omission in a test rendering, such as a missing shadow or a reflection appearing beyond transparent glass, or in a reflection, raising your raytrace depth could fix the problem.

- Black areas that appear where you wanted to see transparency or a reflection are another sign that you need to raise your raytrace depth.

In other cases, the raytrace depth can be left at default values, and will not affect your rendering. For example, if there are no cases of reflection or transparency in your scene, and the raytrace depth does not limit anything, then it will not affect your rendering time.

9.59 A trace depth of 2 (left) prevents you from seeing through the second plate, whereas a trace depth of 8 (right) lets you see through all the plates.

9.4 GLOBAL ILLUMINATION

Global illumination is illumination that takes into account light transmitted from other objects. (Contrast global illumination with *local illumination*, in which no other objects are taken into account.) In real life, objects can be illuminated by indirect light, which is light that has reflected off another surface, instead of coming directly from a light source. For example, if a bright light were aimed at the ceiling of a room, light reflected from the ceiling would indirectly illuminate the floor and walls.

Figure 9.60 shows a 3D scene where you would expect the light aimed at the ceiling to softly illuminate the rest of the room. However, an ordinary renderer or raytracer (without using any of the global illumination functions discussed here), would render only an illuminated ceiling and bright upper walls. The rest of the room would be left dark.

A more realistic result was achieved in Figure 9.61, which shows a rendering of the same scene, this time with global illumination activated in the renderer.

There are a number of different types of global illumination, including radiosity, photon mapping, and caustics. You can also achieve similar results in many cases by using a manual simulated radiosity style of lighting.

9.4.1 RADIOSITY

Radiosity is an approach to rendering indirect light, in which light is transmitted between surfaces by diffuse reflection of their surface color. Radiosity can be calculated progressively, so that light can bounce as

9.61 Activating global illumination in a renderer fixes the problem, and correctly calculates the indirect light. (Rendered with photon-mapped global illumination, which is explained later.)

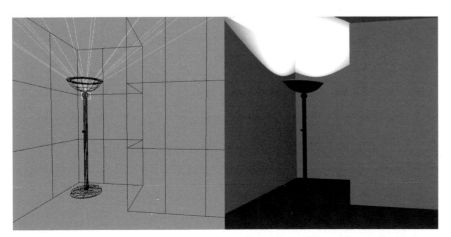

9.60 Disappointing results are achieved when a light hits a ceiling without reflecting back to illuminate the rest of the room.

many times as needed to create a refined, accurate simulation of real lighting. The number of bounces in a progressive radiosity solution is only limited by the amount of time available to compute the radiosity solution.

A phenomenon called *color bleeding* can be seen in many radiosity renderings. Figure 9.62 shows a radiosity rendering with light reflecting off a red cube. The red diffuse color of the cube is transmitted via reflected light onto other surfaces in the scene.

Radiosity is usually calculated by storing shading information for each vertex of the polygonal objects in a scene. Figure 9.63 shows how the scene is subdivided during the radiosity calculation. More vertices are added where additional detail is needed in the shading, such as at the edges of shadows or highlight areas.

A disadvantage of this approach is that the resolution of your geometry is linked with the resolution of your global illumination solution. It is difficult to compute a quick approximation of the lighting for a scene with a high polygon count. The radiosity solution and subdivision of the geometry is also difficult to recompute at each frame of an animated sequence, if major objects in a scene were moving.

9.4.2 PHOTON MAPPING

Another approach to calculating indirect lighting is called *photon mapping*. The same kind of results calculated by conventional radiosity can also be rendered via photon mapping. With photon mapping, a

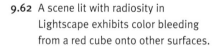

9.62 A scene lit with radiosity in Lightscape exhibits color bleeding from a red cube onto other surfaces.

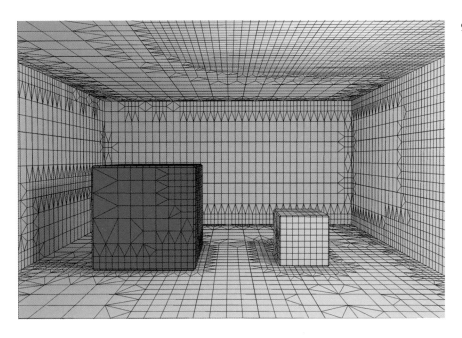

9.63 Polygon meshes are adaptively subdivided by Lightscape based on contrast in the scene.

separate data type, the *photon map*, is created to store the global illumination solution. The resolution of a photon-mapped solution is independent from the resolution of the geometry.

> **NOTE**
>
> The Name Game: Some people define *radiosity* broadly to mean "a rendering principle that calculates diffuse reflection of light and color among surfaces in a scene." Based on this functional definition, photon mapping could be said to be a type of radiosity. However, many computer scientists reserve the word radiosity only for specific algorithms, and refer to photon mapping as "an alternative to radiosity." You are safer using the blanket term *global illumination* when discussing all these indirect lighting processes in general.

For more accurate photon-mapped illumination, you can raise the number of photons emitted from a light. You can also lower the number of photons if you want a quick rendering. Figure 9.64 was rendered with a low number of photons, without any interpolation. The individual photons that bounce through the scene can be seen as paintball-like dots, splattered onto every surface of the rendering. You can see photons that have become red from bouncing off the red cube dotting other nearby surfaces with their reflected light.

The photons in Figure 9.64 were adjusted to see the internal workings of the renderer. Individual photons are not visible under normal circumstances, and usually nobody can tell from your final rendering whether you used a photon-mapped or conventional radiosity solution.

9.64 A photon-mapped global illumination solution depends upon a number of photons bouncing between surfaces. There is no texture mapping in this scene—all dots are photons.

Photon mapping presents an easy one-step solution to adding indirect light to a scene. Starting from only one direct light source, as shown on the left side of Figure 9.65, the rendering software can calculate all the indirect lighting to produce the final solution rendered on the right side of the figure.

9.4.3 CAUSTICS

The beginning of this chapter noted two different ways light can reflect off a surface. Diffuse reflection and specular reflection need to be addressed by a full global-illumination solution. Generally, radiosity solutions only address diffuse reflection of light, whereas photon-mapped solutions calculate a mixed reflection.

The results of specular light transmission are called *caustics*. Caustic patterns are perhaps best known for creating the shimmering light patterns

9.65 A scene without global illumination (left), and with global illumination activated (right) in a Mental Ray rendering.

seen on the bottom and walls of swimming pools, as shown in Figure 9.66. However, caustics are actually a much broader category of effects than just the shimmering light that bounces off water.

Caustics are not a rendering technique or specific algorithm, they are a description of an effect. In just the same way that color bleeding is an effect of diffuse light transmission, caustics are an effect of specular light transmission. Photon mapping is a rendering technique that can calculate caustics, and other techniques may be used in the future as more programs add support for rendering them.

Caustics are often the brightest, most noticeable part of the indirect lighting in a scene, so caustics are sometimes used by themselves, without activating a full global-illumination solution. Figure 9.67 includes examples of several types of caustics at work, including the transmission of reflected and refracted light.

Figure 9.68 shows exactly what caustics add to the scene. The light bouncing off the mirror, refracting though the glass vase, and reflecting off the vase onto the top of the dresser, are all added due to caustics.

9.66 Patterns reflected off water are one of the most recognizable caustic effects, although they are also among the easiest to simulate without true caustic rendering.

9.67 Caustics are used to simulate light reflecting off the mirror, and refracting through the vase.

9.68 A conventional raytraced image (left) does not include caustics. The addition of caustics (right) add realistic glints of light coming from the mirror and vase.

Caustics calculate light that remains focused, instead of diffusely scattering, which makes caustics a more straightforward task to compute than a full global illumination solution. Caustics can render much more quickly than full global illumination. The rendering time required by most caustic effects is roughly equivalent to the amount of extra rendering time required to add raytracing effects to your scene, such as a reflective mirror or refractive glass. Full global illumination, on the other hand, can increase rendering times to a much greater degree than ordinary raytracing. You can use caustics more liberally than full global illumination.

When you start looking for them, you will see that caustics are all around you in the real world.

- Light that refracts through a lens, magnifying glass, or prism is a caustic effect. You often see refracted caustics on top of a table next to glasses and bottles.

- Beams of light reflecting off a mirror are caustics, and so are all the glints reflected off a disco ball.

- Any shiny or highly specular surface creates caustic effects when hit by a bright light. On a sunny day, a car's chrome bumper or a building's window will create caustic patterns on the ground.

- The throw pattern of lights with built-in reflectors, including flashlights and car headlights, are broken up with caustic patterns from the reflected light. (In 3D this is usually more efficiently rendered by putting a map on the light, however.)

- Caustic patterns are reflected onto walls near water surfaces, or refracted into shimmering patterns on the bottom of swimming pools. (This kind of pattern can also be created by texture mapping.)

Much like raytracing, caustics run the risk of appearing cheesy if overused. However, in a more subtle combination, caustics can add greatly to the lighting of a scene.

You can think of caustics as a dirty, imperfect kind of light, because caustics are be more varied and broken-up than light coming directly from a light source or a diffuse reflection. The interaction of light between objects in your scene can add an extra touch of realism to an environment that you could not achieve through direct lighting alone.

9.4.4 SIMULATED RADIOSITY

If you don't have the software support or rendering time to render a project with true global illumination, but you want to achieve some of the same looks, you can light your scene in a style called simulated radiosity.

Simulated radiosity is a process of adding extra fill lights to your scene to simulate reflected light in areas where you think it should appear. Fill lights used for this purpose are sometimes called *bounce lights*.

Suppose that the main source of light in a room were sunlight coming though a window. Starting at the top of Figure 9.69, the direct light from the sun is clearly insufficient to light the room. A standard fill light is added (in the second panel), to illuminate the interior. The lower three panels of Figure 9.69 show the effect of adding extra bounce lights to the scene.

The first bounce light is added underneath the floor. It is a point light, tinted red to reflect the color of the floor. Without casting shadows, it can shine up through the floor to illuminate the room from below. The point light is placed directly underneath the area that the sunbeam hits, as shown in Figure 9.70.

The second and third bounce lights (also shown in Figure 9.70) are spot lights, shining through the walls from the outside. One is behind the back wall, positioned to match the location of the sunbeam on the back wall. The other is positioned behind the exterior window wall, to simulate light bounced off that wall and off the window ledge. There are several guidelines you should keep in mind when adding bounce lights like this:

- Bounce lights should always be set to attenuate or decay with distance, so that they cast the brightest reflected light near the surface, and they don't inadvertently overlight a distant wall or ceiling.

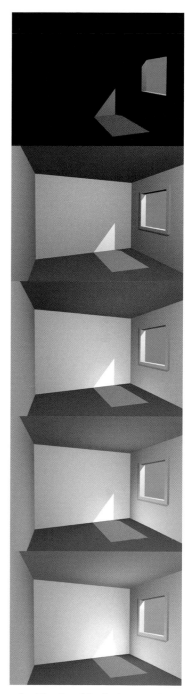

9.69 Simulated Radiosity: Starting with a key light from the sun (top panel) and a fill light (second panel), the process of simulated radiosity involves adding extra bounce lights under the floor (middle panel), and through the walls (lower panels) to simulate indirect light.

9.70 Bounce lights are added below the floor and behind the walls to simulate indirect lighting.

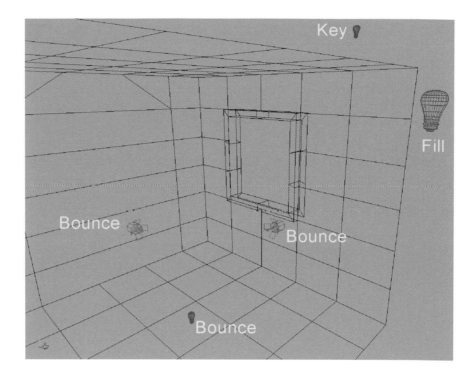

- Bounce lights usually do not need to cast shadows. Avoiding shadows makes them render faster, and allows them to shine through floors and walls.

- Bounce lights should not cast specular highlights. Bounce lights should only add diffuse illumination to your objects, because tightly focused specular highlights could give away the location of a bounce light, instead of simulating light from an illuminated area.

- Spotlights are often the best kind of source for a bounce light, so that it can be aimed and adjusted in the direction that light would bounce off a surface.

The simpler the geometry of the scene, the easier the simulated radiosity approach will be to achieve. With each extra object, surface, and corner, the number of bounce lights required to create realistic lighting increases exponentially. To work efficiently on a deadline, you usually need to focus on the brightest or most prominent areas to add bounced lighting. You will have to stop working when it looks good enough, even if some small areas do not have reflected light simulated perfectly.

9.4.5 USE IN ANIMATION

Global illumination techniques that add light to the diffuse shading of models are non-view-dependent. This means that a stored solution can be used from many different camera angles, and still enhance the realism of the scene.

The most popular, established use for conventional radiosity is in realistically lighting and rendering architectural spaces. The only animation needed by architects to previsualize a building design is usually a fly-through, with the camera gliding through a space. None of the objects or lights need to move in a fly-through, so the same radiosity solution, computed once and stored per each vertex of the geometry, can be used for each frame of the sequence.

Photon-mapped solutions can also be stored, so that a photon map computed once can be reused for every frame of an animation. However, for fully animated sequences in which more than the camera is moving, you might want to invest the extra time and have the photon map rebuilt at every frame.

Recomputing a photon map at every frame adds to your rendering time, but can produce beautiful interactive lighting effects between moving objects. Figure 9.71 shows an example of this—a door is keyframed to swing open, and all the lighting in the room changes as light pours through the opening door.

9.4.6 WHICH APPROACH IS BEST?

Global illumination solutions are the "power tools" of realistic lighting, and can save users a great deal of time in lighting a scene realistically, even if they have the skills and experience to be able to set up their own simulated radiosity instead.

Today, it is more popular to use simulated radiosity in a production, instead of rendering with a full global illumination solution, because a

9.71 A simple animation of a door swinging open creates a complex and subtle lighting animation with global illumination. (View the animation file online at 3dRender.com/light/bluedoor.mov, if you want to see the shot in motion.)

9.72 When sunlight is available, reflectors are frequently used in place of lighting instruments on film shoots.

full global illumination solution can take far too long to render for most productions. In addition, it is only recently that major brands of 3D-animation software added global illumination capabilities to their renderers.

Over the next few years, more productions may turn toward global illumination solutions for everyday productions. Computers are always becoming faster, so that every year more ambitious rendering tasks can be handled for the same cost. Meanwhile, the quantity of shots being delivered in 3D productions continues to increase, leaving less time for experienced 3D artists to work on lighting each shot.

Some professional 3D artists seem to live in fear that their hard-earned experience and knowledge may be made obsolete or irrelevant by future software versions. They sometimes deride global illumination, saying that it "does your lighting for you." While it is true that global illumination allows beginners to light scenes with unprecedented realism, having more powerful illumination tools available only adds to your options, and does not take away your creative control over the scene.

Photographers and cinematographers in the real world are accustomed to using indirect lighting as a part of their work, and routinely take advantage of the capability to reflect light off natural surfaces or specially adjusted reflectors. Reflectors like the ones shown in Figure 9.72 are carefully aimed to bounce sunlight at actors, fill in harsh shadows, and decrease the key-to-fill ratio of sunny days.

The combination of faster computers and the need to increase an artist's productivity in lighting scenes will inevitably force a reevaluation of traditional trade-offs between operator time and processor time. Full global illumination will become expected for any realistic scene, and eventually clients will demand a subtle level of interactive lighting that is usually skipped by today's standards.

9.5 EXERCISES

1. Starting with the cover of this book, check three or four different surfaces to see what kind of specular highlights they exhibit. Be sure to view the surfaces from different angles, to see how the highlights travel. What is the shape of the highlights? Are there any cases of multiple highlights or mixed highlight types? Which surface shows the biggest highlights, and which has the brightest?

2. Examine any of your (or somebody else's) previous 3D renderings. Do the specular highlights look like realistic and appropriate reflections of a light source? If raytraced reflections are also used, does the position and brightness of the specular highlight make it blend convincingly into the reflection?

3. Find a surface that you normally consider blank, or devoid of texture, such as a wall or the side of a monitor. How can you tell by sight what material it is made of? For example, how would you tell when looking at the surface whether it was paper, or plastic, or plaster? What kinds of texture mapping would you use to represent the surface, and how would you create it?

4. Look around in the room you are in now, and see if you can spot any reflected light. Which surfaces in the room are lit directly, and which are lit indirectly?

5. Next time you are in a space that has mirrors, glass, water, or shiny surfaces (such as a bathroom or outside of a building on a sunny day), see how many caustic effects you can find around you, and see if you can locate their source.

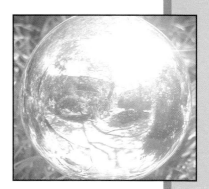

CHAPTER] 10

COMPOSITING

FILM AND TELEVISION production companies are continually asked to render scenes that seem to be beyond the limits of their software and hardware. To complete ambitious 3D renderings with the required complexity, quality, and speed, almost all professional productions are rendered in multiple layers or passes, and finished though *compositing*. Compositing is the art of combining multiple images into a unified final scene. Multipass rendering and compositing allow for more efficient rendering, increased creative control, convincing integration with live-action footage, and rapid revisions to your renders.

10.1 RENDERING IN LAYERS

Rendering in layers is the process of rendering different objects in your scene separately, so that a different image is rendered for each layer. The simplest case is to separate animated subjects from background environments. For example, the background layer of the sample scene in Figure 10.1 is the planet surface, and the foreground layer is the spaceship.

To set this up, start with a full scene with all of the objects visible. Assembling all of the objects in one scene will ensure that all layers will match in scale, lighting, and camera angles. After arranging the entire scene, sort your objects into separate layers.

10.1 A sample scene is composited to add the spaceship (from Figure 10.3) over the background environment (from Figure 10.2).

NOTE

Don't have any compositing software yet? See http://3dRender.com/light/compositing/ for an index of all the software companies that supply it.

To render the background layer, shown in Figure 10.2, simply hide the foreground layer objects. If the background layer is not moving, and the camera is not moving, then you need to render only one frame of the background. In your compositing program, the animated foreground can be composited over your static background. If the background is animated, or the camera is moving, then render all of the frames of your background layer.

In a more complex scene, instead of simply hiding the foreground layers during background rendering, you might save a separate version of your scene with the other layers deleted. This can save even more memory and rendering time.

To complete the scene, foreground layers are rendered with the background hidden or deleted. The foreground shown in Figure 10.3 is rendered along with an alpha channel to guide the compositing. The white area of the alpha channel shows where the foreground element will be added. The black areas of the alpha channel indicate areas that will show through to the background layer. For more complex scenes, many foreground layers can be rendered, each with its own alpha.

Why bother to render in layers? Rendering in layers clearly involves more set-up work than rendering all the objects in the scene at once. However, there are several advantages to rendering in layers, some of which can end up saving you valuable time:

- For high-quality character animation, most of your final revisions and rerenders are likely to apply to the character, not the background. In this case, the character can be quickly rerendered as a foreground layer, without rerendering the full scene.

10.2 The background of the sample scene is rendered separately.

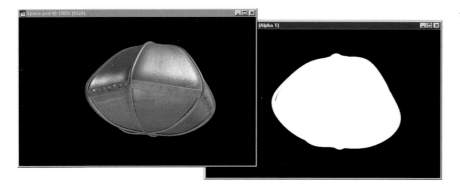

10.3 The foreground layer is another rendering, rendered with an alpha channel to guide compositing.

- For extremely large scenes, rendering in layers makes possible projects that would overload your computer's memory if all objects had to be rendered at once.

- For static background layers, if the camera is not moving, you need only to render one frame to composite behind your entire animated shot.

- For a soft-focused background, you need only to blur the background layer in your compositing program, instead of needing to render a slow depth-of-field effect in 3D.

- For maximum rendering efficiency, different layers can be rendered using different software settings. For example, you might use more antialiasing, motion blur, or raytracing on some important layers. More distant objects, or objects that you plan to blur in post, might be rendered in a manner more optimized for speed.

- Separately rendered elements can be reused in multiple places and times. When compositing layers, you might repeat a flock of birds more than one place in the sky or recycle soft-focused foreground shrubbery between shots.

- To work around bugs, limitations, or incompatibilities in your software, split different effects into different render layers. For example, if you use an effect that does not render through a transparent surface, you could render the effect as a separate layer and then composite the transparent foreground layer over it. If you have created a character's hair via a plug-in that works only with some types of shadows and not others, then you don't have to compromise the lighting of your entire scene if you render the hair in a different layer.

Almost every rendering system has limitations that are best resolved by rendering in layers. In some situations, rendering in layers is more efficient. To achieve even greater efficiency and control, complex professional scenes are usually also rendered in passes.

10.2　RENDERING IN PASSES

Rendering in passes is the process of rendering different attributes of your scene separately. The seven most common types of passes you can render are as follows:

- Beauty pass

- Highlight pass

- Reflection passes

- Shadow passes

- Lighting passes

- Effects passes

- Depth maps

Each of these passes can be created as separate renderings. By combining and adjusting different passes in a compositing program, a scene can be tweaked interactively without being rerendered, and subtle effects can be precisely fine-tuned or matched to a filmed background plate.

10.2.1　BEAUTY PASS

A *beauty pass* (sometimes called *diffuse pass* or *color pass*) is the main, full-color rendering of your subject, including diffuse illumination, color, and color maps, as shown in Figure 10.4. A beauty pass usually will *not* include reflections, highlights, or shadows; these are usually rendered as separate passes.

A beauty pass is usually rendered along with an alpha channel of your subject, to be used later for compositing your subject over a background. Different objects in your scene can have different beauty passes if, for example, you want to render different subjects or elements in the environment separately.

To render an object's beauty pass, often a modification to its materials or shaders will be necessary, to block any reflections or specular highlights. Some software may have pass-management features that simplify this process, but editing your subject's materials in order to show only diffuse illumination is something that is possible to achieve in almost any rendering software. A shortcut in many programs is to set your lights to emit only diffuse illumination when rendering your beauty pass (instead of editing each individual material's specularity).

10.2.2 HIGHLIGHT PASS

Highlight passes (sometimes called *specular passes*) isolate the specular highlights from your objects. You can render highlight passes by turning off any ambient light and setting the object's diffuse shading and color mapping to pure black. The result, as shown in Figure 10.5, will be a rendering of all the specular highlights in the scene, without any other types of shading.

Isolating your specular highlights into a separate pass is optional. Use a separate highlight pass for more important renderings, where you care

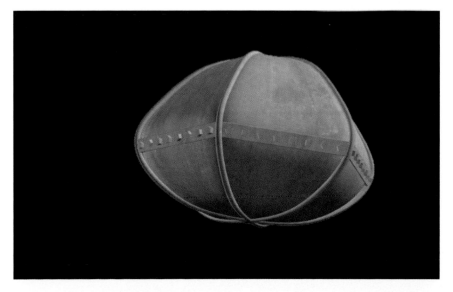

10.4 The beauty pass is rendered without reflections, highlights, or shadows.

10.5 The highlight pass shows only the highlights on the surface, over a black color.

NOTE

LightWave users may want to use Adrian's Nifty Special Buffer Saver from www.1410.com.au/adrian/ sbs.htm to help isolate specular highlights, reflections, and many other elements from the buffers created for a rendering.

the most about quality. For less important elements, you might simply include some specularity along with your beauty pass.

Rendering a separate highlight pass allows you more creative control over how the highlights are rendered. In Figure 10.5 a bump map was added to vary and soften the highlights. The bump map was not there in rendering the beauty pass; it was applied only for the highlights. You may also move your lights to different positions if it makes better highlights. Naturally, the lights should come from the same general angle as the lighting is used in the beauty and shadow passes, but there's nothing wrong with cheating a little bit to make a better-looking rendering.

Highlight passes can be composited over your beauty pass with an Add or Screen operation. This way, lighter areas of your highlight pass will brighten your beauty pass, black areas of your highlight pass will have no effect, and no alpha channel is necessary.

During your composite, having highlights as a separate pass will allow control over their color and brightness so that you can adjust the highlights to match the rest of your composited scene. Don't clip large areas of your highlights into pure white. Your highlight pass will work best if highlights run through different shades of gray, which will allow it to look realistic when composited with different intensities.

Separately rendered highlights can also be used to control visual effects, such as glows, added in compositing. Adding a blurred copy of your highlight pass will create glows around your highlights, as shown in Figure 10.6. This way, glows do not take any test renders to adjust, and they can be adjusted in context with the final composite.

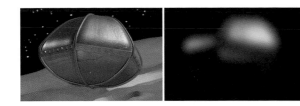

10.6 A composited image (left) can be enhanced with a blurred copy of the highlight pass (middle) to produce a soft glow around the highlights (right).

As discussed in the previous chapter, specular highlights are closely related to reflections, and may be partially or wholly replaced by reflections. If your light sources are visible in a reflection, you might sometimes skip the highlight pass. If your reflection does not include visible reflections of the lights themselves, adding together a highlight pass and a reflection pass can more completely simulate reflected light on the object.

10.2.3 REFLECTION PASSES

A *reflection pass* includes reflections of other objects or the surrounding environment. To isolate reflections, usually all you need to do is turn off ambient, diffuse, and specular shading from a surface so that only reflections appear, as in Figure 10.7.

You do not need any lights to illuminate an object when rendering the reflections on its surface. If your reflections come from reflection maps, you can remove all the lights in your scene when rendering a reflection pass. If raytraced reflections show other objects, some lights may still be needed for the other objects, unless they are constant-shaded or incandescent.

Often, your reflection pass will show reflections of objects from other layers or passes. If you are using reflection maps, this requires that you

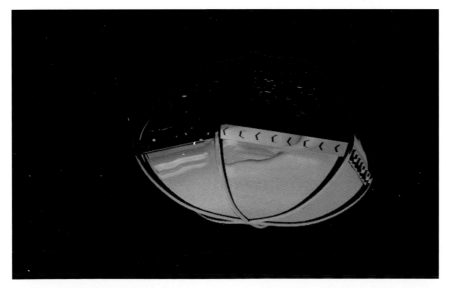

10.7 The reflection pass shows only the reflections of the surrounding environment, from a purely reflective object.

NOTE

3D Studio MAX users can use the free Utility Material from Blur Studio (www.blur.com) to render an object's reflections without rendering the original object.

have previously rendered a reflection map of your surrounding objects, but you don't need those objects to be present after creating the map. If you are using raytraced reflections, then you need to designate the reflected objects to be visible in reflections (sometimes called *secondary rays*) but not directly visible to primary rays.

In many cases, you will get the best results by blurring your reflection pass slightly in your compositing program. If you're going to be blurring the reflection pass, you can usually save rendering time by turning off antialiasing. Even if your reflection pass doesn't look perfectly refined when rendered, it will still look good after it's blurred in your compositing program.

10.2.3.1 COMPOSITING REFLECTIONS

To composite the passes of a reflective object, a reflection pass is generally dissolved with the underlying beauty pass, before the highlight pass is added on top. A reflection pass may use its own alpha channel, but it can also share the alpha channel from the beauty pass. If you render reflection passes without antialiasing, use the alpha from the beauty pass.

The intensity of the beauty pass, reflection pass, and highlight pass are all reduced when they are blended in the composite, as shown in Figure 10.8. The exact proportions of each are judged visually. As you adjust the passes, compare the highlight pass to the light sources in the scene, and compare the reflection pass to the surrounding environment, to make sure your levels look appropriate to your object and its surroundings. This part of compositing is an art—not a science—and you need to trust your eyes.

10.8 A balanced composite combines the beauty pass, highlight pass, and reflection pass.

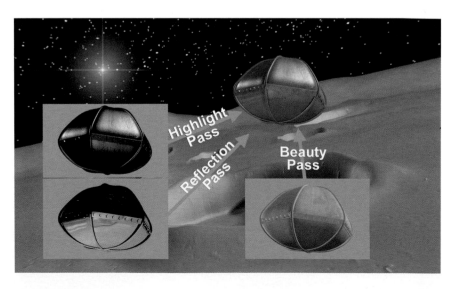

10.2.3.2 ADDING REFLECTIONS TO REAL OBJECTS

Sometimes, your 3D object will cast a reflection onto a real-world surface, such as a shiny floor, countertop, or water surface. The cast reflection should be rendered as a separate reflection pass.

If the surface showing the reflection is another 3D object, then that object needs only to be made visible and reflective to render the pass. If the surface showing the reflection is a real-life surface, then you will need to build a 3D model of that surface and position it to align with the live-action plate, as with the grid in Figure 10.9.

For the effect of rippling water, you might add a bump map to a reflective water surface object, which distorts a reflection, as shown in Figure 10.10.

10.9 A grid matches the water surface to receive a reflection.

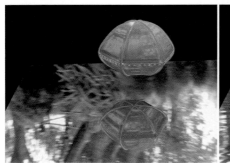

10.10 Bump mapping on a reflection surface distorts the reflection to simulate water ripples.

The alpha channel output by most renderers will default to showing the shape of an entire reflective object, rather than the shape of the reflection itself. For example, the alpha channel could show the shape of the rectangular plane, instead of the reflection that was cast onto the plane. If the alpha channel cannot be fixed in rendering your reflection pass, you may be able to produce a mask by using a luminance key function in your compositing software to isolate the reflection from a black surrounding area. As a last resort, you could render a second reflection pass—reflecting solid white objects against black backgrounds—to use in place of the alpha channel.

When keying the reflection over a surface, adjust it in your compositing program to match the tones of existing reflections on the surface, as in Figure 10.11. Reflections that have too much color and contrast can look unrealistic, so color correction is usually necessary to match any real background sequence.

10.2.4 SHADOW PASSES

A *shadow pass* is a rendering that shows the locations of shadows in a scene. A shadow pass often appears as a white shadow region against a black background, as in Figure 10.12. Common variations on this include renderings with black shadows against white backgrounds and renderings with the shadow shape embedded in the alpha channel. These variations can all work equally well in compositing.

10.11 A 3D reflection is keyed over water.

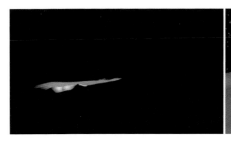

10.12 A shadow pass (left) indicates a ship's shadow cast on the ground and is used to darken the corresponding area of the final composite (right).

To render shadows cast from one object onto another, the object casting the shadows needs to be invisible to primary rays in your rendering but still cast shadows into the scene (this is sometimes called a *shadow object*.) The surface receiving the shadow, such as the ground, still needs to be visible.

To ensure an accurate shadow pass, make sure there is no ambient or incandescent light in the scene. The only light source in the scene should be the one light that is casting the shadow. To further isolate shadows, sometimes a light is used with a negative brightness, as well as a negative shadow brightness, to create white shadows over a uniform black background. This avoids any shading variation in the background, because the background area remains pure black, even beyond the edge of the light's beam.

Shadows often look best when the shadow pass is blurred slightly during compositing. If you are rendering a shadow pass that will be blurred later anyway, you might turn off antialiasing on the shadow pass, turn down shadow samples on an area light, or use a lower resolution shadow map.

10.2.4.1 ATTACHED SHADOWS

Attached shadows are shadows a surface casts onto itself. For example, a character's nose can cast an attached shadow onto other parts of his face. A bumpy or hilly terrain can also have attached shadows, as shown in Figure 10.13, especially if your light comes from the side.

If you want to control the intensity and color of the shadows separately during your composite, attached shadow passes need to be rendered separately from cast shadows. If you don't want to render an attached shadow pass, attached shadows can sometimes be rendered as a part of the object's beauty pass. In other cases, attached shadows can be skipped entirely. For example, no attached shadows were rendered on the spaceship in the sample scene.

> **NOTE**
>
> 3D Studio MAX users can use the free Cast Shadows Only Material from Blur Studio (www.blur.com) to render cast shadow passes, and may also use the free Render Layers script from www.gfxcentral.com/ bobo/ to help with multiple passes.

10.13 The attached shadow pass for a terrain is rendered separately (left) and used to darken areas of the final composite (right).

10.2.4.2 **DOUBLED SHADOWS**

A common problem in compositing visual effects shots is doubled shadows. As shown in Figure 10.14, *doubled shadows* occur where a shadow pass further darkens an area that was already shadowed from the same light source. When combining two shadow passes that represent the occlusion of the same light, be sure to composite the passes first in a lighten-only or darken-only mode, and then use the merged shadows to darken the background plate.

Doubled shadows can also be a problem when adding a shadow pass to a shadowed area of a live-action background plate. Especially for exterior scenes where the sun provides a single source for shadows, doubled shadows would look highly unrealistic. The shadow pass must not darken areas that are already darkened by a real shadow. The real shadow needs to be masked out so that your shadow pass darkens only the areas that weren't already in shadow. Your shadow pass should appear to extend the area of the real shadow, extending its area with the same shadow tone.

Adding shadows to a real scene is sometimes a lot of work. Luckily, all that needs to be done in 3D is to render each shadow pass separately, and most of the work is left to the compositing process.

Some 3D artists have the unfortunate habit of trying to render cast shadows into the alpha channel of the same pass as their 3D objects. Because of all the issues that can arise in compositing shadows and all of the adjustments that need to be made to achieve convincing shadow

10.14 Poor compositing can result in doubled shadows, with the same light being removed twice from the same area (left, note where the two shadows overlap). Properly composited shadows merge into a unified area where the objects block the same light source (right).

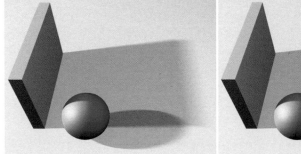 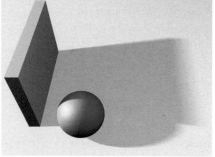

tones, this technique would not actually save time or make compositing any easier.

10.2.5 LIGHTING PASSES

A *lighting pass* is an optional part of multipass rendering that adds a great deal of flexibility and control to the compositing process. Instead of rendering a beauty pass all at once, you could instead render multiple lighting passes, as shown in Figure 10.15. An individual lighting pass shows the influence of one light (or one group of lights) on an element, with other lights hidden or deleted.

The three passes can be added together during compositing. Use the *Add* or *Screen* mode in your compositing program in just the same way that you would composite a highlight pass. During the composite, you can separately tweak the brightness and color of each of the lighting passes to produce different lighting effects, as shown in Figure 10.16.

You probably won't have time to render separate lighting passes from each light on each element in your scene. Separating lighting passes is best reserved for special situations where they will be of the most use during compositing:

- A back light or rim light to an object could be rendered in a separate lighting pass, instead of being a part of your beauty pass. Isolating the rim light could allow the rim light to be separately adjusted when building the final composite.

- Any light that might be blocked by a shadow pass, while allowing other lights to fill in the shadow area, should be rendered as a separate lighting pass.

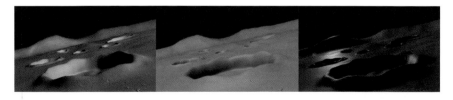

10.15 Lighting passes were rendered separately for the key light (left), fill light (center), and backlight (right).

10.16 During compositing, manipulation of the color and intensity of each lighting pass allows lighting adjustments without rerendering.

- Any kind of global illumination, such as radiosity or caustic effects, could be isolated from the direct lighting passes so that the global illumination could be brightened, darkened, or tinted without a recalculation.

- Animated lighting effects are sometimes motivated by a source seen in another pass or live-action plate. For example, a flash of light received from an explosion could be rendered as separate lighting passes. This allows the animated lighting to be precisely matched in color and timing to the element that motivates it.

- Lights with highly saturated colors can be isolated into a separate lighting pass. This allows the hue, intensity, and saturation of the colored light to be edited independently.

When rendering separate lighting passes, try to err on the side of less-saturated light colors. If you need to increase the saturation during the composite, you can, but you wouldn't want to use such a boldly saturated color that the red, green, or blue would be underexposed and difficult to boost.

10.2.6 EFFECTS PASSES

Depending on the needs of your project, *effects passes* may sometimes be rendered in a scene. An effects pass is a separate rendering of a visual effect or a mask for a visual effect. An effects pass might be an optical effect, such as a light glow or lens flare, or a particle effect, such as a cloud of smoke or plume of jet exhaust.

10.2.6.1 OPTICAL EFFECTS

Optical effects are phenomena such as lens flares or streaks radiating from a light, which simulate effects that could occur in a camera's lens or film plane. During compositing, optical effects should always be added last, superimposed over other elements.

Optical effects are especially important to isolate as a separate pass. By themselves, they are quick to render. However, you wouldn't want to repeatedly rerender a more complex scene just to see different adjustments to a lens flare!

Optical effects are a popular part of many computer graphics scenes. Visible rays radiating from the star seemed like an obligatory component in making the example scene for this section. However, if you don't want your work to look like a computer graphics demo, you are usually best off to avoid conspicuous optical effects. Rendering optical effects separately at least enables you to diminish or delete the effect later, if you change your mind about its importance in your scene.

10.2.6.2 PARTICLE EFFECTS

The appearance of particles can be modified and enhanced by rendering them separately in their own pass. You can use rendered particles as masks to control different image processing effects, manipulate their color and opacity, and combine them in different ways with the background image.

Figure 10.17 shows a simple cloud of particles. By using the particle cloud as a mask for a distortion effect, the background is distorted by the particles, as though the particles were causing refraction. Finally, the particles are colored green and keyed over the background, behind the ship that emitted them.

When particles are widely distributed throughout a scene, some of them may appear in front of other objects, and some of them behind other objects. There are three main strategies for dealing with this problem:

- Render multiple layers of particles, separating foreground particles, mid-ground particles, and background particles. The particle layers may be separately emitted, or split via clipping planes.

- Render your particles with solid-black copies of other objects, which will block some of the background particles.

- Render particle systems and integrated objects along with depth maps (see the next section) for use in depth-based compositing.

Rendering multiple layers of particles is usually the simplest of these choices, and it allows the most flexible control over particle appearance and compositing.

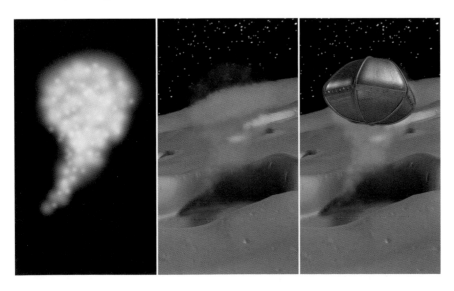

10.17 A simple particle system is rendered as an effects pass over a black background (left) and used as a mask for glass distortion and Gaussian Blur filters applied to a background layer (center) to simulate refractive smoke in the final composite (right).

10.2.7 DEPTH MAPS

A *depth map* (also called *Z-Depth* or a *depth pass*) is a pass that stores depth information at each point in your scene. Some productions use depth maps rendered in a special depth map file format. Other productions use *simulated depth maps,* which are rendered as standard image files just like any other pass but are designed to serve the same purpose as a true depth map.

A depth map is an array of values, measuring the distance from the camera to the closest subject being rendered at each pixel. A depth map of the space scene is shown in Figure 10.18. Brighter shades of gray represent parts of the scene that are closer to the camera.

10.2.7.1 TYPES OF DEPTH MAPS

A true depth map is not an image. The value stored for each pixel location is not a color or shade, but a floating-point accurate number representing the camera-to-subject distance. If a true depth map is converted into a viewable grayscale image, with only 256 levels of gray, then the accuracy is limited, compared to the original distance measurements.

True depth maps output by a renderer do not include antialiasing, because they store only one distance per pixel. You may have to render your images and depth maps at a higher resolution, and then scale down the final composite, in order to achieve correctly antialiased output from a depth-map-based composite. To produce antialiased output from a scene's depth, you can make a rendering that is sometimes called a *simulated depth map*. Simulated depth maps are really the output of a regular rendering. They do not involve floating-point distance measurements. To set up a simulated depth map rendering, all of the objects in your scene

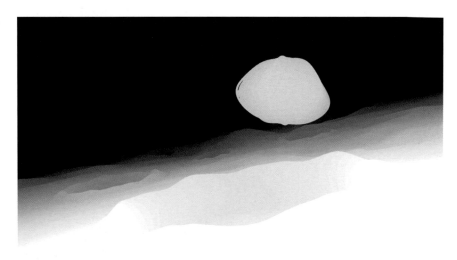

10.18 Brighter tones are closer to the camera in this grayscale representation of a depth map.

need to be given a flat, constant white color, with no shading. Then, a *depth-fading* or *fog* effect needs to be activated, to fade your scene toward black at greater distances from the camera. The results will be something like Figure 10.18.

10.2.7.2 USES FOR DEPTH MAPS

Rendered depth information can be used in different ways during compositing.

If you have two rendered scenes, each of which was rendered with a matching depth map, then a *depth-based composite* can merge the two scenes based on the depth at each pixel. Different objects or particles in the renderings can occlude each other or appear in the foreground or background based on their own distance from the camera.

Depth maps were once used with standalone programs for rendering particles. To composite particle renderings with the objects rendered in another program, depth maps were rendered with both the particles and the objects so that particles could correctly appear in front of or behind different objects. This approach has fallen out of favor because it did not support antialiasing, did not work correctly with transparent objects, and did not allow lighting and shadows to interact between particles and geometry. Particle support built in to the main renderer of most programs has largely replaced this approach.

Another way you can use a depth map is as a mask for any kind of image-processing effect. Figure 10.19 used the rendered depth map (from Figure 10.18 earlier) to mask a blur of the background and to tint the background with a cool, gray color. This enhances the sense of depth

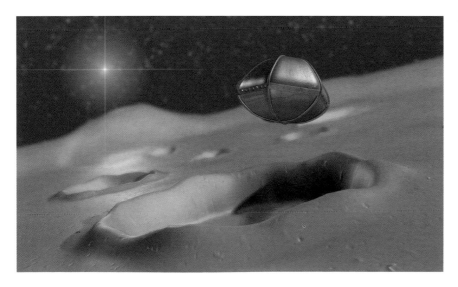

10.19 A depth map is used as a mask for blurring and color-correcting operations that simulate depth.

in the scene through simulating a camera's limited depth of field and also simulates atmospheric perspective as though looking through dust that dulled the color of the distant rocks.

Depth maps are worth rendering for any environment that needs a lot of atmospheric or depth-of-field effects to be simulated during compositing. Simulated depth maps, rendered as a separate pass with depth fading or fog, usually work best for this purpose because their antialiasing will match the other passes.

10.2.8 THE ORIGINS OF PASSES

There is a misconception among some users that rendering in passes is a new technique, only done in certain high-end 3D programs. Rendering in passes has actually been a part of 3D rendering from the first uses of computer graphics in film. In fact, visual effects have been created in passes since before the first 3D effects shots.

The word *pass* originated in *motion-control photography*. Motion-control photography is primarily used in filming miniature models for visual effects. A motion-control camera can repeat the exact same motions several times, moving on a computer-controlled arm or motion base. Each time it repeats its motions through a scene, it's called a *pass*. For example, in filming a model of a spaceship, the first pass through the scene could be a beauty pass, shooting a fully-lit shot of the model. For the next pass, the camera could be loaded with high-contrast film, the lighting could be changed, and the camera could film a matte pass (the equivalent of an alpha channel.) For a third pass, lights might be turned on inside of the model's windows so that a lighting pass could be filmed. Prior to the development of digital compositing systems, all of these passes used to be printed together optically on film.

10.2.9 PASS-MANAGEMENT FEATURES

Any 3D rendering software that is used professionally in film and television productions can be made to render in passes. In most cases, passes are simply created as modified versions of a 3D scene. For example, to isolate a highlight pass, save a version of the scene that has pure black diffuse shading, no ambient light, and renders only specular highlights over a black background. 3D software does not need any special features to support this kind of pass rendering, because all passes are set up manually by the user.

Recently, new pass-management features that can speed and simplify rendering in passes have appeared in some high-end programs, as shown in Figure 10.20. The advantages of having pass-management features

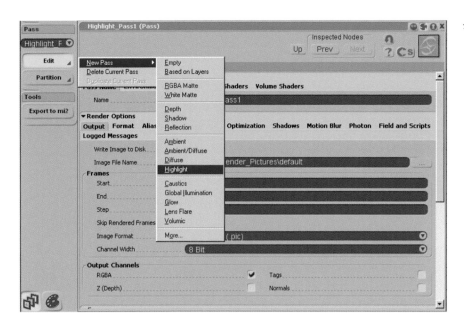

10.20 Pass-management features in Softimage|XSI streamline the definition of different passes and allow a scene to be instantly switched between pass configurations.

built in to the software are that many pass descriptions can be preconfigured for rapid set-up and that different versions of the scene do not need to be saved separately for each pass. Even after making changes to other aspects of a scene, such as to the animation, all of the passes are still renderable from the same scene.

Another approach to pass management is to render multiple passes and scene layers into one multilayer file, such as RPF (Rich Pixel file Format), the expanded version of the earlier RLA format files output by 3D Studio MAX. If you are sure that the compositing software can make use of the RPF format, then it can be used to convey images, Z-Depth, and other information that allows for effects and lighting changes, all in a single file.

Pass-management features in 3D software are a case of the developers following their users. Advanced 3D effects have always been accomplished by layering different passes over a background plate, even before software developers started to notice and build in compositing-related rendering features.

10.3 LIGHTING TO MATCH BACKGROUND PLATES

A *background plate* is usually a sequence of frames digitized from live-action film or video, into which you will add your computer graphics elements. In some projects, your background plate could also be a matte painting, a previously rendered 3D scene, or a composite of multiple elements.

Many 3D programs have an option to view background plates within an animation window (sometimes called an *image plane* or *rotoscope background*), showing how your subject will be aligned with the background. After your 3D scene is aligned with the camera angles from the real-world shot, you face the challenge of matching the lighting from the real-world environment. Matching the direction, color, and tone of the light sources in the real scene is essential to integrating your 3D rendered passes with the photographed background plate.

10.3.1 REFERENCE BALLS AND LIGHT PROBES

A set of reflective and matte balls can be ideal reference objects to help measure the position and color of lights on a location. Mirrored balls are sold as lawn ornaments and as housings for ceiling-mounted security cameras. For a ball with a matte finish, plaster is ideal, but a Styrofoam ball from a craft store could be more portable and affordable. You may need to paint the ball gray and attach a piece of wire to hold it in place.

10.3.1.1 MATTE BALLS

A picture showing the matte ball in a lighting environment, as shown in Figure 10.21, can be great for choosing the color of light reaching your subject from each direction. Ideally, this image should be shot with the same camera as your final background plate and digitized in the same session with the same color correction.

For the most accurate color matches, bring the ball image into a paint program and pick specific RGB color values from the image of the ball, as shown in Figure 10.22. These RGB colors can then be assigned directly as colors for your lights from corresponding directions.

When developing the scene's lighting, you can import the ball image as a background image in your 3D program and create a 3D sphere in front of the image. Using your 3D sphere as a reference, adjust infinite or directional lights from each direction to make the shading of the 3D sphere match the shading of the ball in the background plate.

Studying the colors reaching a point in a real-world environment is a great exercise for anyone working in 3D lighting. Even if you don't need to match the lighting of a background plate right now, this process could be worth trying a few times, just to get a better feel for the colors of real-world lights.

10.21 A matte-finished gray ball is positioned between a fire and window to probe different colors in the scene.

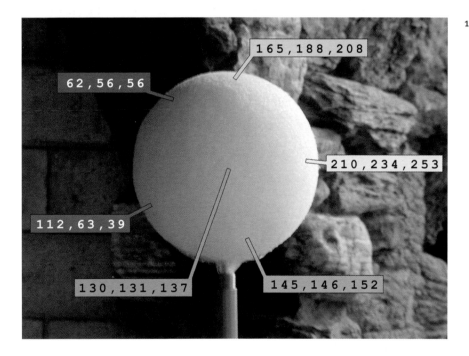

165,188,208

62,56,56

210,234,253

112,63,39

130,131,137

145,146,152

10.22 RGB colors chosen from the reference ball will give an accurate color match to 3D lights.

10.3.1.2 **MIRROR BALLS**

A picture of a reflective ball in an environment helps you more precisely determine the angle and relative brightness of each light, and guides you in creating highlights and reflections for your object (see Figure 10.23). As you know, reflections are view–dependent, so it is vital that the reflective ball be shot from the same camera position as your final background plate.

10.23 A mirror ball captures a reflected image of the surrounding environment for reference or for use as a reflection map.

As with the matte ball image, the reflective ball image can be brought into your 3D program. If you make a shiny 3D sphere, you should be able to see highlights from your brighter lights and match these to the highlights in the reflective ball.

An added bonus to having a picture of a reflective sphere in your environment is that you can use it to develop a reflection map for your object, as shown in Figure 10.24. In many programs, the best way to project your acquired image is as a planar projection onto the side of a large sphere surrounding your 3D scene; make the sphere render reflections only.

10.3.1.3 LIGHT PROBE IMAGES

The traditional approach to matching natural light from a real environment is to use an array of infinite or directional lights, as described earlier. After each light is properly adjusted to match the color and brightness from each direction, this approach can produce realistic renderings and seamless lighting matches.

10.24 The captured reflection map matches a 3D object's reflections to the environment.

Another approach to re-creating a real-world lighting environment is to use a *light probe image* recorded on the same location as your background plate. A light probe image is an image that captures the lighting from all angles around a subject, which can be created by photographing a reflective ball at the shooting location. The light probe image can then be used to illuminate objects with all the recorded colors and tones of real-world light. From only one light probe image, illumination will reach 3D objects from all angles, as though the light source were a giant sphere wrapped around the entire 3D scene.

Unlike ordinary photographs of a reflective ball, light probe images are *high dynamic range (HDR) images*, meaning that they can capture an exposure latitude greatly exceeding the range of one visible image. To photograph light probe images, cameras are programmed to shoot a series of images at different exposure settings, exposing for the brightest light sources all the way down to the darkest, as shown in Figure 10.25. Without using HDR images, all of the brighter lights in a scene might appear clipped as pure white highlights, with no record of their relative brightness or color. By using HDR images, a light probe image can accurately record the color and relative brightness of every light source.

10.3.2 OTHER APPROACHES

You can't always use probes and reflective balls on the set of every production. You can't expect every production to stop and wait for you to

> **NOTE**
>
> Information about High Dynamic Range images can be found on the Internet at www.cs.berkeley.edu/ ~debevec/ and fiatlux.berkeley.edu/ mkhdr/. The first commercial software to support illumination with HDR images is NewTek's LightWave 3D (www.newtek.com).

10.25 A High Dynamic Range (HDR) image will indicate accurate colors at multiple levels of exposure.

set up special reference shots. Sometimes you won't even be able to visit the location where background plates are photographed.

Even if you do get to measure the lighting with different kinds of balls, the lighting in the scene may change without being remeasured. Balls in one location in a scene also may fail to give you the information you need about lighting in another point—you'd need an infinite number of probes to fully measure the light at every point in space.

If you can go to the set or shooting location, you can use other techniques to assist in matching the lighting:

- **Bring a camera to the set.** Take reference pictures of the set and the lighting around it. Take flat-on pictures of walls or floors for possible use in texture mapping. Take wide-angle or panoramic pictures to create reflection maps.

- **Bring a measuring tape to the set.** Ask early in the production if you can have blueprints to the set, but don't trust the original plans to be accurate. Bring a measuring tape and record enough information so that you could build an accurate 3D model of the set if necessary.

- **Watch for changes during the course of the production.** In a studio, lights are adjusted, and even the walls and set pieces are moved between shots. Outside, the weather and time of day create more changes.

If you cannot go to the shooting location, or your background plate comes from stock footage or other sources, you still can match the lighting using other techniques:

- **Study shadows in the background plate.** When you have matched their length and direction in 3D, your lights will be in the right places.

- **Use an object in the background plate to find light colors.** Try to find a white or gray object in the background plate from which you can pick RGB values.

- **Try to find reference objects in the background plate that can be made into a matching 3D model.** By aligning the 3D model with the real object, you can compare how illumination and highlights hit your 3D model until it receives the same illumination as the background plate.

Every production will create different challenges, but with this basic set of tricks, you should be able to match the lights from any background plate.

10.4 WORKING WITH A COMPOSITOR

As a 3D artist in a professional environment, you might not do all of your own compositing. Often there will be a full-time compositor assembling effects shots that contain your 3D rendered elements, as well as live-action images and other types of plates.

In commercial production facilities, it makes good economic sense to finish your 3D work and move a project into compositing as soon as possible, making changes and experiments in the compositing stage. 3D-rendering projects are often billed on a per-project basis, while compositing services are billed per hour of use.

The speed of the compositing process is generally fast enough that clients can supervise compositing sessions, and request and evaluate changes as the work is done. This speed and degree of client involvement is not yet possible in 3D (thankfully!), making clients happier to work and request changes in the 2D compositing stage, even if they are paying by the hour.

Give more flexibility to the compositor, and a shot is less likely to need rerendering in 3D. Here are a few things you can do in rendering to give the compositor more flexibility include the following:

- **Keep animated objects within the frame.** There could be times when you need to reposition your object within the frame, to re-animate its position or track it to a 2D camera move. For any element that a compositor might want to reposition, try to frame your 3D shot so that your animated subject is not cropped off at the edge of the frame. Even if the compositor needs to scale the object up, it is better than losing a part of the model that should have been visible.

- **Render "clean" footage, and save post effects for compositing.** Most 3D programs have options to add effects such as glows, blurs, film grain, and lens flares to your 3D rendering. In most cases it is best to render without these effects and instead add them in a compositing program. It is not cost-effective to redo a raytracing just to test different levels of film grain, when the film grain could have been added to the rendered image in 2D more quickly and interactively.

- **Err on the side of motion that is too slow if speed changes might be needed to an element.** Motion can be sped up more easily than slowed down. To speed up footage, frames can simply be thrown away or dissolved together. To slow down footage, new

NOTE

For more information on compositing in general, check out the books The Art and Science of Digital Compositing by Ron Brinkmann (Morgan Kaufmann) or Digital Compositing In Depth by Doug Kelly (Coriolis). New Riders tells me their own [digital] Compositing & Post will be out in 2001—until then, though...

frames would need to be created, often by repeating existing frames, which can make motion jerky.

- **Use your full exposure latitude.** If you didn't read Chapter 7, "Exposure," before this chapter, please read it now! Vital issues in compositing are matching the black levels, colors, and brightness of the background plate. Compositors will have the most flexibility if they use the full exposure latitude available, so that banding artifacts don't appear during color correction.

- **Avoid clipping.** Areas of your rendering that are overexposed to pure white or underexposed to pure black lack image information and cannot be effectively brightened or darkened during compositing. Keep your shading within a range of tones that will allow for further adjustment.

- **Render more passes.** As a general statement, a scene rendered in more separate passes is easier to manipulate than a scene rendered in only a few passes. For example, if a light source is rendered in a separate lighting pass, then that light can be brightened, dimmed, or tinted by the compositor without rerendering in 3D.

Compositing is a complex craft in its own right and worthy of study by any digital artist. Ideally, you should try to get your first compositing experience working on student, personal, or low-budget projects, where a 3D artist becomes a jack-of-all-trades. Even if you are doing your own compositing on a personal computer, compositing can grow into a great timesaver, a powerful problemsolver, and an important part of your creative process.

10.5 EXERCISES

1. Download a multilayer Photoshop file from http://3dRender.com/
   light/compositing/ and review the functions of the different passes.
   See if you can improve the images by adjusting the color, blending,
   or level of blur on the layers of the file.

2. Rent a movie such as Disney's *Dinosaur*, in which 3D renderings
   have been composited over live-action background plates.
   Examining a still frame, ask yourself the following:

   How well do the composited shadow passes match and merge
   with the shadows that already existed in the background plate?

   Do the black levels and dark tones of the 3D elements match
   the live action?

   Is the level of color saturation consistent?

3. Load any 3D scene that you previously rendered in a single pass
   and then try splitting it up into multiple layers and passes. Try to
   improve each aspect of your rendering as you render it separately,
   such as achieving the most realistic highlights you can in your
   highlight pass. Composite the results in a paint or compositing
   program, adjust the layers, and see how much you may have
   improved upon your original rendering.

A Final Word

I hope you learned as much from reading this book as I did in writing it. It gave me the chance to put into words issues, techniques, and concepts that in the past I had known only through doing, and to share a bit of what I've learned so far in my career. I'll continue to support the CG community and write more articles and tutorials on my web site, www.3dRender.com. I welcome you to send feedback through 3dRender.com—whether you have questions, suggestions, comments, complaints, or corrections. Please feel free to get in touch with me. Happy rendering!

Jeremy Birn
www.3dRender.com

INDEX

3D Studio MAX 3 Fundamentals
Michael Todd Peterson
0-7357-0049-4

3D Studio MAX 3 Magic
Jeff Abouaf, et al.
0-7357-0867-3

3D Studio MAX 3 Media Animation
John Chismar
0-7357-0050-8

3D Studio MAX 3 Professional Animation
Angela Jones, et al.
0-7357-0945-9

Adobe Photoshop 5.5 Fundamentals with ImageReady 2
Gary Bouton
0-7357-0928-9

Bert Monroy: Photorealistic Techniques with Photoshop & Illustrator
Bert Monroy
0-7357-0969-6

CG 101: A Computer Graphics Industry Reference
Terrence Masson
0-7357-0046-X

Click Here
Raymond Pirouz and Lynda Weinman
1-56205-792-8

<coloring web graphics.2>
Lynda Weinman and Bruce Heavin
1-56205-818-5

Creating Killer Web Sites, Second Edition
David Siegel
1-56830-433-1

<creative html design>
Lynda Weinman and William Weinman
1-56205-704-9

<designing web graphics.3>
Lynda Weinman
1-56205-949-1

Designing Web Usability
Jakob Nielsen
1-56205-810-X

[digital] Character Animation 2 Volume 1: Essential Techniques
George Maestri
1-56205-930-0

Essentials of Digital Photography
Akari Kasai and Russell Sparkman
1-56205-762-6

Fine Art Photoshop
Michael J. Nolan and Renee LeWinter
1-56205-829-0

Flash 4 Magic
David Emberton and J. Scott Hamlin
0-7357-0949-1

Flash Web Design
Hillman Curtis
0-7357-0896-7

HTML Artistry: More than Code
Ardith Ibañez and Natalie Zee
1-56830-454-4

HTML Web Magic
Raymond Pirouz
1-56830-475-7

Illustrator 8 Magic
Raymond Pirouz
1-56205-952-1

Inside 3D Studio MAX 3
Phil Miller, et al.
0-7357-0905-X

Inside 3D Studio MAX 3: Modeling, Materials, and Rendering
Ted Boardman and Jeremy Hubbell
0-7357-0085-0

Inside Adobe Photoshop 5.5
Gary David Bouton and Barbara Bouton
0-7357-1000-7

Inside Adobe Photoshop 5, Limited Edition
Gary David Bouton and Barbara Bouton
1-56205-951-3

Inside AutoCAD 2000
David Pitzer and Bill Burchard
0-7357-0851-7

Inside LightWave 3D
Dan Ablan
1-56205-799-5

Inside LightWave 6
Dan Ablan
0-7357-0919-X

Inside trueSpace 4
Frank Rivera
1-56205-957-2

Inside SoftImage 3D
Anthony Rossano
1-56205-885-1

Maya 2 Character Animation
Nathan Vogel, Sherri Sheridan, and Tim Coleman
0-7357-0866-5

Net Results: Web Marketing that Works
USWeb and Rick E. Bruner
1-56830-414-5

Photoshop 5 & 5.5 Artistry
Barry Haynes and Wendy Crumpler
0-7457-0994-7

Photoshop 5 Type Magic
Greg Simsic
1-56830-465-X

Photoshop 5 Web Magic
Michael Ninness
1-56205-913-0

Photoshop Channel Chops
David Biedny, Bert Monroy, and Nathan Moody
1-56205-723-5

<preparing web graphics>
Lynda Weinman
1-56205-686-7

Rhino NURBS 3D Modeling
Margaret Becker
0-7357-0925-4

Secrets of Successful Web Sites
David Siegel
1-56830-382-3

Web Concept & Design
Crystal Waters
1-56205-648-4

Web Design Templates Sourcebook
Lisa Schmeiser
1-56205-754-5

COLOPHON

Digital Lighting & Rendering was produced with the help of Microsoft Word, Adobe Photoshop, and QuarkXPress on a variety of systems, including a Macintosh G3. With the exception of the pages that were printed for proofreading, all files—both text and images—were transferred via email or ftp and edited onscreen.

All the body text was set in the Bembo family, and all the headings and figure captions were set in the Meta Plus family. The Zapf Dingbats and Symbol typefaces were used throughout the book for special symbols and bullets.

This book was printed at Graphic Arts Center in Indianapolis, Indiana. Prepress consisted of PostScript computer-to-plate technology (filmless process). The interior pages were printed sheetfed on 70# Sterling Ultra Litho Satin. The cover was printed on 12 pt. Carolina, coated on one side.